Studies in State and Local Public Finance

A National Bureau
of Economic Research
Project Report

Studies in State and Local Public Finance

Edited by Harvey S. Rosen

The University of Chicago Press

Chicago and London

Harvey S. Rosen is professor of economics at Princeton
University and a research associate of the National Bureau of
Economic Research. He is the author of *Public Finance*.

The University of Chicago Press, Chicago 60637
The University of Chicago Press, Ltd., London

Library of Congress Cataloging-in-Publication Data

Main entry under title:

Studies in state and local public finance.

(National Bureau of Economic Research project
report)
    Bibliography: p.
    Includes indexes.
    1. Finance, Public—United States—States—Addresses,
essays, lectures.   2. Local finance—United States—
Addresses, essays, lectures.   I. Rosen, Harvey S.
II. Series.
HJ275.S76   1986   336.73   85-30904

ISBN 0-226-72621-5

Relation of the Directors to the
Work and Publications of the
National Bureau of Economic Research

1. The object of the National Bureau of Economic Research is to ascertain and to present to the public important economic facts and their interpretation in a scientific and impartial manner. The Board of Directors is charged with the responsibility of ensuring that the work of the National Bureau is carried on in strict conformity with this object.

2. The President of the National Bureau shall submit to the Board of Directors, or to its Executive Committee, for their formal adoption all specific proposals for research to be instituted.

3. No research report shall be published by the National Bureau until the President has sent each member of the Board a notice that a manuscript is recommended for publication and that in the President's opinion it is suitable for publication in accordance with the principles of the National Bureau. Such notification will include an abstract or summary of the manuscript's content and a response form for use by those Directors who desire a copy of the manuscript for review. Each manuscript shall contain a summary drawing attention to the nature and treatment of the problem studied, the character of the data and their utilization in the report, and the main conclusions reached.

4. For each manuscript so submitted, a special committee of the Directors (including Directors Emeriti) shall be appointed by majority agreement of the President and Vice Presidents (or by the Executive Committee in case of inability to decide on the part of the President and Vice Presidents), consisting of three Directors selected as nearly as may be one from each general division of the Board. The names of the special manuscript committee shall be stated to each Director when notice of the proposed publication is submitted to him. It shall be the duty of each member of the special manuscript committee to read the manuscript. If each member of the manuscript committee signifies his approval within thirty days of the transmittal of the manuscript, the report may be published. If at the end of that period any member of the manuscript committee withholds his approval, the President shall then notify each member of the Board, requesting approval or disapproval of publication, and thirty days additional shall be granted for this purpose. The manuscript shall then not be published unless at least a majority of the entire Board who shall have voted on the proposal within the time fixed for the receipt of votes shall have approved.

5. No manuscript may be published, though approved by each member of the special manuscript committee, until forty-five days have elapsed from the transmittal of the report in manuscript form. The interval is allowed for the receipt of any memorandum of dissent or reservation, together with a brief statement of his reasons, that any member may wish to express; and such memorandum of dissent or reservation shall be published with the manuscript if he so desires. Publication does not, however, imply that each member of the Board has read the manuscript, or that either members of the Board in general or the special committee have passed on its validity in every detail.

6. Publications of the National Bureau issued for informational purposes concerning the work of the Bureau and its staff, or issued to inform the public of activities of Bureau staff, and volumes issued as a result of various conferences involving the National Bureau shall contain a specific disclaimer noting that such publication has not passed through the normal review procedures required in this resolution. The Executive Committee of the Board is charged with review of all such publications from time to time to ensure that they do not take on the character of formal research reports of the National Bureau, requiring formal Board approval.

7. Unless otherwise determined by the Board or exempted by the terms of paragraph 6, a copy of this resolution shall be printed in each National Bureau publication.

(Resolution adopted October 25, 1926, as revised through September 30, 1974)

Contents

Acknowledgments

This volume, consisting of papers presented at a conference held at Halloran House in New York City, 15–16 June 1984, presents research carried out as part of the National Bureau of Economic Research's project on government budget and the private economy. The National Bureau has undertaken this project with the support of the Carthage Foundation, the J. M. Foundation, the Lilly Endowment, Inc., the John M. Olin Foundation, Inc., and the J. Howard Pew Freedom Trust.

The many people whose advice and assistance have helped to make this volume possible include National Bureau directors Moses Abramovitz, Morton Ehrlich, and Don Wasserman; National Bureau research associate David F. Bradford; and National Bureau research affiliate Daniel Frisch.

The opinions expressed in this volume are those of the respective authors. They do not necessarily reflect the views of the National Bureau of Economic Research, or any other organization.

Harvey S. Rosen

1   Introduction

Harvey S. Rosen

In fiscal year 1981–82, the federal government's nondefense direct expenditures were $450 billion. In comparison, state and local government expenditures were $485 billion (Tax Foundation, Inc., 1983, 18). It's a small difference, not what one would have guessed in light of the relatively small amount of attention given by academics to state and local public finance. Given its size, the state and local government sector is clearly deserving of serious and sustained study.

Another reason for studying state and local public finance systems is their tremendous diversity. This diversity provides a set of "natural experiments" that can be exploited to discern the effects of government policy upon the private sector, and how government behavior itself is determined. Justice Brandeis once observed: "It is one of the happy incidents of the Federal system that a single courageous state may, if its citizens choose, serve as a laboratory, and try moral, social and economic experiments without risk to the rest of the country." These experiments provide grist for the economist's mill.

In light of these considerations, several years ago the National Bureau of Economic Research established a project on state and local public finance. A conference was held in June of 1984. Six of the papers presented at that conference, and the comments of the discussants, are contained in this volume. Although the papers cover a diverse array of topics, they share an empirical orientation and a concern with policy issues.

The first two papers, by James Poterba and by Roger Gordon and Joel Slemrod, focus on the role of tax-exempt bonds in local public

Harvey S. Rosen is professor of economics at Princeton University, and a research associate of the National Bureau of Economic Research.

finance. Poterba examines the yield differential between taxable and municipal securities. He considers alternative theories of how the differential is determined, and describes their implications for how changes in federal tax policy would affect the differential. His econometric work suggests that expected tax changes have an important effect on the yield spread between taxable and tax-exempt securities. On the basis of these results, he discusses the likely effects of several changes in municipal borrowing practices, and concludes that increased use of short-term borrowing instruments would reduce the cost of debt finance to state and local governments.

Roger Gordon and Joel Slemrod examine the arbitrage opportunities created by the differences between (1) the tax-exempt rate that a community faces when it borrows; (2) the taxable rate that a community can earn, free of tax, when it invests; and (3) the after-tax rate of return that the residents of the community can receive on their savings. Do community financial managers take advantage of such wedges to benefit their residents? Gordon and Slemrod provide a careful discussion of the economic and institutional considerations that might affect a community's propensity to do so. Their econometric results suggest that communities do actively engage in tax arbitrage.

The next three papers, by Michelle White, Kenneth Small and Clifford Winston, and Daniel Feenberg and Harvey Rosen, concern several different aspects of state and local tax policy. White is concerned with the important controversy concerning whether or not local taxation affects firms' location decisions. She begins by discussing alternative theories of property taxation, and the implications of each for the controversy. Her empirical work takes advantage of California data collected about the time that Proposition 13 was enacted. Proposition 13 generated exogenous (to the localities) changes in property tax levels, making them uniform throughout the state. However, other attributes of the business climate stayed about the same. Therefore, by examining location decisions before and after Proposition 13, one can study firm location decisions without having to correct for things like differential production costs. White's econometric results suggest that property taxes are a significant influence on decisions by retailing and service firms, but not manufacturing firms.

The paper by Small and Winston is concerned with a quite different tax problem: efficient road-use charges for trucks. Currently, neither federal nor state policy seriously attempts to align motor vehicle taxes with the damage the vehicles inflict on highways. Small and Winston estimate the welfare effects of instituting nationwide marginal cost pricing for heavy highway vehicles. Their analysis recognizes that a change in the current tax regime to one in which rates are based on weight per axle would induce trucking firms to use different types of trucks, and in some cases induce shippers to switch to other forms of transportation (e.g., rail). They find as a conservative estimate that by moving to marginal cost pricing, a welfare gain of $1.2 billion per year could be realized accompanied by a 17% reduction in highway maintenance and repair expenditures.

The purpose of the paper by Feenberg and Rosen is to provide consistent characterizations of state income and general sales-tax systems over time. For the period 1977–83, they compute revenue elasticities with respect to income, and marginal and average tax rates at various income levels. Such measures, which have not heretofore been available, should provide policymakers and academics with a basis for making interstate and intertemporal comparisons of tax structures. One of their findings is that if the income and general sales taxes are viewed as a single system, the average income elasticity of the revenue across states is about 1.1. This figure has not changed much over the period 1977–83. However, averages tend to mask considerable heterogeneity, both with respect to progressivity of the systems in a given year and how they have evolved over time.

The last paper in the volume, by Steven Craig and Robert Inman, examines some issues concerning the structure of U.S. federalism. They study the ramifications of the structure of federal to state grants in aid, and examine the possible allocative consequences of the "new federalism" program suggested by the Reagan administration in 1982. Craig and Inman specify and estimate a four-equation budgetary model of state spending for education, welfare, other expenditures, and revenues. An important result is that federal dollars which flow into a state via grants in aid are allocated disproportionately away from education and welfare, and toward other expenditures. When the grants come in the form of matching aid, this tendency is mitigated, but not as much as might be expected. Craig and Inman predict that if the Reagan plan were implemented, spending on welfare would be reduced, as would the size of the public sector as a whole.

Taken as a group, the papers in this volume raise important and difficult problems in state and local public finance, and make considerable progress in solving them. One is nevertheless impressed by the number of questions that are introduced and not answered in the essays. What is the optimal subsidy for locally provided capital? Can agency theory be used to explain local managers' responses to the arbitrage possibilities created by the tax treatment of municipal debt? What is the dynamic pattern of firms' responses to changes in local tax systems? What is the relation between a state's tax structure and the size of its public sector? It is hoped that this volume will stimulate research on these and related questions.

References

Tax Foundation, Inc. 1983. *Facts and figures on government finance 22nd biennial edition 1983*. Washington, D.C.

2 Explaining the Yield Spread between Taxable and Tax-exempt Bonds: The Role of Expected Tax Policy

James M. Poterba

The early 1980s was a period of turbulence in the municipal bond market. Interest rates on tax-exempt securities reached record heights, both in nominal terms and relative to comparably risky taxable bonds. Between January 1980 and January 1982, the yield differential between prime long-term municipal bonds and U.S. Treasury obligations fell from 375 to 175 basis points. The yield spread on short-term bonds also declined, but by a smaller amount. The income tax rate at which an investor would be indifferent between holding long-term taxable or tax-exempt securities declined dramatically, from 35% to less than 15%. During the same period, voter resistance to higher taxes, recession-induced service demands, and reductions in federal grants increased state and local borrowing by nearly 50%, even though many jurisdictions postponed capital expenditures because of high interest rates.

The escalation of tax-exempt interest rates has been attributed to many factors. Increased municipal risk, an increased supply of tax-exempt securities such as industrial revenue bonds, falling marginal tax rates among personal investors, and changes in commercial bank behavior have all been advanced as possible explanations.[1] The shrinking yield differential between taxable and tax-exempt securities has germinated many proposals designed to reduce the real cost of debt finance by altering municipal borrowing practices. Proposals include

James M. Poterba is assistant professor of economics at the Massachusetts Institute of Technology and a faculty research fellow at the National Bureau of Economic Research.

This research is part of the NBER project on state and local public finance. I am indebted to Fischer Black, Roger Gordon, Doug Holtz-Eakin, Harvey Rosen, Myron Scholes, Mark Wolfson, and especially Lawrence Summers for helpful discussions. Leslie Papke and Ignacio Mas provided excellent research assistance. Financial support from the NBER is gratefully acknowledged.

increased use of short-term debt, issuing "put bonds" that grant the bondholder the right to terminate his debt contract after a fixed number of years, and use of floating-rate long-term bonds. There has also been renewed interest in the long-standing plan for replacing the current income tax exemption for municipal interest with a federal subsidy to state and local borrowing. The likely impact of these proposals on municipal interest costs is controversial, largely because of disagreement over the forces behind the recent increase in tax-exempt interest rates.

There are several competing theories of how equilibrium yields are determined in the municipal bond market. One view holds that commercial banks are the marginal holders of municipal debt, since they are the only class of investors who are able to borrow at the after-tax interest rate and invest the proceeds in tax-exempt securities. This view implies that only the tax rates facing commercial banks should affect the municipal-taxable yield spread. A second view, which has developed from research on a theory of corporate capital structure proposed by Merton Miller (1977), also relates the yield spread to corporate tax rates. In Miller's model, changes in the relative supplies of corporate debt and corporate equity ensure that the marginal investor choosing between holding taxable and tax-exempt debt faces an interest tax rate equal to the statutory corporate rate. The model predicts that changes in investor tax rates should have no effect on the relative prices of taxable and tax-exempt bonds, although they might affect the equilibrium quantities of different securities.

A third and more traditional view, described by Mussa and Kormendi (1979) and Hendershott and Koch (1977), holds that the municipal bond market is segmented by maturities. Different classes of investors hold long- and short-term bonds, with banks predominating at short maturities and households purchasing most long-term debt. Under this view, personal tax changes should affect the yield spread on long-term bonds, but should have little impact on the relative yields on short-term taxable and tax-exempt bonds.

This paper examines the impact of changing tax expectations on the taxable–tax exempt yield spread. In particular, it tests the hypothesis that downward revisions in expected personal tax rates can lower the yield spread between taxable and tax-exempt debt. Only the third model predicts that such changes should affect relative bond prices. By examining data from four events that substantially altered tax rates—the 1964 Kennedy-Johnson tax cut, the Vietnam War tax surcharge, the 1969 Tax Reform Act, and the 1981 tax cut—this study provides new evidence that *both* personal and corporate tax changes affect the relative yields on taxable and tax-free bonds. These results help distinguish among the competing models of municipal market equilibrium, and illuminate questions about how various policy changes would affect municipal borrowing costs.

The findings also suggest that expected tax changes explain a sizable fraction of the recent narrowing in the taxable–tax exempt yield spread. The passage of the 1981 Economic Recovery Tax Act was contemporaneous with a 25% reduction in the yield spread between long-term municipal and taxable bonds. Although tax reforms cannot explain the entire increase in tax-exempt yields relative to taxable yields during the early 1980s, they appear to have had a significant effect.

This paper is divided into five sections. The first chronicles movements in municipal borrowing costs during the last three decades. The second section presents the three competing models of municipal debt pricing in greater detail and identifies the predictions of each regarding the impact of tax changes on yield spreads. The third section describes my data set and explains the procedure that was used to identify periods of changing tax expectations. The fourth section presents empirical evidence on the effects of tax changes during the last two decades on the taxable–tax exempt yield spread. The concluding section reviews the implications of my results for proposals to reform municipal borrowing policies.

2.1   Recent Movements in Municipal Borrowing Costs

This section describes recent movements in the yield spread between taxable and tax-exempt interest rates. Monthly interest rate data were obtained from Salomon Brothers' *Analytical Record of Yields and Yield Spreads*. These data, derived from yield curves for par bonds with current issue characteristics, are calculated on the first of each month. The differential between taxable and tax-exempt yields can be described by the implicit tax rate, θ^I, which would characterize an investor who was indifferent between the two yields. This tax rate is defined by $(1 - \theta^I)R = R_M$, where R is the yield on a taxable bond and R_M is the yield on a comparably risky tax-exempt security.

The implicit tax rates reported here are calculated from yields on newly issued Treasury securities and prime-grade general obligation tax-exempt bonds. Both securities are close to riskless.[2] "Prime" is the highest rating awarded to municipal bonds by Salomon Brothers. The restriction to general obligation bonds is also important, since many recent events such as the Washington Public Power Supply System default have altered the perceived riskiness of revenue bonds issued by states and localities. These developments should have had a much smaller effect on the market for general obligation bonds, which are backed by the "full faith and credit" of the issuing government.

Table 2.1 reports annual average values of the implicit tax rates on one-, five-, ten-, and twenty-year bonds for the period 1955–83. The series show pronounced declines in the implied tax rates on both long- and short-maturity bonds between 1979 and 1982. The twenty-year implied tax rate declined by more than twenty percentage points during

Table 2.1   **Tax Rates Implied by Taxable and Tax-exempt Bond Yields, 1955–83**

	Treasury bonds versus prime-grade municipals			
Year	20-year Maturity	10-year Maturity	5-year Maturity	1-year Maturity
1955	.244	.341	.406	.414
1956	.219	.279	.333	.413
1957	.151	.222	.296	.380
1958	.189	.262	.326	.412
1959	.222	.290	.376	.433
1960	.227	.293	.364	.422
1961	.190	.284	.397	.476
1962	.256	.353	.423	.468
1963	.261	.351	.412	.465
1964	.265	.327	.375	.442
1965	.264	.316	.346	.426
1966	.227	.266	.316	.336
1967	.239	.286	.325	.370
1968	.226	.282	.330	.405
1969	.133	.214	.278	.344
1970	.101	.259	.353	.387
1971	.130	.292	.390	.405
1972	.154	.331	.388	.435
1973	.282	.339	.374	.453
1974	.282	.300	.366	.424
1975	.217	.266	.364	.408
1976	.276	.361	.424	.475
1977	.322	.406	.439	.507
1978	.346	.408	.436	.493
1979	.355	.417	.429	.497
1980	.308	.400	.439	.485
1981	.229	.323	.395	.463
1982	.154	.249	.336	.424
1983	.206	.281	.372	.445
Averages:				
1955–59	.205	.279	.348	.411
1960–69	.229	.297	.357	.415
1970–79	.247	.338	.396	.448
1980–83	.224	.313	.386	.454

SOURCE: Salomon Brothers, *Analytical Record of Yields and Yield Spreads* and author's calculations.

this period. The tax rates implied by short-term yields declined less dramatically, from 50 to 42%. These changes are larger than those observed in any other three-year period in the postwar era.

The table also shows that in every year the implicit tax rate on short-term bonds was substantially higher than that on any of the long-term bonds. The divergence was most pronounced in the late 1960s and early 1980s, when the difference between the implicit tax rates on one- and twenty-year bonds exceeded twenty-five percentage points. There are also persistent differences in the *levels* of long- and short-term municipal interest rates. Throughout the postwar period, long-term tax-exempt interest rates have exceeded short-term rates, often by as much as 50%. The perennial upward slope in the tax-exempt term structure is the motivation for some recent proposals to increase state and local short-term borrowing.

Several warnings about the use of implied tax rates must be issued before drawing strong conclusions from the data in table 2.1. First, if there are differential expected capital gains on municipal and Treasury bonds, then the implied tax rates will not reflect marginal interest tax rates.[3] If the expected capital gain on a taxable bond is larger than that on a comparable tax-exempt bond, then their yields to maturity will be closer than they would be assuming equal capital gains. This will bias the implied tax rate toward zero.

Tax reforms are one source of capital gains and losses. If tax rates are expected to decline, then the value of tax exemption will diminish and the holders of tax-exempt bonds will experience capital losses. The implied tax rate on long-maturity bonds will therefore be below the current tax rates facing investors. The yield spread between short-term taxable and tax-exempt bonds should depend on current tax rules, while the spread at longer maturities depends on the expected path of tax rates over a longer horizon.

A second problem in comparing the yields on different bonds arises because long-term bonds provide their holders with the opportunity to engage in tax-trading strategies. Investors should therefore require a lower coupon yield than on short-maturity bonds of comparable risk. This contaminates inferences about the term structure of implied tax rates, and it may also contaminate the estimated yield differential between taxable and tax-exempt bonds of the same maturity. Constantinides and Ingersoll (1984) find that the tax-timing option on municipal securities is worth substantially less than the option on taxable bonds, primarily because there are no tax advantages associated with establishing an above-par basis in a municipal bond. The implied tax rate calculated from yields to maturity will therefore *underestimate* the actual tax rates on investors, with larger biases for longer-maturity bonds. These biases can cause large errors in the levels of implied tax rates calculated from long-term yield data. However, the *changes* in implied tax rates, which I focus on, may be less subject to these biases.[4]

A third difficulty with implied tax rates is caused by differential risk. If prime municipals are riskier than Treasury bonds, then the estimated marginal tax rates are biased downward. Moreover, there may be a larger risk differential between long-term municipal and Treasury bonds than between short-term bonds of these types, implying that the bias is greater on long-maturity bonds. If the perceived riskiness of municipal securities has increased in recent years because of near-defaults or taxpayer revolts, it could account for declining implicit tax rates. However, the change in default probabilities required to explain the recent narrowing of the yield spread is implausibly large.[5]

This paper focuses on the effects of expected tax changes in explaining monthly changes in the taxable–tax exempt yield spread. The next section outlines several models with different predictions about which tax rates determine the taxable–tax exempt yield spread. Subsequent sections provide empirical evidence on how announcements of impending tax reform influence the relative yields of taxable and tax-exempt bonds.

2.2   Alternative Models of Municipal Bond Market Equilibrium

The prices of taxable and tax-exempt bonds are determined in a financial general equilibrium. Any analysis of the relative yields on taxable and municipal bonds must therefore specify the behavior of firms and governments that supply these assets as well as the investors who demand them. This section discusses three competing theories of the determination of the taxable–tax exempt yield spread. They generate different predictions regarding how changing tax expectations should affect the implied tax rates calculated from yields to maturity.

2.2.1   The Bank Arbitrage Hypothesis

The first model was developed by Eugene Fama (1977) and has subsequently received favorable empirical support from Skelton (1983). Fama noted that one class of investors, commercial banks, can operate simultaneously in both the taxable and tax-exempt bond markets. Unlike most other investors, banks are permitted to deduct interest payments from their taxable profits even while investing in tax-exempt securities. If the tax-exempt yield, R_M, exceeds the after-tax cost of bank borrowing $(1 - \tau)R$, where τ is the corporate tax rate and R is the taxable interest rate, then commercial banks will issue taxable bonds or notes and purchase municipal securities. By demanding municipal bonds, banks will drive up prices and lower yields until $R_M =$

$(1 - \tau)R$. Alternatively, if municipal yields are below this level, banks will reduce their holdings of municipal bonds and use the proceeds to extend other loans. Since banks have held large amounts of municipal debt for most of the past three decades, and currently own more than one-third of outstanding state and local debt, they have ample reserves to undertake these portfolio adjustments. This model suggests that while the yield spread between taxable and tax-exempt bonds should be stable, the monthly changes in commercial bank holdings of municipal debt could be quite volatile.

There seems little doubt that banks undertake the tax arbitrage transactions described above, especially with short-term bonds.[6] Beek (1982) reports that 52% of the tax-exempt debt held by commercial banks is of less than one-year maturity,while 92% of bank holdings has maturities of less than five years. The role of banks in performing tax arbitrage with long-term bonds is more doubtful, and may be restricted by institutional limitations and other factors. Skelton notes that

> banks may deduct the interest payments on debt obligations incurred in the normal course of business while receiving tax-exempt coupon payments . . . however, liabilities with maturities in excess of three years are considered to be potential contributions to capital and as such are subject to scrutiny of the tax authorities. In addition, long term debt issues by banks must be approved by the Comptroller of the Currency and the FDIC who, as a rule, limit such financing to one third of total capital. This special opportunity for banks, therefore, is limited to the short end of the maturity spectrum. [Skelton 1983, 346]

Even if banks cannot issue long-maturity debt, of course, they should be able to undertake arbitrage in the long-term market by issuing short-term securities while purchasing long-term bonds. This exposes them to some real interest rate risk, but this is a type of risk that they are frequently called upon to hedge.

The bank arbitrage analysis implies that changes in the stock of municipal debt outstanding will have no impact on the relative yields of taxable and tax-exempt debt. Changes in security volume will require more or less borrowing or lending by banks, but the relative yields will not change. In this model, we do not have to explain the debt-supply behavior of states and localities in order to determine equilibrium prices.

Tax changes, however, can affect the yield spread. A temporary reduction in the corporate tax rate will lead to a substantial narrowing of the short-term yield spread but only a small change in long-term yields. A reduction in expected future corporate tax rates would reduce the current yield spread on long-maturity bonds, with no effect on short-term yields. More importantly, the model suggests that personal tax rates are *irrelevant* for determining municipal interest rates.

The bank arbitrage model suggests that, absent any variation over time in expected corporate tax rates, divergences in the yields on taxable and tax-exempt bonds at varying maturities must be attributable to the risk characteristics of the different securities. Fama (1977) argues that although yields to maturity on comparably rated corporate and municipal bonds frequently imply tax rates *below* the corporate tax rate, especially at long maturities, this is due to inadequate risk comparison. He suggests that since bondholders are less able to enforce restrictive covenants against municipal than against corporate borrowers, and since local government assets are virtually impossible to seize during bankruptcy, tax-exempt bonds are riskier than corporate debt. These factors, combined with uncertainties about future political actions, induce higher yields on long-maturity municipal bonds than on top-quality corporate debt.

One piece of evidence against this explanation of long-term yield differentials was provided by Gordon and Malkiel (1981). They compared the yields on long-term corporate bonds and industrial revenue bonds that were backed by the same firms. These bonds were similar in all respects except their tax treatment, with the industrial revenue bonds providing tax-exempt interest. The yields on these securities suggested implied tax rates of about 25%, substantially lower than the prevailing corporate tax rate. Differential risk cannot explain this divergence.

The bank arbitrage model is appealing for its simple account of equilibrium pricing in the municipal bond market. However, it may be of limited relevance for describing future developments in this market. Table 2.2 shows the holdings of municipal debt by commercial banks, households, and property and casualty insurance companies during the period since 1955. Commercial banks' share of the tax-exempt market has declined in each of the last eleven years. Their holdings have declined precipitously since 1980, falling from 42% of the outstanding stock to just over 33% at the beginning of 1984. As a result, households have become increasingly important as holders of municipal debt.

The recent decline in commercial bank activity in municipal debt is attributable to three factors. First, changes in the availability of other sources of tax-sheltered income, particularly the rise in leasing since 1980, have reduced commercial banks' reliance on tax-exempt bonds as a device for lowering tax liability. Second, bank profits were depressed in 1981 and 1982; this diminished the need for tax-exempt income. Finally, the Tax Equity and Fiscal Responsibility Act of 1982 limited banks' interest deductions to 85% of the carrying costs of their municipal bond investments. This reduced the attractiveness of the tax arbitrage described above, and led to increased investment in other assets. The future role of commercial banks in the municipal market remains uncertain.

2.2.2. The Miller Model

The second model of the municipal market was developed by Merton Miller (1977), primarily to analyze questions about corporate capital structure. It emphasizes the role of corporations as suppliers of debt and equity in determining the pattern of equilibrium yields. To highlight the role of tax clienteles, I shall present the model in a world of certainty.

First, consider the situation in which there are no municipal bonds. Firms earn a fixed pretax return R on their investments. If a firm is financed exclusively with debt, then the after-tax return received by its owners is $(1 - m)R$, where m is the investors' tax rate on interest income. Since for tax purposes interest payments are deductible from corporate profits, corporate profits tax liability equals zero. By comparison, if the firm were financed with equity, shareholders would receive an after-tax return of $(1 - \tau)(1 - \tau_e)R$, where τ_e is the effective marginal tax rate on equity income and τ is the corporate tax rate. If shareholders face different marginal tax rates, then those for whom $(1 - m) > (1 - \tau)(1 - \tau_e)$ will hold debt while those for whom $(1 - m) \leqslant (1 - \tau)(1 - \tau_e)$ will invest in equity. This condition can be rewritten as $\tau \gtrless (m - \tau_e)/(1 - \tau_e)$. In equilibrium, investors will be completely specialized in holding either debt or equity.

Aggregate corporate financial policy is determined by the relationship (Debt/Equity) $= \eta$, where

$$(1) \quad \eta = \frac{\text{Net Worth Held by Investors with } (m - \tau_e)/(1 - \tau_e) < \tau}{\text{Net Worth Held by Investors with } (m - \tau_e)/(1 - \tau_e) \geqslant \tau}.$$

The relative returns on debt and equity satisfy

$$(2) \quad (1 - \tau_e^*)R_{eq} = (1 - m^*)R$$

where the pretax equity return is $R_{eq} = (1 - \tau)R$. The marginal tax rates facing investors who are indifferent between debt and equity are indicated by asterisks; they satisfy $(1 - \tau_e^*)(1 - \tau)R = (1 - m^*)R$. Corporations adjust their debt-equity ratios to ensure that all investors for whom $(1 - \tau_e)R_{eq}$ exceeds $(1 - m)R$ are able to hold equity, and all those for whom $(1 - m)R \geqslant (1 - \tau_e)R_{eq}$ can hold debt.

Tax-exempt debt, M, can be introduced into this framework.[7] If there are no taxes on equity income and there is no uncertainty, then municipal debt and corporate equity are perfect substitutes and they must have the same return. This return must equal $(1 - \tau)R$. If there are taxes on equity income, then investors who hold municipals will be

Table 2.2 Trends in the Ownership of Municipal Bonds

Year	Share of outstanding debt held by:			Share of net change in municipal debt absorbed by:		
	Commercial banks	Households	Property and casualty insurance companies	Commercial banks	Households	Property and casualty insurance companies
1955	.282	.422	.091	.003	.684	.160
1956	.264	.435	.099	.029	.647	.213
1957	.262	.432	.104	.248	.378	.156
1958	.282	.405	.106	.462	.146	.129
1959	.261	.430	.111	.053	.752	.183
1960	.250	.435	.114	.173	.489	.177
1961	.270	.422	.119	.463	.371	.201
1962	.316	.388	.122	1.009	−.043	.166
1963	.346	.368	.122	.809	.085	.133
1964	.362	.373	.118	.666	.385	.073
1965	.387	.363	.113	.699	.245	.056
1966	.389	.382	.114	.325	.903	.159
1967	.443	.335	.119	1.195	−.342	.199
1968	.478	.305	.117	.896	−.133	.105
1969	.447	.352	.116	.005	.993	.119

Year						
1970	.464	.340	.117	.993	−.064	.146
1971	.505	.297	.122	.721	−.001	.204
1972	.513	.277	.135	.477	.156	.297
1973	.500	.280	.147	.377	.359	.253
1974	.494	.290	.148	.305	.517	.138
1975	.472	.304	.149	.045	.434	.195
1976	.443	.303	.155	.172	−.028	.510
1977	.441	.276	.178	.361	−.115	.623
1978	.432	.255	.208	.382	−.152	.673
1979	.426	.256	.223	.320	.305	.372
1980	.420	.257	.230	.434	.217	.302
1981	.413	.265	.228	.151	.503	.178
1982	.386	.290	.215	.035	.538	.079
1983	.345	.333	.194	−.014	.609	.035
Averages:						
1955–59	.270	.425	.102	.159	.521	.168
1960–69	.369	.372	.117	.624	.295	.139
1970–79	.469	.288	.158	.415	.141	.341
1980–83	.394	.282	.219	.126	.472	.166

NOTE: The first three columns report the fraction of state and local obligations outstanding at the end of each year which are held by each class of investor. The last three columns report the ratio of the change in each investor class's holdings to the total change in debt outstanding. Data are drawn from the flow of funds accounts.

those for whom $R_M \geq (1 - m)R$ and $R_M \geq (1 - \tau_e)(1 - \tau)R$. Figure 2.1 summarizes the relationship between an investor's tax rate and his portfolio composition, assuming that equity tax rates are a linear function of those on interest income.[8] The diagram makes clear that municipal bondholders are investors who, in the absence of tax-exempt debt, would have held equity. There is a critical value of τ_e at which, given R_M, investors will be indifferent between holding tax-exempt debt and taxable equity. The value of τ_e such that $(1 - \tau_e)R_{eq} = R_M$ will be defined as τ_e^{**}; it corresponds to the "marginal investor" in municipal bonds. Given a stock of municipal debt M, the relative yield on taxable and tax-exempt debt is determined by finding τ_e^{**} such that the total wealth held by investors with $\tau_e \geq \tau_e^{**}$ and $\tau < (m - \tau_e)/(1 - \tau_e)$ equals M. Municipal and corporate bond yields are then related by

$$(3) \qquad R_m = (1 - \tau_e^{**})R_{eq} = (1 - \tau_e^{**})(1 - \tau)R.$$

In this model, changes in the stock of municipal debt have two effects. First, an increase in M will lower the value of τ_e^{**}, since more investors must be induced to hold municipal debt instead of equity. This will reduce the yield spread between taxable and tax-exempt debt, since

$$(4) \qquad R - R_M = (\tau + \tau_e^{**}(1 - \tau))R.$$

In addition, changing the supply of municipal debt will lead to offsetting adjustments in corporate debt-equity ratios. The precise nature of this

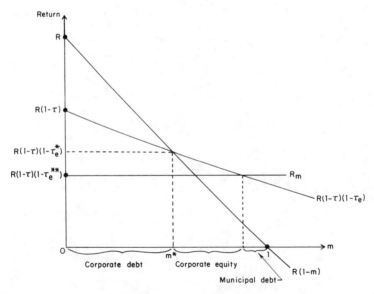

Fig. 2.1   Asset choice in the Miller Model

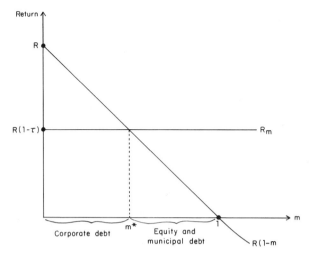

Fig. 2.2   Asset choice in the Miller Model I ($\tau_e = 0$)

effect depends crucially on whether issuing municipal bonds induces a change in the level of private savings. Assuming that total savings are unaffected by an increase in the stock of municipal debt, each dollar of municipal debt displaces one dollar of corporate equity. The corporate debt-equity ratio will satisfy

$$(5) \qquad \frac{D}{E} = \eta(1 + \frac{M}{E}).$$

Increasing the stock of municipal debt will therefore raise the corporate debt-equity ratio.

If issuing municipal bonds induces a change in private savings, then the effect on the corporate debt-equity ratio is unclear. If all additional savings come from investors for whom $(1 - \tau) \geq (1 - m)/(1 - \tau_e)$, investors who hold equity in equilibrium, then the debt-equity ratio will rise by less than it would in the fixed-savings case. If, however, there is increased savings from individuals for whom $(1 - \tau) \leq (1 - m)/(1 - \tau_e)$, then the debt-equity ratio might decline by more than the amount predicted in (5).

In considering the effect of tax changes on the yield spread, it is helpful to distinguish between two versions of the Miller model. They will be labelled Miller Model I and Miller Model II. The first model, which was presented by Miller (1977) and subsequently supported by Trzcinka (1982) and others, holds that the effective tax rate on equity income is zero. This case, which is a special case of the $\tau_e \neq 0$ model, is shown graphically in figure 2.2. If the equity tax rate is zero, then the previous conclusions with respect to changing the stock of municipal debt no longer obtain. Provided M is less than the total wealth of individuals for whom $(1 - m) \leq (1 - \tau)$, changes in the stock of tax-exempt debt will have no effect on R_M. Since $\tau_e^{**} = 0$, $R_M = (1 - \tau)$ R regardless of relative security supplies. As in the bank arbitrage model, changes in the personal tax code will have no impact on the yield spread between taxable and tax-exempt debt. Corporate tax changes will, however, alter the yield spread between taxable and tax-exempt bonds.

The predictions of this model are therefore identical to those of the bank arbitrage model. The mechanism that ensures that $R_M = (1 - \tau)$ R is different, however. This provides one way of distinguishing between the two views. When there are changes in the tax rates or rules applying to banks, but not other firms, the bank arbitrage model predicts that there will be changes in the taxable–tax exempt yield spread. Miller Model I makes no such prediction.

The second version of the Miller model, which I have already described above, allows for the possibility that equity tax rates are positive. This view is supported by the observation that since part of the return to equity holders is through dividend payments, $\tau_e = (1 - \alpha)z + \alpha m$, where α is the firm's payout ratio, z is the effective tax rate on capital gains, and m is the dividend tax rate. In many cases the dividend and interest tax rates are equal. Even if capital gains are untaxed, therefore, the dividend tax burden should make τ_e greater than zero. Although Miller and Scholes (1978, 1982) have argued that the interaction of various tax code provisions makes the effective dividend tax rate zero, their view seems contradicted by evidence on both the tax status of investors (Feenberg 1981) and some findings on the behavior of share prices and corporate dividend decisions (Poterba and Summers 1985).

In Miller Model II, a change in either the corporate tax rate or the provisions of the personal tax code affecting the tax rate on equity income will alter the yield spread between taxable and tax-exempt bonds of comparable risk. A change in the stock of tax-exempt debt could also affect the yield spread, as described above. Increased municipal borrowing reduces τ_e^{**} and thereby narrows the yield spread.

The strict predictions described above about investor specialization in only one asset depend crucially upon that assumption of perfect certainty. When corporate debt, equity, and tax-exempt bonds are all risky assets, portfolio choices will not be determined solely by tax considerations. Auerbach and King (1983) discuss these issues in greater detail.

2.2.3   The Preferred Habitat Model

The bank arbitrage model and both Miller models ignore the agency and transactions costs associated with corporate and municipal finance.

Firms often incur costs from issuing debt rather than equity.[9] Maturity matching, in which firms, states, and localities attempt to incur liabilities with maturities roughly equal to those of their assets, also appears to be a prevalent practice. These market imperfections may restrict movement to equilibrium in the models described above.

A final view of municipal market equilibrium, the "preferred habitat" model, holds that states and municipalities have distinct maturity preferences when issuing different types of debt. Legal restrictions and other factors lead to the use of long-term bonds when financing capital expenditures, and the use of short-term debt primarily to smooth fluctuations in revenues. Other institutional constraints and a desire for maturity matching on the part of lenders lead different classes of investors to hold short- and long-term municipal bonds. Thus, the markets for short- and long-term municipal debt are not linked by any operative arbitrage mechanism, either on the part of suppliers (states and localities) or demanders of debt.

This view explains the divergence in the implied tax rate on short- and long-term bonds as due to the varying tax rates facing the demanders of municipal debt of different maturities. Mussa and Kormendi (1979) present a clear description:

> Commercial banks are the dominant holders of short-term municipal bonds and also hold short-term taxable instruments with essentially the same risk and other characteristics. The yield differential between short-term municipal bonds and comparable short-term taxable instruments is close to the corporate tax rate of 48 percent, since this is the yield differential that offsets the tax advantage of short-term municipal bonds for the dominant holder of such bonds. For long-term municipal bonds, the yield differential is not set by the tax rate for commercial banks. Banks hold long-term municipal bonds, but they do not hold any significant amount of long-term corporate bonds. Hence, the investor who is just balancing between long-term municipal bonds and long-term corporate bonds cannot be a bank but must be some other investor. For this investor, the equalizing yield differential is not 48 percent but only about 30 percent. [Mussa and Kormendi 1979, 7]

This model suggests that the short-term municipal market behaves according to the bank arbitrage model, while at long maturities Miller Model II is a more accurate description of the market.

Under this view, the effect of changing the stock of outstanding debt will depend upon the maturity at which it is issued. Short-term bond issues will not change the implied tax rate on short-maturity municipal debt, while long-term bonds may have an impact on the relative pricing of taxable and tax-exempt securities. The model's predictions with regard to tax changes are also a mix of the previous results. Corporate tax changes will affect both the short- and long-term yield spread between taxable and tax-exempt debt. The effect of personal tax changes, however, will be confined to the long-term yield spread.

The "preferred habitat" model provides an account of why the implied tax rates on long- and short-term municipal debt may differ. However, it also emphasizes our lack of understanding of municipal financial policy, since it raises a puzzle: Why do municipalities issue long-term debt? If the upward-sloping tax-exempt term structure is partly due to the maturity preference of municipal bondholders, and high tax bracket investors prefer short-maturity bonds, then states and localities could reduce their borrowing burden by issuing short-term securities. One explanation of their failure to do this is that there are substantial transactions or administrative costs associated with rolling over short-maturity debt, or raising taxes to pay off principal during a liquidity crisis. This argument is more persuasive in the case of small townships or municipalities than for cities and states with ongoing financial needs, since the latter are involved in frequent debt issues.

A second reason for the reluctance to use roll-over short-term debt may be that interest payments over the course of a year become uncertain. This could impede budgeting, create situations in which tax revenues would not fully cover expenses, or require more frequent changes in tax rates than under a system with fixed-rate long-term finance. Finally, the municipalities' fear of credit rationing cannot be ignored. Prior to the New York City crisis in 1974–75, 53% of state and local debt issues were at short maturities. This declined to 35% in 1976 and 1977, and it has not exceeded 40% since then.[10] Beek (1982) suggests that the danger of being unable to refinance a short-term bond issue is frequently a reason for issuing long-term debt.

Table 2.3 provides a summary of the three views of municipal market equilibrium that have been described in this section. It outlines their

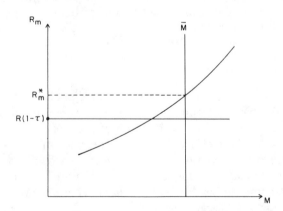

Fig. 2.3   The demand curve for municipal debt, different equilibrium models

Table 2.3   **Summary of Alternative Models of Municipal Market Equilibrium**

| | Effect on taxable–tax exempt yield spread (by maturity) | | | | | |
| | Increasing stock of municipal debt | | Raising corporate tax rates | | Raising personal tax rates | |
Equilibrium model	Short	Long	Short	Long	Short	Long
Bank arbitrage model	none	none	↓	↓	none	none
Miller Model I ($\tau_e = 0$)	none	none	↓	↓	none*	none*
Miller Model II ($\tau_e \neq 0$)	↑	↑	↓	↓	↓	↓
Preferred habitat model	none	↑	↓	?	none	↓

*Some personal tax changes could have an effect by eliminating the provisions of the tax code which Miller and Scholes (1978) argue permit investors to reduce their equity tax burden to zero.

predictions for how tax changes and changes in the stock of municipal debt affect yield spreads. The shape of the demand curve for municipal debt under each of the competing hypotheses is shown in figure 2.3. The horizontal demand curves for municipal securities correspond to either the bank arbitrage model or Miller Model I. The upward-sloping demand curve reflects either the preferred habitat model at long maturities or Miller Model II. The next two sections develop empirical tests that try to distinguish between these views.

2.3 Empirical Methods

The competing views of the municipal market can be tested by examining the reaction of long- and short-term yield spreads to changes in expectations about tax policy. Changes in current corporate tax rates should affect short-term yield spreads under all views. Miller Model II and the preferred habitat theory suggest that movements in expected personal tax rates should show up in long-term yield differentials, while the bank arbitrage model and Miller Model I suggest that only changes in future corporate rates should affect long-term yields. This section describes my procedure for analyzing the impact of expected tax changes on yield spreads.

2.3.1 Asset Pricing Framework

In equilibrium, newly issued T-period bonds with a par value of one dollar and a tax-exempt coupon C^m will sell at par if

$$(6) \qquad 1 = \sum_{j=0}^{T} (1 + \rho)^{-j} C^m + (1 + \rho)^{-T}$$

where ρ is the nominal after-tax discount rate applied to the bond's income stream. Similarly, a taxable bond selling at par must satisfy the condition

$$(7) \qquad 1 = \sum_{j=0}^{T} (1 + \rho)^{-j}(1 - \theta_j^e)C^t + (1 + \rho)^{-T}$$

where C^t is the taxable coupon and θ_j^e is the expected marginal tax rate of the marginal holder of this bond in period j. This tax rate could change over the life of the bond in either of two ways. The tax code might change, altering θ_j for the bond's initial owner, or the owner of the bond might change, as when a household purchases a long-term new-issue bond and sells it to a bank when its remaining maturity is five years. For bonds that are sold at par, the yield to maturity (y) equals the coupon rate, so $y^t = C^t$ and $y^m = C^m$.

The asset pricing equations can be linearized, following standard procedures from term-structure studies, to calculate the effect of a tax change on each bond's yield to maturity. My analysis assumes that the discount rate, ρ, is unaffected by the tax change. This is an oversimplification, since major reforms in either the corporate or personal tax system are likely to affect the after-tax return available to investors.[11] The yield to maturity on a tax-exempt bond must equal ρ, so by assumption the tax change will have no effect on the required municipal coupon rate. Changes in expected tax rates will, however, affect the required coupon on taxable bonds selling at par. By differentiating (7), we find

$$(8) \qquad \frac{dy^t}{d\theta_j^e} = \frac{dC^t}{d\theta_j^e} = \frac{(1 + \rho)^{-j}C^t}{\sum_{k=0}^{T} (1 + \rho)^{-k}(1 - \theta_k^e)} = w_j.$$

The change in the taxable yield to maturity from one period to the next is

$$(9) \qquad dy^t = \sum_{j=0}^{T} w_j d\theta_j^e .$$

The implied tax rate computed by comparing taxable and tax-exempt yields at maturity T is defined to be θ_T^t, where

$$(10) \qquad \theta_T^t = (y_T^t - y_T^m)/y_T^t .$$

Changes in the implied tax rate can be linked to changes in expected future tax rates using (9):

$$(11) \qquad d\theta_T^I = \frac{y_T^m}{(y_T^t)^2} \cdot dy_T^t = \sum_{j=0}^{T} z_j d\theta_j^e$$

where

$$(12)$$
$$z_j = \frac{(1 - \theta_T^I)(1 + \rho)^{-j}}{\sum_{k=0}^{T} (1 - \theta_k^e)(1 + \rho)^{-k}} = \frac{C^t(1 - \theta_T^I)(1 + \rho)^{-j}}{1 - (1 + \rho)^{-T}} = \frac{C^m(1 + \rho)^{-j}}{1 - (1 + \rho)^{-T}}.$$

In the special case of a consol, the expression for $d\theta^I$ becomes

$$(13) \qquad d\theta_\infty^I = \rho \sum_{j=0}^{\infty} (1 + \rho)^{-j} d\theta_j^e$$

which is just a discounted sum of changes in expected future tax rates.

The change in the implied tax rate can also be written in terms of holding period returns on taxable and tax-exempt bonds. In the fixed discount rate case, the price of a taxable consol is $P_\infty^t = 1/y_\infty^t$ and the expression for θ_∞^I becomes

$$(14) \qquad \theta_\infty^I = 1 - \frac{y_\infty^m}{y_\infty^t} = 1 - \frac{P_\infty^t}{P_\infty^m}.$$

Therefore the change in the implied tax rate is proportional to the return on the taxable consol, since

$$(15) \qquad d\theta_\infty^I = - \frac{dP_\infty^t}{P_\infty^t} \cdot \frac{P_\infty^t}{P_\infty^m}.$$

where dP_∞^t/P_∞^t is the holding period return. If the discount rate were allowed to vary, $d\theta_\infty^I$ would be proportional to the difference in the holding period returns on municipal and taxable consols.

If it were possible to obtain reliable estimates of $\{d\theta_j^e\}_{j=1}^T$ then (11) would provide a basis for empirical investigation. We could estimate regression models of the form

$$(16) \qquad \Delta\theta_T^I = \alpha + \beta \left[\sum_{j=0}^{T} z_j \Delta\theta_j^e\right] + \epsilon$$

to test whether changes in expected personal or corporate tax rates altered the yield spreads on taxable and tax-exempt bonds. Alternative measures of θ_j^e could be constructed from forecasts of the future course of personal, and corporate, tax policy. Evidence that changes in expected personal tax rates influenced the taxable–tax exempt yield spread would contradict the bank arbitrage model and Miller Model I.

The dependent variable in equation (16) is readily observable; it is the change in the implied tax rate between two periods. Unfortunately, the independent variable depends upon the path of tax expectations over a long horizon. These are difficult, if not impossible, to measure. Several problems are particularly acute. First, it is necessary to distinguish between permanent and temporary tax reforms. Transitory tax changes will have smaller effects on long-term yields than permanent changes, and it is therefore essential to specify the horizon over which investors expect tax reforms to persist. Second, the marginal tax rates that determine θ^I may depend on both the tax code and the *distribution of wealth* by tax brackets. Changes in the highest marginal personal tax rates, without any movement in lower bracket rates or in the distribution of wealth, might have no effect on the yield spread. Forecasting the distribution of wealth across tax rates is also rather difficult. A final problem in constructing $\Delta\theta_j^e$ is predicting the debt-supply behavior of municipal governments. A smaller yield spread between taxable and tax-exempt yields, possibly induced by tax reform, might reduce the total amount of municipal debt marketed by states and localities. In some models this could change the tax rate of the marginal investor. Since there is at present little evidence on how municipal debt supply responds to interest rates, these predictions would again be subject to great uncertainty.

Rather than trying to construct a measure of $\sum_{j=0}^{T} z_j \Delta\theta_j^e$ for each month, this paper adopts a simpler but less powerful testing strategy. By examining news accounts of tax policy debates, it is possible to identify months when investors should have revised their expectations of future tax rates. These months can be classified into those in which there would have most likely been positive and negative revisions. Indicator variables for these months are then included in regression models for the movements in implied tax rates at various maturities. If changes in expected future personal tax rates do affect the yield spread, then these indicator variables should have significant effects and their signs should accord with the direction of movement in tax expectations.

The principal empirical difficulty that arises in implementing this procedure is deciding what tax expectations were *before* news arrived. The passage of a tax bill raising interest income tax rates might increase expected future tax rates. However, if investors expected the increase in tax rates to be larger than those that were actually approved, then the final passage of a higher-taxes bill might in fact *reduce* expected future tax rates. There is no easy way to resolve problems of this type, and the results presented below should therefore be interpreted with some caution. The remainder of this section describes how tax policy "events" were identified and their effects on expectations assessed. It then discusses the econometric specification of my estimating equations.

2.3.2 Data Description: Tax Policy Events

To identify tax policy events during the last thirty years, I searched through the annual indexes to the *New York Times* and read the sections on Federal Income Taxation and Government Bonds. My first reading was confined to items that appeared in boldface type. Whenever a potentially significant tax policy announcement was encountered, I searched backward in time to see if previous months had contained similar but less highly publicized information. My search revealed numerous events that could have changed expectations of tax rates, and it was necessary to make subjective judgements about which ones to investigate further. I pursued those that seemed most important by examining the *Congressional Quarterly Weekly Report* for each year to look for related events that might not have been reported in the *New York Times.* The resulting series of monthly tax events should provide a rough chronology of times when tax policy was expected to change.

The set of tax events I considered most significant, along with a brief description of each, is reported in table 2.4. The events vary in their character and importance. Some are proposed IRS rulings on the tax treatment of municipal interest payments, others are developments during congressional debates, and still others are announcements of plans for far-reaching changes in the tax structure. The events I consider to be of the greatest significance with respect to tax expectations are identified with an asterisk; they are the principal events I analyze in the next section. However, further results involving all of the tax events are reported in the appendix.

The important tax events divide into five major groups: those surrounding the Kennedy-Johnson tax cut; the Vietnam War tax surcharge; the 1969 Tax Reform Act's proposed changes in the tax treatment of municipal interest; the Reagan tax cut; and several changes in the tax treatment of banks. While it is difficult to obtain information on the relative importance of the different tax events, a brief account of each is provided below.

The 1964 tax cut had been discussed by officials in the Kennedy administration beginning in 1962 and was proposed in the 1963 State of the Union speech. It reduced the top marginal tax rate on individuals from 91% to 70%, although its effect on tax rates below the maximum was less dramatic. The weighted average marginal dividend tax rate series computed by Estrella and Fuhrer (1983) declined by 6.5 percentage points between 1963 and 1965. The 1964 Act also lowered corporate tax rates from 52% to 48% over a two-year period. Both

Table 2.4   **Tax Policy Events, 1955–84**

Month	Tax policy event	Bank arbitrage/ Miller Model I	Preferred habitat/ Miller Model II
		Predicted effect on implied tax rate	
May 1959	Rep. Wilbur Mills proposes to hold hearings to broaden the tax base.	–	–
*May–June 1962	Treasury Secretary Dillon and President Kennedy advocate reductions in tax rates, especially at top rates.	0	–
September 1962	Keogh-Smathers bill signed into law allowing self-employed individuals to maintain tax-favored retirement plans.	0	–
*January 1963	President Kennedy proposes tax cut in State of the Union message.	–	–
January 1964	President Johnson asks Congress for urgent action to pass tax-cut proposal.	–	–
February 1964	Tax cut passes Congress and is signed into law; top marginal tax rates reduced from 91% to 70%.	–	–
*January 1967	President Johnson asks for a tax surcharge to stem inflation and finance Vietnam War.	+	+
May 1968	Surtax plan passes Congress.	+	+
*June 1968	Final passage of surtax plan.	+	+
*March 1969	Several members of House Ways and Means Committee announce intention of changing the taxation of municipal interest.	–	–
*July 1969	House Ways and Means Committee passes minimum tax provision including municipal interest in tax base.	–	–
*September 1969	Senator Russell Long and Finance Committee members express opposition to House treatment of tax-exempt interest in minimum tax provision.	+	+
December 1969	Passage of 1969 Tax Act with surtax extended for part of 1970.	+	+
July 1974	House Ways and Means Committee passes bill reducing top marginal tax rate on unearned income to 50%.	0	–

Table 2.4   (continued)

| Month | Tax policy event | Predicted effect on implied tax rate | |
		Bank arbitrage/ Miller Model I	Preferred habitat/ Miller Model II
January 1978	Carter proposes tax reforms that would raise tax rates on high-income groups.	0	+
*June 1980	At a major press conference, candidate Reagan explains his 30% tax reduction plan with across-the-board tax cuts.	0	−
*November 1980	Election of Ronald Reagan raises the probability of major tax reductions.	0	−
*December 1980	IRS rules that commercial banks may not deduct interest expenses on borrowing used for holding municipal debt.	(−)	0
*January 1981	IRS reverses ruling on bank tax treatment regarding municipal interest.	(+)	0
*February 1981	Reagan proposes tax cut.	0	−
*August 1981	Tax cut passes with provisions for IRAs, Keoghs, and All-Savers certificates, reduces maximum marginal tax rate on unearned income to 50%.	0	−
*August 1982	TEFRA restricts access to tax-deferred savings vehicles, changes interest deduction rules on banks, makes municipal interest subject to tax for some Social Security recipients	(+)	+

NOTE: These tax events were identified by scanning the pages of the *New York Times Index* and the *Congressional Quarterly Weekly Report*. Events preceded by an asterisk are those that were considered to be most significant in their effects on tax expectations. The events in December 1980, January 1981, and August 1982 have no effect under Miller Model I, but have the effect indicated in parentheses for the bank arbitrage model.

Miller models as well as the bank arbitrage view therefore predict that these changes should have affected the relative pricing of taxable and tax-exempt debt.

President Johnson's Vietnam War surtax was first proposed in January 1967, but it did not receive congressional approval until June 1968.

There was a 5% surtax on both corporate and individual income tax liability in 1968, a 10% surtax in 1969, and a 2.5% surtax in 1970. I focus principally on the proposal of the surtax in 1967, and its effect on tax expectations. Okun (1971), in his study of consumption responses to the surtax, argues that "influenced in part by the history of the Korean war 'temporary' taxation, American citizens typically were skeptical that the tax surcharge would actually expire in a short time" (p. 178). This suggests that the surtax may have had larger effects than would ordinarily be associated with a three-year tax increase. Since the surtax altered both individual and corporate tax rates, it is again difficult to distinguish between the different models using this tax reform.

The third set of tax events that impinge upon municipal bond yields involve the Tax Reform Act of 1969. Early in 1969, several members of the House Ways and Means Committee indicated informally their intention of reforming the tax treatment of municipal interest payments. The Treasury Department proposed a plan for a minimum tax, which included interest on municipal bonds in the definition of income subject to minimum tax. The Ways and Means Committee passed legislation to this effect in July, and revised tax treatment of municipal interest seemed likely until September, when Senate hearings began and Senator Russell Long and members of the Senate Finance Committee made their intention of preserving tax-exempt interest well known. The popular wisdom at the time held that the escalation of municipal interest rates was principally due to the tax reforms. The *New York Times,* in a September 1969 article, concluded that

> some of the [increase in municipal interest rates] has been caused by the general tightness in the money and capital markets. . . . More of the increase, however, appears to result from investor worries over the possibility that municipal bonds won't carry a tax advantage as attractive as they do now. Tax reform legislation has significantly undermined the traditional method for financing state and local capital needs. [7 September 1969, p. III–12]

While the immediate prospect for tax reform declined after the final provisions of the 1969 Act became clear, there were still discussions of some reform plans for some time afterward.

The 1969 reform discussion is important because it did not propose any changes in corporate tax rates. The minimum tax was to be applied to *individuals,* not firms, and corporate tax rates were largely unaffected by the Tax Reform Act. If the Miller Model I or the bank arbitrage hypothesis is correct, then there should be no change in the implied tax rates on municipal bonds as a result of the tax proposals. Miller Model II and the "preferred habitat" model, however, would both predict substantial movements in interest rate spreads as a result of these changes.

The next major tax change is President Reagan's tax cut of 1981. Ronald Reagan had discussed tax reform during the election campaign of 1980, and in a June press conference he made clear that if elected he would introduce across-the-board cuts in marginal personal tax rates. The news media at the time concluded that, regardless of the election's outcome, some type of significant tax reduction would be likely. The final tax bill reduced the highest marginal tax rate on unearned income from 70% to 50% and instituted a tax reform plan that would reduce tax rates by 26% over three years. Two of the most important 1981 tax developments, from the standpoint of the municipal bond market, did not occur until near the time of the tax bill's passage. These changes were the extension of the IRA eligibility to individuals enrolled in private pension plans, and the one-year All-Savers program. The former altered the long-run prospects for the attractiveness of municipal bonds as a source of tax sheltered income. The latter drew short-term money from municipal bond funds into savings institutions. The importance of these events led me to focus on August 1981 in my analysis of the 1981 tax cut.[12]

The 1981 tax changes were also directed primarily at the individual tax rate, and they did not substantially affect the marginal tax rates facing firms. Both the bank arbitrage model and the Miller Model I would predict no effects from the 1981 reforms, while the Miller Model II and the preferred habitat model would predict substantial movements in implied tax rates.

The final set of tax events concerns the tax treatment of banks. The first occurred in December 1980, when the IRS issued Revenue Procedure 80–55, which stated that banks would henceforth be unable to deduct interest paid on governmental time deposits that were collateralized by tax-exempt securities. If implemented, this rule would have substantially reduced the attractiveness of holding municipal debt for commercial banks (see Madeo and Pincus 1983). The rule was subsequently reversed in January 1981 after the Reagan administration took office. These two months should be characterized by changes in short-term yield spreads under all views, and long-term responses under the preferred habitat model and the bank arbitrage hypothesis. In both Miller models, corporate financial adjustments determine the equilibrium pattern of bond prices, so the tax treatment of banks is irrelevant. A less important event affecting the attractiveness of bank participation in the municipal market occurred with the passage of TEFRA in 1982, when banks were restricted to deducting only 85% of their interest payments on borrowing used to hold municipal bonds.

Determining the magnitude and direction of expectational changes is not the only problem with an "event" study of this type. We also must measure *when* expectations changed. The equations reported in the next section all assume that expectations change during the month I have labeled as the "tax event." An alternative approach would recognize that in many cases information builds gradually over time. This could be implemented by defining indicator variables for the month labeled as the tax event and either the month before or the month afterward. I experimented with these different approaches, and found that the qualitative character of my results was unaffected by them.

2.3.3 Econometric Specification

Subsections 2.3.1 and 2.3.2 have described how tax events affect the municipal yield spread. However, to provide reliable evidence on whether or not tax changes affect municipal yields, we must control for a variety of other factors that also induce movements in the yield spread. The relative riskiness of taxable and tax-exempt debt is the most important such factor.

Two techniques are used in controlling for changing risk. First, just as in the case of tax policy events, the *New York Times Index* was scanned for evidence of important events that would have affected the perceived riskiness of municipal securities. These events, which are detailed in table 2.5, included the New York City financial crisis of 1974–75 and the passage of Proposition 13 in 1978. For each risk event, an indicator variable was defined and included in the regression for changes in the implied tax rates. Increases in municipal riskiness should reduce θ^I, since higher tax-exempt interest rates would be demanded by investors. Many of the risk events proved insignificant when added to the regression equations, and they are not reported in the tables in the next section.

The relative riskiness of municipal securities also depends on other factors such as the economy's position in the business cycle and the share of state and local revenues provided through federal revenue sharing. The change in the unemployment rate, ΔUNEMPR, and the change in the share of federal grants in state and local expenditures, ΔFEDGRANT, were therefore included in some specifications. To allow for any systematic changes in the composition or riskiness of tax-exempt debt issued at different moments in the calendar year, I also included a set of monthly dummy variables in the regression equations. January was the only month that ever showed a substantial or significant coefficient, and since there are other anomalies of security behavior that are known to occur in January, I retained the January variable but left all other monthly variables out of the final specifications.[13]

The equations in the next section also include two other variables. The first, ΔSLSHARE, is the change in the fraction of total outstanding credit market debt that is accounted for by state and local obligations.

Table 2.5   **Events Affecting Municipal Bond Risk**

Month	Risk event	Predicted effect on implied tax rate
January 1970	President Nixon announces plan for revenue sharing in State of Union address.	+
November–December 1970	Expansion of size of proposed revenue-sharing plans (REVSHARE).	+
March 1972	House Ways and Means Committee approves revenue-sharing bill.	+
November–December 1974	First indications of financial distress by New York City (NYC1).	−
September 1975	Height of New York City financial crisis (NYC2).	−
June 1978	Passage of Proposition 13 in California.	−
March–May 1983	Rising concern over impact of WPPSS default and Washington State Supreme Court ruling absolving utilities of liability (WPPSS).	−

NOTE: These events were identified by examining the *New York Times Index* sections for government bonds. A more complete discussion of the two New York events may be found in Advisory Commission on Intergovernmental Relations (1976) and Hoffland (1977). The names in parentheses are used to describe these variables in subsequent tables that report regression results.

In Miller Model I and the bank arbitrage model, the quantity of state and local debt outstanding should have no impact on the implied tax rate, because offsetting changes should occur in corporate capital structures. In Miller Model II and the preferred habitat model, there could be an effect on the implied tax rate. The variable ΔSLSHARE is included as a test of these predictions.

The final variable I include is Δ(VOLATILITY), the change in an estimate of interest rate volatility. This is measured as the change in a thirty-six-month rolling estimate of the variance of tax-exempt interest rates at the maturity of the implied tax rate. It is designed to capture the changing value of the "tax trading" options on taxable and tax-exempt bonds.

The basic equation which I estimated for one-, five-, ten-, and twenty-year maturity bonds is:

$$
\Delta\theta_t^I = \beta_0 + \beta_1\Delta UNEMPR_t + \beta_2\Delta FEDGRANT_t
$$
$$
(17) \quad + \beta_3\Delta SLSHARE_t + \beta_4\Delta(VOLATILITY)_t + \beta_5 JANUARY
$$
$$
+ \sum \delta_j RISK_{jt} + \sum \gamma_k TAX_{kt} + \epsilon_t
$$

The set of variables RISK$_{jt}$ are indicator variables for risk events, and TAX$_{kt}$ are indicators for tax policy changes.

Before considering the results, two estimation issues should be mentioned. First, the data on yields to maturity are sometimes subject to errors of measurement. Salomon Brothers *estimates* the yield that would be required on a T year bond selling at par. The estimates are based on a yield curve calculated from actual bond sales. For municipals, which are typically sold in blocks including bonds of varying maturities, the yield curve may give slightly erroneous estimates for some yields. Since the dependent variable in (17) depends on the difference in yields in two consecutive months, errors in the yield data will induce a moving average error. The reported equations were all corrected for MA(1) errors using a maximum-likelihood procedure.

Second, the residuals from OLS estimation of (17) were clearly heteroscedastic over time. To allow for changing error variances, the sample was divided into twelve subsamples of equal length, twenty-nine months, and the error variance was assumed to be constant within each of these months but allowed to vary between them. The White Test reported in each column of the tables is a test (White 1980) against heteroscedasticity of this form; it always allows us to reject the null of homoscedasticity. The reported equations were estimated using a feasible GLS procedure.[14]

2.4   Regression Results

This section reports the results of analyzing the movements in implied tax rates for short- and long-term bonds during the months of major tax policy changes. Table 2.6a reports results for bonds with maturities of ten and twenty years. Results for one-year bonds are reported in table 2.6b. This section first analyzes which tax events appear to have affected the bond market substantially, and then returns to the question of which equilibrium model these results support. The tax policy events are discussed in chronological order, focusing on those events that were marked with an asterisk in table 2.4. Full sets of regression results for all tax and risk events are reported in the appendix.

2.4.1   Tax Policy Events

The initial discussions of a tax cut in 1962 seem to have induced little movement in the taxable–tax exempt yield spread. When President Kennedy asked for the tax cut in his State of the Union address in January 1963, however, there was a coincident decline in the implied long-term marginal tax rate of nearly four percentage points. This is evident in the implied tax rates on ten- and twenty-year bonds. By comparison, the yields on one-year bonds hardly responded to the

Table 2.6a   Changes in Implicit Tax Rates on Long-Maturity Bonds

Variable	Twenty-year maturity			Ten-year maturity		
	Model 1	Model 2	Model 3	Model 1	Model 2	Model 3
Constant	-0.13	-0.21	-0.21	-0.21	-0.29	-0.28
	(0.12)	(0.12)	(0.12)	(0.13)	(0.14)	(0.14)
May–June 62	-1.02	-1.00	-1.01	-1.07	-1.02	-1.01
	(0.92)	(0.93)	(0.93)	(1.35)	(1.34)	(1.34)
Jan. 63	-3.89	-3.24	-3.27	-4.49	-3.86	-3.90
	(1.36)	(1.38)	(1.38)	(1.95)	(1.95)	(1.95)
Jan. 67	4.44	4.62	4.65	6.25	6.45	6.48
	(1.29)	(1.32)	(1.32)	(1.68)	(1.69)	(1.69)
June 68	0.23	0.28	0.27	-0.10	-0.00	-0.00
	(2.48)	(2.42)	(2.42)	(2.35)	(2.33)	(2.33)
Mar. 69	-4.74	-4.50	-4.49	-3.25	-2.99	-3.00
	(2.48)	(2.43)	(2.42)	(2.35)	(2.33)	(2.33)
July 69	-6.25	-6.64	-6.60	-5.32	-5.41	-5.38
	(3.86)	(3.86)	(3.84)	(4.34)	(4.36)	(4.35)
Sept. 69	12.88	12.39	12.44	9.42	9.26	9.34
	(3.86)	(3.86)	(3.85)	(4.34)	(4.36)	(4.35)
June 80	-4.08	-3.30	-3.11	-0.03	0.81	0.97
	(1.86)	(1.84)	(1.86)	(2.15)	(2.15)	(2.18)
Nov. 80	0.11	-0.60	-0.36	-0.16	-0.74	-0.67
	(1.86)	(1.84)	(1.87)	(2.15)	(2.14)	(2.18)
Dec. 80	-3.61	-3.45	-3.26	-2.90	-2.70	-2.66
	(1.86)	(1.85)	(1.88)	(2.15)	(2.15)	(2.18)
Jan. 81	-0.42	-0.93	-0.76	-0.76	-1.02	-0.93
	(1.90)	(1.88)	(1.92)	(2.19)	(2.19)	(2.22)
Feb. 81	0.58	0.16	0.34	0.50	0.25	0.37
	(1.86)	(1.84)	(1.88)	(2.15)	(2.15)	(2.18)
Aug. 81	-6.62	-6.73	-6.24	-6.32	-6.23	-5.90
	(3.29)	(3.16)	(3.14)	(2.52)	(2.48)	(2.45)

Table 2.6a   (continued)

Variable	Twenty-year maturity			Ten-year maturity		
	Model 1	Model 2	Model 3	Model 1	Model 2	Model 3
Aug. 82	3.71	4.38	4.04	4.10	4.74	4.58
	(3.29)	(3.16)	(3.15)	(2.52)	(2.48)	(2.43)
REVSHARE	3.99	4.76	4.77	3.79	4.31	4.29
	(2.73)	(2.74)	(2.73)	(3.07)	(3.09)	(3.08)
NYC1	-8.40	-6.51	-6.65	-3.13	-1.02	-1.17
	(3.82)	(3.80)	(3.80)	(3.62)	(3.69)	(3.71)
NYC2	-3.75	-3.87	-3.82	2.58	2.42	2.45
	(2.70)	(2.61)	(2.61)	(2.55)	(2.52)	(2.52)
WPPSS	-0.81	-0.50	-0.74	-1.32	-1.21	-1.35
	(1.90)	(1.84)	(1.83)	(1.46)	(1.45)	(1.43)
JANUARY	2.04	2.10	2.10	2.07	2.06	2.06
	(0.43)	(0.43)	(0.43)	(0.46)	(0.46)	(0.46)
ΔUNEMP	—	-1.45	-1.34	—	-1.31	-1.15
		(0.61)	(0.62)		(0.66)	(0.68)
ΔSHARESL	—	-7.27	-7.57	—	-4.48	-4.67
		(3.79)	(3.81)		(3.96)	(3.97)
ΔFEDGRANT	—	-0.11	-0.13	—	0.01	-0.00
		(0.34)	(0.34)		(0.36)	(0.36)
ΔVOLATILITY	—	—	-1.34	—	—	-1.34
			(1.98)			(2.10)
θ	0.32	0.36	0.37	0.39	0.40	0.41
	(0.05)	(0.05)	(0.05)	(0.05)	(0.05)	(0.05)
R^2	0.23	0.25	0.25	0.18	0.20	0.20
D.W.	2.02	2.02	2.01	2.01	2.00	2.00
SEE	0.98	0.97	0.97	0.96	0.95	0.95
White Test	38.47	40.42	40.42	43.31	44.29	44.62

NOTE: All equations are estimated for the period 1955:1–1983:12, a total of 348 monthly observations. Equations are estimated allowing for a first-order moving average error structure, with MA parameter θ, with a correction for heteroscedasticity. Standard errors are shown in parentheses.

Table 2.6b   **Changes in Implicit Tax Rates on One-Year Bonds**

Variable	Model 1	Model 2	Model 3
Constant	−0.15	−0.24	−0.22
	(0.16)	(0.17)	(0.17)
May–June 62	0.67	0.72	0.71
	(1.08)	(1.02)	(1.02)
Jan. 63	−0.11	−0.11	−0.66
	(1.62)	(1.57)	(1.57)
Jan. 67	10.15	10.40	10.60
	(2.03)	(2.07)	(2.08)
June 68	−1.05	−0.93	−1.10
	(2.89)	(2.94)	(2.94)
Mar. 69	−5.96	−5.42	−5.41
	(2.89)	(2.94)	(2.95)
July 69	1.93	1.86	2.20
	(3.75)	(3.67)	(3.62)
Sept. 69	4.11	3.63	4.29
	(3.75)	(3.67)	(3.63)
June 80	−3.59	−3.66	−3.09
	(2.71)	(2.82)	(2.69)
Nov. 80	0.08	−0.42	−1.25
	(2.71)	(2.82)	(2.69)
Dec. 80	−4.89	−5.56	−6.26
	(2.71)	(2.83)	(2.70)
Jan. 81	3.36	2.99	2.80
	(2.78)	(2.88)	(2.75)
Feb. 81	2.37	2.16	2.58
	(2.71)	(2.82)	(2.69)
Aug. 81	−6.46	−6.91	−6.79
	(3.06)	(3.07)	(3.05)
Aug. 82	4.26	4.34	3.19
	(3.06)	(3.07)	(3.06)
REVSHARE	1.69	2.07	1.78
	(2.65)	(2.61)	(2.58)
NYC1	0.12	−1.67	−1.23
	(5.75)	(5.92)	(5.88)
NYC2	1.21	1.06	0.47
	(4.06)	(4.09)	(4.06)
WPSS	−1.99	−1.26	0.02
	(1.77)	(1.80)	(1.85)
JANUARY	0.47	0.61	0.74
	(0.62)	(0.62)	(0.62)
ΔUNEMPR	−	0.64	1.04
		(0.87)	(0.87)
ΔSHARESL	−	−10.76	−11.30
		(5.63)	(5.62)

Table 2.6b   (continued)

Variable	Model 1	Model 2	Model 3
ΔFEDGRANT	–	0.28	0.20
		(0.53)	(0.53)
ΔVOLATILITY	–	–	– 8.63
			(3.70)
θ	0.38	0.38	0.38
	(0.05)	(0.05)	(0.05)
R^2	0.14	0.15	0.16
D.W.	1.93	1.94	1.94
SEE	0.97	0.97	0.97
White Test	54.47	54.43	54.94

NOTE: All equations are estimated for the period 1955:1–1983:12, a total of 348 monthly observations. Equations are estimated allowing for a first-order moving average error structure, with MA parameter θ, with a correction for heteroscedasticity. Standard errors are shown in parentheses.

proposed tax cut; the implied tax rate on one-year bonds changed by less than one percentage point. This suggests that the market reacted to changing expectations about the long-run course of tax policy, but recognized that because of implementation lags, reforms were not likely to occur immediately. The magnitude of the implied tax rate change, four percentage points, is close to the proposed change in corporate tax rates and somewhat smaller than the change in measures of personal tax burden such as weighted average dividend or interest income tax rates. Since the tax bill proposed by President Kennedy reduced both personal and corporate tax rates, all of the equilibrium models proposed in section 2.2 predict movements in implied tax rates. The finding that bond prices adjusted supports the notion that tax expectations affect the yield spread, but does not help distinguish between the competing views.

The bond price effects of the initial announcement of President Johnson's surtax plan are also pronounced. In January 1967 the implied long-term tax rate rose by over 4%. This coefficient is statistically significant at all standard levels. President Johnson's proposed surtax, in spite of its explicitly temporary nature, had as large an impact on the yield spread as the announced 1963–64 tax cut; this is somewhat puzzling. It may suggest that taxpayers perceived the far-reaching Kennedy reforms to be no more than a transitory event, or that they suspected that the surtax might last for a long while. The short-term municipal market also reacted to the tax-cut plan, again by "too much" to be explained by tax expectations alone. The implied tax rate on one-year bonds rose by more than ten percentage points in January 1967.

This may reflect the expectation of bondholders that a large tax increase would be enacted swiftly, as part of an emergency war finance program. Even if it were expected to pass immediately, however, the magnitude of the short-term yield effect is larger than can plausibly be attributed to taxes alone. Like the 1964 change, the 1967 reform affected both personal and corporate tax rates and it therefore has little power to distinguish between the different models of municipal yield determination.

The tax reform discussions of 1969 provide more convincing evidence that personal tax changes affect yield spreads in the tax-exempt bond market. The initial proposals for changing the tax status of municipal interest, in March 1969, coincided with sharp declines in the implied tax rates in all markets. The tax rate computed from twenty-year bonds fell by 4.5 percentage points, while that on ten-year bonds fell by 3%. Short bonds also responded dramatically, with the tax rate changing by almost six percentage points.[15] The subsequent action by the Ways and Means Committee in July 1969 had a pronounced effect on the long-term market, inducing between five- and seven- point reductions in the long-term implied tax rate, but had virtually no impact on one-year implied tax rates. In the short- term market, the implied tax rate actually rose by two percentage points during that month. The turn-about in expectations that occurred in September 1969 once again caused dramatic effects in the long-term bond market but only small movements in short-term yields. The implied tax rate on twenty-year municipal bonds rose by twelve percentage points in September; that on ten-year securities jumped nearly 10%. By comparison, short-term implied tax rates rose by only 4%.

Unlike the previous tax events, the 1969 legislative developments can help to resolve the differences between the competing models of municipal market equilibrium. All of the proposals to implement a minimum tax focused only on changing the *personal* tax code. In both the bank arbitrage model and Miller Model I, these proposals should have had no effect on the relative yields on taxable and tax-exempt debt. The finding of major changes in long-term yields coincident with these tax developments suggests that Miller Model II or the preferred habitat model may provide a better explanation of long-term yield determination than either of the models that focuses on the corporate tax rate.

The fourth major tax reform, the Reagan tax cut of 1980–81, also seems to have affected the yield spread between taxable and tax-exempt debt. However, relatively few of the events I identified prior to the passage of ERTA in 1981 had substantial effects. In June 1980, for example, when candidate Reagan announced his tax-reform plans at a press conference, the implied tax rate on twenty-year municipal bonds declined by nearly four percentage points. This could be attributed to tax expectations; however, this explanation is weakened by the finding that ten-year implied tax rates hardly declined during that month. Similarly, the effect of Reagan's electoral victory in November 1980 is weak. The signs of the coefficients on long-term implied tax rates are mixed, and none of the coefficients is close to statistically significant. The Reagan budget proposal in February 1981 evoked a similarly small response from the long-term bond market; most of the estimated coefficients are positive, not negative, as would be predicted by either of the models that focuses on personal taxes. These insignificant results during three periods when tax expectations may have changed constitute some support for the bank arbitrage model and Miller Model I. Alternatively, they may show that bond market participants considered *passage* of a tax reform plan unlikely until President Reagan's stunning victory in the House at the end of July 1981.

Support for the importance of personal tax variables comes from the coefficients on the August 1981 indicator for the passage of ERTA. All of the long-term implied tax rates decline substantially, with twenty-year bonds showing a drop of six percentage points in the value of θ^l. Smaller but statistically significant effects are recorded on the other long-term implied tax rates. Like the 1969 discussions of minimum tax, most of the provisions of the 1981 bill were directed at personal, not corporate, tax reform. The bill cut the top marginal tax rate on unearned income from 70 to 50% and also extended access to tax-exempt saving vehicles. The finding that municipal bond yields changed therefore provides some evidence for Miller Model II and the preferred habitat view. Short-term yields also rose substantially during August 1981, reducing the implied tax rate. This was probably due to the introduction of one-year All-Savers certificates, which drew funds away from commercial banks and money market mutual funds and into savings and loan institutions. This reduced commercial banks' demand for tax-exempt bonds.

The final tax events concern the tax treatment of banks. The tax event in December 1980 is the proposed IRS ruling to disallow interest deductions for bank loans that were collateralized with municipal securities. Under the bank arbitrage hypothesis, this development should have substantially lowered the implied tax rate in both long and short-term markets, since it ended the attractiveness of this form of tax-exempt income for many banks. Under both Miller models this change should have had no effect, and under the preferred habitat model, the change should have affected only short-term yields. The evidence suggests a pronounced effect on the one-year implied tax rate, a change of between six and seven percentage points, as well as small but statistically less significant effects on longer-term implied tax rates. When the change was rescinded in January 1981, however, only the short-term yield spread responded in any significant fashion. This suggests that bank participation in the municipal market is a more significant force in setting short- than long-term bond prices.

The evidence from the passage of TEFRA in August 1982, while more difficult to interpret, also suggests a role for banks. The 1982 law reduced the share of interest payments that banks could deduct on loans used to hold municipal bonds from 100% to 85%, lowering the attractiveness of holding municipal debt. Coincident with the law's passage is a widening of the yield spread between taxable and tax-exempt debt. The difficulty in interpretation arises because the law also instituted other changes that might have affected non–bank investors' demand for municipals. The law effectively taxed some Social Security recipients on municipal interest and placed restrictions on future issues of Industrial Revenue Bonds. This *could* have raised the expected future marginal tax rate on municipal interest and thereby raised the implied tax rate calculated on long-term bonds. These developments seem to support the importance of banks, especially at short maturities, in determining the yield spread.

The results in this section are summarized in table 2.7. They do not provide universal support for any single theory of how municipal interest rates are determined. However, the evidence from the 1969 Tax Reform hearings and the passage of ERTA in 1981 supports either Miller Model II or the preferred habitat hypothesis at long maturities. The absence of strong reactions to events during the 1980 election campaign and the subsequent introduction of the tax bill support the two views that regard personal taxes as irrelevant. The dramatic reaction in December 1980 to the changed IRS ruling on commercial bank deductability of taxable interest payments, especially at short maturities, supports the bank arbitrage and preferred habitat views. The preferred habitat model therefore receives the most widespread support in the data.[16]

The results on tax changes and long-term yield spreads can provide some information on the source of recent changes in the yield spread between taxable and tax-free securities. The implied tax rate on long-term bonds declined by over twenty percentage points between 1980 and 1982. Adding up the five coefficients on the tax events during the 1980–81 period suggests a total tax-related effect of about eight percentage points, between one-third and one-half of the total. This calculation is based on twenty-year bonds; analysis of ten-year bonds suggests that 24.5% of the decline may be attributable to taxes. These estimates are probably lower bounds for the true effect of taxes on yield spreads, since they neglect all of the changes that may have taken place between my "event months." Nonetheless, they suggest a sig-

Table 2.7   **Summary of Empirical Findings**

Tax Change	Predictions of Model for Implied Tax Rate:				Observed
	Bank Arbitrage Model	Miller Model I	Miller Model II	Preferred Habitat Model	
1962–63 tax cut proposal					
– short term	↓	↓	↓	↓	0
– long term	↓	↓	↓	↓	↓
1967/8 surtax					
– short term	↑	↑	↑	↑	↑
– long term	↑	↑	↑	↑	↑
1969 tax act hearings					
– short term	0	0	↓	0	↓
– long term	0	0	↓	↓	↓
1981 tax cut					
– short term	?	?	↓	?	↓
– long term	0	0	↓	↓	↓
Changes in bank taxation					
– short term	↓	↓	↓	↓	↓
– long term	↓	↓	↓	0	↓

SOURCE: Results reported in tables 2.6a and 2.6b and discussed in the text.

nificant influence of tax policy on the relative yields on taxable and tax-exempt debt.

Before examining the results for other variables included in the specifications, two important caveats should be noted. First, my event variables may have dated incorrectly the points at which expectations of market participants changed. This should bias my results on tax policy effects toward zero. Secondly, however, the low power of the event-study approach and its susceptibility to spurious factors must be emphasized. I have surely not controlled for all of the nontax influences on the tax-exempt bond market, and the results should therefore be interpreted with some caution.

2.4.2   Other Explanatory Factors

Adding variables designed to measure changes in relative riskiness over time, such as the change in the unemployment rate, did not change the conclusions about tax policy at all. The estimated coefficients for the tax event months change slightly between the three different specifications that are reported for each maturity in tables 2.6a and 2.6b, but they always suggest the same conclusions. The coefficients on the change in the unemployment rate indicate that an increase in unemployment reduces the implied tax rate on long-term bonds. If the unemployment rate rose by one percentage point during a one-month period, this would induce between a one- and two-percentage-point reduction on the implied tax rate for long-term bonds. This is consistent with the standard notion that Treasury securities are riskless but that the perceived default probability on municipal bonds, even highest-grade municipals, rises during economic downturns. This effect seems unimportant for short-maturity debt, where the coefficient on ΔUNEMPR is positive but statistically insignificant. The other variable that controls for risk, the share of state and local revenues financed through federal grants, proved insignificant in all of the estimated equations. Experiments with other risk measures, such as the yield spread between BAA and AAA corporate bonds or good- and prime-rated municipals, produced similarly insignificant results.

The indicator variables designed to measure risk events generally had their predicted signs, but most were statistically insignificant. The variable for the expansion of revenue sharing suggested a one-percentage-point reduction in the implied tax rate because of risk reduction. Both of the New York City indicator variables have statistically insignificant effects; this is not surprising given Hoffland's (1977) report that most of the municipal market jitters engendered by the New York City crisis affected state and local bonds in lower rating classes. The WPPSS default in early 1983 also had some effect on the implied yield spread, inducing a large (two-point) but statistically insignificant reduction in the implied tax rate. Again, this is not unexpected since most of the effect of the WPPSS default was on revenue bonds, not the general obligation securities used to construct my implied tax rates.

The volatility variable that was included to capture changes in tax-timing values had a negative sign in all of the estimated equations. The hypothesis that it has no effect is often impossible to reject, however, and the pattern of coefficients across different maturities is also surprising. The volatility effect through the tax-timing option should be smallest for short-maturity bonds, but the coefficient on the volatility variable is larger for short- than for long-maturity implied tax rates. Large standard errors make inferences about these coefficients difficult, however.

The final variable I included, the "supply effect" measure of the share of state and local debt in the outstanding stock of credit market debt, has a significant or nearly significant negative coefficient in nearly all of the estimated equations. This suggests that increases in the outstanding stock of municipals will lower the implied tax rate between taxable and tax-exempt bonds, providing strong evidence against both the bank arbitrage model and Miller Model I, both of which predict the irrelevance of relative supplies. A one-percentage-point increase in the quantity of municipal debt would be predicted to reduce implied tax rate on twenty-year bonds by approximately 4.7 percentage points. The estimated effects of the same change for other maturities vary between three and seven percentage points. These results are consistent with the preferred habitat model and Miller Model II, both of which allow changes in the stock of municipal debt to change the tax rate of the marginal holder of municipal bonds. Unfortunately, the lack of data on the outstanding stock of debt at different maturities precluded testing more precise hypotheses, such as whether larger issues of short-term debt depress the short-term implied tax rate.

2.5 Conclusions

This paper provides evidence that the yield spreads between long-term taxable and tax-exempt bonds respond to changes in expected future tax rates. The finding that changes in expected tax rates on individual investors alter the yield spread casts doubt on some of the theories of municipal bond pricing that have been advanced in recent years. It supports the conclusion that the municipal market is segmented, with different investor clienteles at short and long maturities.

These results shed some light on the likely effects of two proposed changes in municipal borrowing practices. The first reform calls for increased state and local use of short-term borrowing with a concommitant reduction in long-term bond issues.[17] This proposal is motivated by the upward-sloping nominal term structure of tax-exempt interest rates. In 1983, for example, the average yield on one-year prime municipal bonds was only 60% of that on twenty-year bonds. Short-term tax-exempt rates were also lower relative to comparable taxable rates. In spite of this interest rate differential, only 31% of municipal borrowing in 1983 was at maturities of less than one year, and less than 6% of the outstanding stock of state and local debt was short-term.

The potential savings from increased short-term borrowing depend crucially upon the causes of the recent increase in, and generally elevated level of, long-term tax-exempt interest rates. If long-term yields are high because of risk, which would be the explanation of the upward-sloping term structure in either the bank arbitrage model or Miller Model I, then heavier use of short-term debt would yield little reduction in borrowing costs over the life of state and local capital projects. However, the preferred habitat theory suggests that some savings might occur. If yield differentials are due partly to different tax rates facing investors in different market segments, then increased short-term borrowing could reduce borrowing costs. The findings in this paper provide some support for this view. Further research is needed to disentangle the contributions of risk, tax expectations, and other factors to the shape of the tax-exempt term structure, and to provide estimates of the expected savings from increased short-term borrowing.

A second reform proposal is the so- called taxable bond option, which would allow states and localities the option of issuing taxable debt while receiving a subsidy, equal to a fixed fraction of the bond issue, from the federal government.[18] Fama (1977) argued that this proposal would not be successful unless the subsidy rate equaled the corporate tax rate, since all deviations from $R_M = (1 - \tau)R$ are due to risk. The results in this paper, however, cast doubt on this conclusion. In either a preferred habitat or Miller Model II scenario, states and localities might choose to issue taxable debt at subsidy rates substantially below the corporate tax rate. Unfortunately, the estimates here do not provide direct measures of the required subsidy level.

These results also inform the debate on corporate capital structure and what determines debt-equity ratios. Evidence on the relative prices of taxable and tax-exempt debt contradicts the frequent assumption that the effective tax rate on equity income equals zero. In the capital structure model advanced by Merton Miller (1977), nonzero equity tax rates imply that few investors will choose to hold equity rather than corporate debt.[19] The observation that corporate capital structures are 75% equity is therefore difficult to explain in this framework.

This paper raises several important questions for future studies of municipal finance. First, the municipal debt supply decision has been left unspecified throughout this analysis. Little is known about how municipal finance officers choose between issuing debt of different maturities. Second, I have discussed plans to change real borrowing costs for states and localities without addressing the normative question of whether such a reduction should be a goal of public policy.[20] States' and localities' capital expenditures are twice subsidized relative to private capital, through both tax-exempt finance and the income-tax deductability of property taxes. However, many of the benefits from provision of public capital, such as schools or roads, accrue to individuals outside the jurisdiction that provides them. The optimal degree of subsidy vis-à-vis private capital may therefore be greater than, or less than, that currently provided. Finally, the evidence presented here suggests that some of the current proposals to reform municipal financing policies could affect the real cost of public borrowing. Numerical estimates of these effects are still needed.

Table 2A.1   Regression Results Including All Tax Events

Variables	Maturity class			
	Twenty years	Ten years	Five years	One year
Constant	−0.14	−0.22	−0.23	−0.14
	(0.12)	(0.13)	(0.14)	(0.17)
May 59	−2.34	−0.85	−0.55	−2.74
	(3.33)	(4.02)	(5.09)	(8.31)
May/June 62	−0.99	−1.10	1.44	0.66
	(0.92)	(1.38)	(1.08)	(1.09)
Sept. 62	1.02	2.10	−0.76	−1.21
	(1.29)	(1.95)	(1.52)	(1.53)
Jan. 63	−4.04	−4.77	−3.16	0.20
	(1.37)	(2.00)	(1.60)	(1.67)
Jan. 64	−0.58	−0.02	−0.60	1.14
	(1.37)	(2.00)	(1.60)	(1.67)
Feb. 64	1.37	0.23	1.93	0.86
	(1.29)	(1.95)	(1.52)	(1.53)
Jan. 67	4.32	6.00	3.67	10.39
	(1.34)	(1.72)	(2.15)	(2.09)
May 68	−1.14	−0.68	−0.33	−2.71
	(2.52)	(2.36)	(2.11)	(2.87)
June 68	0.64	0.25	0.92	0.03
	(2.52)	(2.36)	(2.11)	(2.87)
Mar. 69	−4.76	−3.28	−5.42	−5.94
	(2.52)	(2.36)	(2.11)	(2.87)
July 69	−6.35	−5.38	−5.69	1.93
	(3.94)	(4.35)	(3.73)	(3.79)
Sept. 69	12.93	9.84	11.90	4.13
	(3.94)	(4.35)	(3.73)	(3.79)
Dec. 69	−1.53	−0.56	2.79	0.77
	(3.94)	(4.35)	(3.73)	(3.79)
Jan. 70	−0.28	4.97	2.61	3.80
	(3.97)	(4.37)	(3.77)	(3.85)
REVSHARE	3.83	3.45	3.55	1.31
	(2.79)	(3.07)	(2.64)	(2.68)
Mar. 72	0.04	−0.82	1.94	8.84
	(2.79)	(2.89)	(2.51)	(3.79)
July 74	0.77	0.87	2.53	0.61
	(2.69)	(2.56)	(2.76)	(4.14)
NYC1	−8.18	−3.14	−1.02	−0.17
	(3.81)	(3.63)	(3.90)	(5.87)

Table 2A.1   (continued)

Variables	Maturity class			
	Twenty years	Ten years	Five years	One year
NYC2	−3.67	2.68	0.70	1.30
	(2.69)	(2.56)	(2.76)	(4.14)
Jan. 78	−0.91	−2.68	−3.06	−2.66
	(1.79)	(1.45)	(1.69)	(2.90)
June 78	0.30	−0.13	−0.17	2.12
	(1.74)	(1.37)	(1.61)	(2.82)
June 80	−4.07	0.01	0.77	−3.66
	(1.90)	(2.20)	(2.55)	(2.78)
Nov. 80	0.14	−0.14	0.04	0.21
	(1.90)	(2.20)	(2.55)	(2.78)
Dec. 80	−3.58	−2.96	−4.31	−5.55
	(1.90)	(2.20)	(2.55)	(2.78)
Jan. 81	1.57	1.04	1.07	3.12
	(1.95)	(2.25)	(2.60)	(2.86)
Feb. 81	0.60	0.48	0.48	2.10
	(1.90)	(2.20)	(2.55)	(2.78)
Aug. 81	−6.58	−6.29	−4.80	−6.43
	(3.36)	(2.59)	(2.78)	(3.14)
Aug. 82	3.78	4.18	6.05	4.19
	(3.36)	(2.59)	(2.78)	(3.14)
WPPSS	−0.92	−1.40	−2.17	−2.10
	(1.94)	(1.50)	(1.61)	(1.82)
JANUARY	2.21	2.30	2.12	0.21
	(0.48)	(0.50)	(0.56)	(0.71)
θ	0.34	0.40	0.49	0.39
	(0.05)	(0.05)	(0.05)	(0.05)
R^2	0.23	0.20	0.17	0.16
D.W.	2.00	2.00	1.95	1.89
SEE	1.00	0.98	0.96	1.00
White Test	33.44	40.59	43.71	54.94

NOTE: All equations are estimated for the period 1955:1–1983:12, a total of 348 monthly observations. Equations are estimated allowing for a first-order moving average error structure, with MA parameter θ, with a correction for heteroscedasticity. Standard errors are shown in parentheses. Equations reported here correspond to those in Model I of tables 2.6a and 2.6b in the text.

Notes

1. Arak and Guentner (1983) discuss several of these explanations.
2. Other recent studies such as Trczinka (1982) and Kidwell and Trczinka (1982) have compared the yields on prime municipals with AAA-rated corporate bonds. However, their corporate bond data are only available since 1970, and that would eliminate many interesting tax changes from the sample period. The corporate-municipal yield spread is also more sensitive to varying risk differentials than the yield spread between Treasury bonds and municipals.
3. Schaefer (1977) discusses several problems associated with yields to maturity in situations when the return on a bond is not proportional to its coupon payment.
4. Reference to tables 5 and 9 in Constantinides and Ingersoll (1984) suggests that changes in coupon rates and interest rate volatilities, while they can substantially alter the value of the tax timing option, do not lead to large changes in the relative values of the options on taxable and tax-exempt bonds.
5. Yawitz, Maloney, and Ederington (1985) estimate default probabilities for municipal debt of more than 1% per year. This is inconsistent with the history of municipal defaults, reported for example in ACIR (1976). The annual default probability on a prime municipal would have to have risen by almost 2% between 1980 and 1982 to explain the narrowing taxable–tax exempt yield spread. A newly issued twenty-year bond would therefore have had at least a 35% chance of defaulting during its lifetime; this seems implausibly large.
6. A discussion of commercial bank behavior may be found in Proctor and Donahoo (1983).
7. My discussion of municipal debt in the Miller Model draws heavily on Auerbach and King (1983) and McDonald (1983). A related discussion may be found in Buser and Hess (1984).
8. The figure assumes that $\tau_e = \gamma m$, for some γ. This would be the case if capital gains were untaxed, dividends were taxed at the interest tax rate, and γ were the dividend-payout ratio. Auerbach and King (1983) present a figure similar to my figure 2.1; an error in their diagram relating to the intersection of the tax-exempt and corporate equity return lines is corrected in my figure.
9. Jensen and Meckling (1976) and Buser and Hess (1984) discuss the agency and contracting costs associated with different financial choices.
10. Data on the fraction of tax-exempt borrowing at different maturities was obtained from the "Decade of Municipal Financing" tables published periodically in the *Weekly Bond Buyer*.
11. When the discount rate is allowed to change, the conclusion that municipal bond prices remain constant in the face of a tax change would no longer follow. If there were a fixed world pretax interest rate and the discount rate equaled $(1 - m)$ times this rate, then taxable bond prices would be unaffected by tax changes and municipal bond prices would adjust.
12. The passage of Reagan's tax bill in the House occurred on July 29, 1981. Since the bond market would not have reacted to this news until the thirtieth, and since the Salomon Brothers data would be for yields *reported* on the first of August (i.e., trades from the thirty-first), there is a substantial risk that the information associated with the tax cut is not included in the recorded August 1 yield. That is why I focus on the August event for ERTA; that is also the month during which actual passage occurred.
13. The "January effect" in the municipal bond market causes an increase in the implied tax rate; this would correspond to a decline in the relative price of municipal bonds.
14. The GLS procedure was implemented by estimating separate residual variances for each twenty-nine-month period, using the homoscedastic OLS residuals, and then dividing each observation by the square root of the estimated variance for its data period.
15. The pronounced effect of the personal tax change in the short-term market may be due to the binding nature of Regulation Q during 1969. Skelton (1983) argues that during periods when Regulation Q was binding, banks were not the marginal investors in the short-term municipal market.

16. Campbell (1980) argues against the segmentation view by claiming that bank behavior is uncorrelated with the municipal-taxable yield spread. However, he ignores the simultaneous determination of prices and quantities: under the pure Miller model, the yield spread would not vary but bank behavior would change often, leading to zero correlation!

17. This proposal for short-term borrowing and several related plans are described in Beek (1982).

18. A summary of arguments for and against the taxable bond option, along with much discussion, may be found in Mussa and Kormendi (1979).

19. The principal difficulty with the Miller model is that explaining the large outstanding stock of corporate equity is difficult when only investors for whom $(1 - \tau)(1 - \tau_e) \geq (1 - m)$ should hold equity. With $\tau = .46$ and m reaching its maximum at .50, only very low tax rates on equity are consistent with equity holding.

20. Gordon and Slemrod (1983) discuss some of the issues concerning the size of public capital stock, and assess the distributional effects of changing the tax exemption of municipal bonds.

References

Advisory Commission on Intergovernmental Relations. 1976. *Understanding the market for state and local debt.* Washington, D.C.: ACIR.

Arak, M., and K. Guentner. 1983. The market for tax-exempt issues. *National Tax Journal* 36:145–63.

Auerbach, A., and M. King. 1983. Taxation, portfolio choice, and debt-equity ratios: A general equilibrium model. *Quarterly Journal of Economics* 98:587–609.

Beek, D. C. 1982. Rethinking tax- exempt financing for state and local governments. *Federal Reserve Bank of New York Quarterly Review* 7 (Autumn): 30–41.

Buser, S. A., and P. J. Hess. 1984. Corporate finance and the relative yields on taxable and tax exempt securities. Unpublished manuscript, University of Chicago.

Campbell, T. S. 1980. On the extent of segmentation in the municipal securities market. *Journal of Money Credit and Banking* 12:71–83.

Constantinides, G., and J. Ingersoll. 1984. Optimal bond trading with personal taxes. *Journal of Financial Economics* 13:299–336.

Estrella, A., and J. Fuhrer. 1983. Average marginal tax rates for U.S. household interest and dividend income, 1954–1980. NBER Working Paper no. 1201.

Fama, E. 1977. A pricing model for the municipal bond market. Unpublished manuscript, University of Chicago.

Feenberg, D. 1981. Does the investment interest limitation explain the existence of dividends? *Journal of Financial Economics* 9:265–69.

Gordon, R., and B. Malkiel. 1981. Corporation finance. In *How taxes affect economic behavior,* ed. H. J. Aaron and J. A. Pechman. Washington: Brookings Institution.

Gordon, R., and J. Slemrod. 1983. A general equilibrium simulation study of subsidies to municipal expenditures. *Journal of Finance* 38:585–94.

Hendershott, P., and T. Koch. 1977. *An empirical analysis of the market for tax exempt securities.* New York: Center for Study of Financial Institutions, New York University.

Hoffland, D. 1977. The "New York City Effect" in the municipal bond market. *Financial Analysts Journal* 33 (March/April):36–39.

Jensen, M., and W. Meckling. 1976. Theory of the firm: Managerial behavior, agency costs, and ownership structure. *Journal of Financial Economics* 3:305–60.

Kidwell, D., and C. Trzcinka. 1982. Municipal bond pricing and the New York City fiscal crisis. *Journal of Finance* 37:1239–46.

McDonald, R. L. 1983. Government debt and private leverage: An extension of the Miller theorem. *Journal of Public Economics* 22:303–25.

Madeo, S., and M. Pincus. 1983. Economic consequences of a tax rule. Unpublished working paper, Department of Accounting, Washington University.

Miller, M. H. 1977. Debt and taxes. *Journal of Finance* 32:261–75.

Miller, M. H., and M. Scholes. 1978. Dividends and taxes. *Journal of Financial Economics* 6:333–64.

———. 1982. Dividends and taxes: Some empirical evidence. *Journal of Political Economy* 90:1118–42.

Mussa, M., and R. Kormendi. 1979. *The taxation of municipal bonds.* Washington: American Enterprise Institute.

Okun, A. 1971. The personal tax surcharge and consumer demand, 1968–1970. *Brookings Papers on Economic Activity* 1:1971.

Poterba, J., and L. Summers. 1985. The economic effects of dividend taxation. In *Recent Advances in Corporate Finance,* ed. E. Altman and M. Subrahmanyam. Homewood, Illinois: Richard D. Irwin.

Proctor, A. J., and K. K. Donahoo. 1983. Commercial bank investment in municipal securities. *Federal Reserve Bank of New York Quarterly Review* 8 (Winter):26–37.

Salomon Brothers. 1984. *Analytical Record of Yields and Yields Spreads.* New York: Salomon Brothers.

Schaefer, S. M. 1977. The trouble with yields to maturity. *Financial Analysts' Journal* 33 (July/August):59–67.

Skelton, J. L. 1983. The relative pricing of tax exempt and taxable debt. *Journal of Financial Economics* 12:343–56.

Trzcinka, C. 1982. The pricing of tax-exempt bonds and the Miller hypothesis. *Journal of Finance* 37:907–23.

White, H. 1980. A heteroscedasticity-consistent covariance matrix estimator and a direct test for heteroscedasticity. *Econometrica* 48:817–38.

Yawitz, J., K. Maloney, and L. Ederington. 1985. Taxes, default risk, and yields spreads. *Journal of Finance* 40:1127–41.

Comment   Douglas Holtz-Eakin

The major question addressed by Poterba's paper is: Can we explain recent declines in the taxable versus tax-exempt yield spread by appealing to anticipated reductions in tax rates? The coincidence of Reagan's election and tax cut with a substantial narrowing of the yield spread is a strong temptation for the casual empiricist in us all. Further, this is an important issue from a number of perspectives. For the local public finance specialist, it addresses the efficacy of programs to reduce borrowing costs by substituting short-term for long-term debt. For the profession as a whole, it is another investigation of the importance of expectational effects; effects important to the conduct of macroeconomic policy, the design of efficient taxes over time, and numerous other issues.

To investigate this issue is, at least in principle, straightforward. "All" one need do is specify the economic actors determining demand and supply for tax-exempt debt of different maturities, formulate the mapping from past history to their expectations, and specify the relevant list of exogenous or predetermined variables. After repeating these steps for the markets of other assets (federal debt, corporate debt, equity), the researcher estimates the various supply-and-demand schedules and compares the predicted and observed changes in the yield differential. Unfortunately, this is as infeasible as it is appealing.

Alternatively, one may consult the relevant theoretical work for predictions concerning the determinants of equilibrium in the market for tax-exempt debt. The empirical counterpart is a reduced-form equation linking the yield differential with a list of relevant variables and some measure of expectations. The author follows this latter strategy, the price of which is a less powerful methodology.

The empirical work attempts to discriminate among four alternative hypotheses about the determinants of tax-exempt bond yields at varying maturities. The four theories are: the bank arbitrage model, Miller Model I, Miller Model II, and the preferred habitat model and are clearly presented in section 2.2. The main implications of the models are easily summarized.

Under the bank arbitrage model, short-term and long-term bond yields are determined by the arbitrage activities of banks. As a result, the

Douglas Holtz-Eakin is assistant professor in the Department of Economics at Columbia University.

yield spread depends only upon the corporate tax rate. Movements in the yield curve are the result of expected future changes in the corporate tax rate. Changes in either the personal tax rates or the supply of tax-exempt debt do not affect the yield spread. It is this prediction that is most strongly rejected by the data.

Miller Model I reaches the same conclusions as the bank arbitrage model, but instead because of the debt and equity supply decisions of corporations. Accordingly, it also is treated poorly by the data.

Miller Model II assumes that individuals are unable to circumvent taxes on equity income. As a result, the corporate tax rate, the personal tax code, and the tax-exempt debt supply all influence the equilibrium yield spread.

The final hypothesis, the preferred habitat model, combines the predictions of the previous models. In this view, commercial banks dominate the short-term market, but at longer maturities individual investors are the dominant source of demand. Just as in the bank arbitrage model, neither the personal tax code nor the tax-exempt debt supply affects the equilibrium short-term yield spread. At longer maturities, the yield spread is determined by the tax rate of the marginal investor in tax-exempt bonds. As a result, the yield spread depends directly upon the personal tax code and the municipal debt supply. The latter effect comes from the necessity of attracting investors in lower tax brackets to hold increases in debt.

What are the implications for municipal borrowing costs? If yields are determined either by the bank arbitrage or miller I models, changes in the slope of the yield curve reflect expected reductions in the corporate tax rate. In these circumstances any movement to substitute short-term finance for longer-maturity bonds will be undone by higher refinancing costs in the future. Alternatively, if the slope reflects differing tax rates of clienteles in a segmented market, then real borrowing costs may be reduced by this substitution.

What are the answers? To find out, the author tests whether changes in observed yield spreads or implicit tax rates are correlated with "tax policy events" likely to affect expectations of future personal or corporate tax rates. In doing so, he minimizes the importance of biases in the levels of implicit tax rates by focusing on the changes in the implicit tax rate. While this may reduce confounding expectational effects with either changes in differential risk or tax trading effects, it remains susceptible to changes in the after-tax discount rate. A more troubling drawback is the (unavoidable) use of dummy variables to proxy changes in the future stream of tax rates (see equation (11)). As such, they inevitably introduce a form of measurement error into the analysis. While the author is careful to stress the limitations of his results, the potential biases are worth emphasis.

The regressions argue against either the bank arbitrage or Miller I models. In my view, the strongest indication is the importance of changes in the share of state-local debt in changes in the yield spread at all maturities. Thus, it is possible to eliminate these two hypotheses without any appeal to tax events.

Still, the regressions indicate that tax events are important. The more subtle question is whether tax *expectations* are important, and here I think the results speak clearly. One, albeit crude, way of sorting out the relative importance of expectations versus actions is to compare the effects of policy announcements to those of actual implementation. Of the major tax events analyzed in table 2.6, eight were announcements and six were implementations.[1] Using model 3 results as the guide, we find significant responses to four of the announcements: the Kennedy tax cut, the Vietnam War surcharge, the March 1969 House decision, and the Long announcement opposing taxation of interest on municipal bonds. In contrast, the only policy implementation to show significant effects at all maturities is the passage of the Reagan tax cut. This is the only instance in which a policy implementation, but not announcement, changes the yield spread. It is easy *ex post* to rationalize this as reflecting uncertainty about the final form of the tax bill, but such temptations are an inherent weakness of this method.

A second weakness is apparent in the estimates. It is only a slight exaggeration to say that the evidence presented consists of essentially four episodes: the Kennedy State of the Union address, Johnson's announcement of the surcharge, the March and September 1969 flip-flop on the taxation of interest from municipal bonds, and the August 1981 passage of the Reagan tax program. By this measure, it takes a "big" tax event to move expected tax rates, and most theories that emphasize expectations suggest a continual, subtle reassessment of the future.

This paper raises the hope that it is possible to reduce municipal borrowing costs through changing the mix of debt maturities. One cannot predict the size of the savings, but this may be asking too much. The evidence in this paper supports the importance of expectations, with implications beyond the particular subject. Moreover, municipal bond market performance has been puzzling, and explicit tests of the few available explanations are welcome. Despite any limitations of the methods used, the paper makes an important contribution to testing the relevant hypotheses.

Note

1. The announcements are: May–June 1962, January 1963, January 1967, March 1969, September 1969, June 1980, November 1980, and February 1981.

3 An Empirical Examination of Municipal Financial Policy

Roger H. Gordon and Joel Slemrod

Current U.S. tax law creates a variety of incentives affecting municipal financial policy. Under current law, municipalities can borrow at a tax-exempt interest rate yet can earn the full market rate of return on any assets held. Residents, in contrast, if they borrow or lend as individuals, pay or earn the market rate of return but after personal income taxes. These differences in rates of return create a variety of arbitrage opportunities, allowing communities and residents to borrow at low rates and invest at higher rates.

The purpose of this paper is to examine empirically the financial policy of municipalities in four states (Connecticut, Maine, Massachusetts, and Rhode Island) to see to what degree these municipalities attempt to take advantage of each of the available opportunities to engage in tax arbitrage. Our data come from the 1980 U.S. Census of Population and Housing, and the 1977 U.S. Census of Governments. We find clear evidence that communities do actively engage in such tax arbitrage.

The organization of the paper is as follows. In section 3.1 we explore in more detail the tax incentives affecting municipal financial policy, and then discuss other factors that may also influence financial decisions. In section 3.2 we describe the construction of the data set used in the empirical study, and present tables summarizing the general characteristics of municipal financial policy. In section 3.3 we present and discuss the results of our regression analyses investigating the role of the various factors affecting municipal financial policy. Finally, in

Roger H. Gordon is associate professor of economics at the University of Michigan and a research associate at the National Bureau of Economic Research.

Joel Slemrod is associate professor of economics at the University of Minnesota and a faculty research fellow at the National Bureau of Economic Research.

section 3.4 we comment briefly on the implications of our results for the distributional and efficiency effects of the current tax treatment of municipal financial policy.

3.1 Factors Affecting Municipal Financial Decisions

3.1.1 Tax Factors

Base Case

Based on a simplified view of the current tax law, individuals, when investing as individuals, face a nominal before-tax interest rate of r and an after-tax rate of $r(1 - t)$,[1] where t is their marginal personal income tax rate. Assume that all residents in a community face the same marginal tax rate, that their marginal tax rate will remain constant over time, and that any prospective home buyer in the community will have the same tax rate. (Assume also that if they currently itemize deductions, then they and any buyers will also itemize in the future.)

If an individual's community buys securities, the community can earn a before- and after-tax return of r, while the community can borrow at a tax-exempt interest rate, which we denote by r_m. By construction let $r_m = r(1 - t_m)$. Because of its tax-exempt status, r_m has historically been approximately 70% of the value of r.[2]

Differences between

(1) the community's borrowing rate, r_m,
(2) the community's lending rate, r, and
(3) the residents' borrowing and lending rate, $r(1 - t)$,

create a variety of arbitrage opportunities whereby the community/residents can borrow at a low rate and lend at a higher rate. Three different forms of arbitrage are possible given the three different pairwise differences in the borrowing and lending rates above.

In the first and simplest form of arbitrage comparing rates of return (1) and (2), the community can borrow a dollar through the municipal bond market and invest it in taxable securities, receiving on net $r - r_m = t_m r$. The IRS has been concerned with this form of arbitrage, and in 1969 a section was added to the Internal Revenue Code that attempted to restrict severely the extent of such arbitrage. Specifically, section 103(c) of the Internal Revenue Code states that interest on municipal debt is taxable if a major portion of a debt issue is used directly or indirectly to buy securities earning a materially higher rate of return. Proceeds from a debt issue can be invested temporarily in taxable securities, however, and by statute up to 15% can remain invested for extended periods, as a reserve or replacement fund. The IRS has not been very aggressive in enforcing this statute. Only in 1979 did it rule that a community which has large holdings of taxable securities relative to its outstanding debt is in violation of section 103(c) per se, even if the debt was issued for a clearly different purpose. The interpretation of the statute was less clear in 1977, the year our data were collected. In addition, the IRS has recently allowed communities to borrow in order to invest in taxable securities if the purpose is to raise their bond rating. We will assume for now, however, that the IRS does enforce the statute, so communities are permitted to invest only n percent of any debt issue in taxable securities, and that all communities puruse this arbitrage to the legal limit. Evidence on the extent to which communities engage in this arbitrage is presented below.

A second form of arbitrage available to communities, comparing rates of return (2) and (3), is to raise property taxes now, invest the proceeds in taxable bonds, then use the proceeds from the bonds to lower property taxes in the future. By investing indirectly through the community, individuals earn a rate or return on their investment of r, rather than the rate of return of $r(1 - t)$ available when they invest directly. When they invest an extra dollar through the community, residents gain $r - r(1 - t) = rt$ each year in arbitrage profits.[3] The IRS has not attempted to restrict this second form of arbitrage.

In the third and final form of arbitrage, comparing rates of return (1) and (3), communities/residents attempt to take advantage of the difference between r_m and $r(1 - t)$. Wealthier individuals, for whom $r(1 - t) < r_m$, will want to borrow as individuals and buy tax-exempt securities. In this situation, their municipality plays no role. Individuals in lower tax brackets, however, for whom $r(1 - t) > r_m$, cannot borrow as individuals at the tax-exempt rate in order to invest at $r(1 - t)$—only municipalities can borrow at the tax-exempt rate. But these individuals can have their municipality borrow for them at rate r_m, then use what is borrowed to lower property taxes. The residents can then invest what they save in property taxes and earn a rate of return of $r(1 - t)$. On net they gain $r(1 - t) - r_m$ in arbitrage profits.[4] However, communities are allowed by statute to invest a fraction of what they borrow in taxable securities. Given this, the net gain to residents each year per dollar borrowed becomes

(1) $(1 - n)(r(1 - t) - r_m) + n (r - r_m) = rt_m - (1 - n)t).$

For many communities, the last two forms of arbitrage (raising property taxes and investing in bonds earning r, or lowering property taxes and borrowing at rate r_m) can simultaneously be worthwhile. However, if both are pursued, the community is in effect borrowing at r_m and investing at r, the policy that is restricted by the IRS. Each community must therefore choose to pursue either one policy or the other. Which is preferable? That depends first on the relative gain per dollar change in current property taxes, and second on how aggressively one policy versus the other can be pursued and what offsetting costs are incurred in doing so.

If the community chooses to lower taxes and borrow, what limits the amount of such tax arbitrage that it can undertake? One potential limit is that states set statutory limits on how much municipalities can borrow. Generally, the statutes specify that the outstanding debt in a municipality cannot exceed some percentage of the assessed property value of the community.[5] Commonly, separate limits are set for school bonds and for debt of special districts, so that creating special districts allows more debt to be issued. In addition, some forms of debt are normally entirely exempt from these limits, and states often provide a mechanism to relax binding restriction on debt issues. It therefore seems unlikely that a community would face such a binding limit.

Similarly, states often allow debt to be issued for only certain purposes, e.g., capital expenditures and short-run cash flow needs. These restrictions set some upper limit on debt issues, though communities should have some flexibility in broadening the definition of "capital expenditures" when the restriction is binding. Aggregate data, however, suggest that this constraint is not close to binding on average. For example, Peterson (1978) and Peterson (1981) report the percentage of state and local capital expenditures financed by long-term bonds, by federal aid, and by other local resources for selected years between 1952 and 1977. In these figures, long-term debt issues never exceeded 56% of total capital outlays, and never exceeded 65.4% of nonfederal expenditures on capital outlays. (The average figures were 42.7% and 55.8% respectively.) Unfortunately, it was not possible to test explicitly whether such a constraint was close to binding in any of the towns in our sample.[6]

Some other nonstatutory factor seems to limit the extent to which communities issue debt. One possible factor limiting the amount of borrowing by a community is risk aversion on the part of residents. The real value of the outstanding municipal debt is random, depending on interest rate fluctuations and inflation. Since the relative interest rates on municipal bonds and taxable bonds change substantially over time, as shown in Poterba (chapter 2 of the present volume), borrowing in the municipal market and investing in the taxable market is by no means a fully hedged investment. Risk aversion would limit the size of municipal debt relative to the individual's total wealth, everything else being equal.

Alternatively, the same set of factors appealed to in discussion of corporate financial policy,[7] agency costs and bankruptcy costs, could also play a role in limiting the amount of municipal debt. The only implicit security that lenders have is the tax base of the community, so they would be increasingly reluctant to lend as the outstanding debt grows relative to this tax base.[8] In summary, agency costs and risk aversion each provide an explanation why municipal debt cannot become too large relative to the municipal property tax base, or the total wealth, of the community.

Related factors presumably limit the extent to which residents will invest their wealth through the community. Accounting standards in communities would normally be viewed as lax compared with those of mutual funds, so residents may well fear that municipal employees could divert surplus funds into excess expenditures on municipal services, or invest it poorly. The more money that is invested in the community, presumably the more difficult it would be to guard against such behavior. In addition, the risk individuals face with such investments includes not only the risk in the return on the securities, but also the risk in the value of their property relative to the total tax base of the community, and the risk that any buyer may not adequately take into account the value of the asset being purchased with the house. Individuals would become increasingly risk averse at the margin as more of their wealth depended on the value of their house.

The benefits from pursuing one or the other arbitrage strategy vary with the tax rate of the residents: the gain from investing through the community, rt, grows with t, whereas the gain from borrowing through the community, $r(t_m - (1 - n)t)$, falls with t. In contrast, the offsetting costs limiting the extent of such arbitrage should not depend directly on the tax rate of the residents. We would therefore expect communities with low tax rates to favor issuing municipal bonds, while wealthy communities would prefer to invest through their community. These are two of the principal relationships we will look for in the empirical analysis.

Complicating Factors

In the above discussion, we assumed that the after-tax rate of return to savings for the individual was $r(1 - t)$, and ignored the individual's portfolio problem. However, if individuals can exchange taxable and tax-exempt bonds freely and without constraint, they will do so until they are indifferent at the margin to owning one or the other. For example, at this point the cost of bearing the extra risk in the return on municipal bonds just offsets any gain in expected return. In this situation, they would, as residents, be indifferent to either having the community borrow in the municipal bond market or to raising taxes (assuming $n = 0$). Wealthier individuals (those facing a $t > t_m$) will normally be in just this situation, investing in taxable and tax-exempt securities until they become indifferent.[9] They would then find the riskier return on municipal bonds just equivalent to the return $r(1 - t)$, implying that the gain from having the community borrow an extra dollar, as expressed in equation (1), simplifies to nrt. Poorer individuals, in contrast, cannot sell municipal bonds short as individuals and invest the proceeds in taxable bonds, given existing institutions. Instead, they have their community borrow for them on the municipal market, just as described previously. In summary, the gain to residents from an extra dollar of municipal debt would now equal max(t_m − (1 − n)t, nt)r.

The above discussion also focused on a situation where residents do not itemize. If residents do itemize, then any property tax payment costs residents only (1 − t) percent of the tax payment. Therefore, everything else being equal, lenders can hope to collect 1/(1 − t) times as much from residents when residents itemize, and so would view 1/(1 − t) dollars of debt from a community where residents itemize as equivalent in risk to one dollar of debt from a community of nonitemizers. As a result, both the costs of issuing an extra dollar of debt and the benefits of issuing an extra dollar (see note 3) are reduced by (1 − t) percent when residents itemize. Communities where residents itemize should therefore undertake tax arbitrage to the same extent as communities where residents do not itemize, everything else being equal, but in doing so would issue 1/(1 − t) times as much debt.

This argument assumes that if residents itemize deductions in one year, then they itemize in all years. If not, then individuals face an incentive to shift tax payments toward those years in which they itemize, when the payments are tax deductible. Most new homeowners itemize, but as time passes owners would eventually become increasingly unlikely to itemize. Therefore, new owners would face a strong incentive to pay as much as possible in property taxes while they itemize, and thus ought to avoid having their municipality borrow (and would prefer having it build up a reserve). Similarly, during the years in which the individual does itemize, he would prefer to push his property tax payments toward the years in which his personal income tax rate is highest. Furthermore, an individual who is no longer itemizing, and who is expecting to sell his house in the near future to someone who will be itemizing, would much prefer to keep property taxes as low as possible now and have the municipality go into debt. The buyer can deduct the cost of repaying this debt, and will therefore reduce his bid for the property by only (1 − t) percent of the value of the outstanding debt. The gain to the seller from lowering taxes is the full reduction in taxes, since he does not itemize, and losing (1 − t) percent of the gain through the sale price of his house is an atttractive exchange. By the same argument, an individual in this situation would be reluctant to build up assets in the community.

3.1.2 Nontax Factors

Lumpiness of Capital Expenditures

Conventional wisdom says that lumpy expenditures are more likely to be financed with debt, because it is difficult to adjust property tax rates enough to cover extraordinary capital expenditures. However, this factor does not necessarily imply high debt on average, as communities could built up assets in anticipation of heavy expenditures, and pay off any debt quite quickly. Most large expenditures, e.g., school buildings, are easily anticipated, making this process straightforward. Also, for large communities, any given lumpy capital expenditure would not be so large relative to the total budget, making it easier to pay for the expenditure over a short period of time. There seems to be little reason to expect in the data a strong association between the level of debt and the size of the community's capital stock.

Burden on Current vs. Future Residents

Conventional wisdom also says that bond finance of capital projects and tax finance of current expenditures is more equitable, because under this system payments and benefits coincide in time. If the housing stock is unchanging, however, any difference in the timing of payments and benefits ought to be capitalized in house prices, thus leaving incentives on financial policy unaffected. What current residents avoid paying now through use of debt they end up paying through reduced property values. This is true as long as buyers and sellers are in the same tax bracket, and buyers correctly perceive the fiscal position of the community.

However, new buyers may well misperceive the financial position of the community. For example, buyers are likely to take the property tax rate into account, but may presume that taxes finance constant real expenditures, whereas debt service involves constant nominal expenditures (ignoring refinancing). This consideration leads to a preference for tax finance. On the other hand, keeping the current tax rate low through debt finance may lead buyers to underestimate future tax bills.

If the housing stock is not fixed, then use of debt finance allows more of the cost of current expenditures to be pushed onto property used for new construction. When a house is built, that property becomes a larger share of the property tax base of the community, and so pays a larger share of the property taxes. When taxes are used to finance current expenditures, each property pays based on its current share of the total property tax base. However, when debt finance is used, each property pays based on its share of the property tax base over the next twenty years or so. If a new house is built on a property during that time, then that property pays a larger share of the original expenditures if debt finance is used rather than tax finance.

A community would not necessarily want to increase the tax burden on newly built houses, however. If this tax burden already exceeds the marginal cost of public services to new residents,[10] and if the amount of new constrcution is sensitive to the property tax rate, then shifting taxes further onto new residents may not be desirable.

Heterogeneity of the Community

In the previous section, we made the obviously unrealistic assumption that the community was entirely homogeneous. Modeling the political decision making of a heterogeneous community is complicated, however. The median voter model is often used, and we will appeal to it below in the empirical work, but its characterization of the decision-making process is very naïve. The more heterogeneous the community, the less we would expect our tax story, as applied to the median income voter, to fit the data. Similarly, when relative prices of houses within the community are changing, there is a clear conflict of interest about financial policy, with uncertain outcome.

Transactions Costs of Bond Issues

When municipal bonds are marketed, buyers seek information about the riskiness of the bonds. For large communities, rating services and brokerage houses will collect and provide such information. For smaller communities, however, the available information would be much less reliable. As a result, buyers would not be able to differentiate between safe and risky issues, and thus price them the same, encouraging risky issues and discouraging safe ones, the classic "lemons" problem. Whether or not the market breaks down completely, we would expect our theory to be much less applicable to smaller communities.

Rental Units

Renters favor debt finance if there is rent control with a property tax pass through. If a project is financed by a property tax increase, then a tenant under rent control must pay the full cost immediately. However, if debt finance is used, rental payments each year would go up only slightly. If the tenant expects to move before the debt is fully repaid, then debt finance is clearly preferable.

If market rents are unconstrained, however, then the equilibrium rent is affected by municipal financial policy only through the preferences of landlords—the demand curve for apartments is unaffected by how expenditures are financed, but the supply curve would be affected. Landlords would normally be in high tax brackets, so prefer that the community avoid debt and attempt to build up a reserve of taxable securities. Renter-voters may not perceive these incentives, however.

3.2 Characteristics of the Data Set

In order to investigate the importance of the various factors affecting municipal financial policy, we have assembled what we believe to be a unique set of data. Our data source on government financial policy was the Finance Summary Statistics from the 1977 Census of Governments. This tape provided information for all state and local government units on their revenues and expenditures, plus the book value of various categories of financial assets and liabilities that they held. Our data source on the characteristics of the residents of each community was the 1980 Census of Population and Housing,[11] Summary Tape File 3C. This tape reported a variety of characteristics of the population and the housing stock for all "minor civil divisions" (MCDs) with a population of at least 10,000 in eleven states, and all counties and "places" with a population of at least 10,000.

Unfortunately, the two data sets were not easily matched. To begin with, the identification codes for each observation on the two tapes had no relation. Fortunately, the Census kindly created for us a third tape that matched these identification codes wherever possible. In addition, however, many "places" are not contiguous with any unit of government, while many units of government (e.g., school districts) do not coincide with a "place" or an MCD, the unit of observation on the Census of Population and Housing tape. By necessity, our study had to be confined either to MCDs and those places that coincided with units of government, or to counties. Our judgment was that the population of each county would be very heterogeneous, and the variation in average characteristics across counties would be too small to allow much to be learned from county data. Our study therefore focuses on data for MCDs and places.

In many states, however, school districts and special districts are very important, and these districts can issue debt in their own right. Residents should not care whether debt is issued by their municipality or by their special district—they are liable either way—so how much debt is issued by MCDs versus special districts should be arbitrary. But matched data is available only for MCDs.

In order to avoid the problem of arbitrary division of financial responsibility, we focused on four states where only a small fraction of the short-term debt and full-faith-and-credit long-term debt was issued by units of government other than MCDs: Connecticut (5%), Maine (32%), Massachusetts (20%), and Rhode Island (1%).[12] Within these states there were 276 usable observations.[13]

For each community, we constructed a measure of its outstanding debt. This figure was defined to equal the book value at the end of the year of short-term debt plus long-term general obligation debt, minus any holdings of state and local bonds. We made no attempt to estimate the market value of the outstanding debt, given the reported book values. Our presumption was that since all data came from the same calendar year, the ratio of market value to book value should be very similar for all communities.[14]

We did not include in our measure of debt the book value of revenue bonds or other nonguaranteed bonds that each community had outstanding. Such bonds are not legal liabilities of the municipal government, and are not paid for out of property tax revenues.

We next constructed a measure for each community of the book value at the end of the year of its holdings of Federal securities and other bonds, notes, mortgages, and financial assets, excluding state and local government securities. A critical issue in constructing this measure was the proper treatment of cash and deposits held in "sinking funds, bond funds, or other noninsurance funds." Such deposits could be held primarily for liquidity purposes soon after bonds are issued or soon before bonds are retired. If they earn less than the interest due on the bonds, as would checking accounts and perhaps savings accounts, then there is no arbitrage reason to borrow to put the proceeds in cash and deposits. However, deposits might also be held in money-market funds or certificates of deposit, and earn a return well above that on municipal bonds. In order to compare the typical rate of return earned on cash and deposits with that earned on other taxable securities, we regressed total interest income divided by the par value of all security holdings (I/S) against a constant and the fraction of total security holdings held in cash and deposits (CD/S). The results were as follows (standard errors are in parentheses):

$$(I/S) = .045 + .015 \ (CD/S).$$
$$(.011) \quad (.013)$$

The estimated rate of return on cash and deposits is 6% per year, almost exactly the interest rate of 5.94% earned in one-year Treasury notes of 1977, and higher than the estimated 4.5% earned on other taxable securities.[15] In most of the results reported below, we therefore included cash and deposits in our measure of taxable security holdings.

We also ignored any assets held in the various insurance and pension funds. It is possible that communities choose to borrow to overfund their insurance and pension funds, contributing more now and less later and earning a market return tax free in the interim.[16] Unfortunately, we had no information about the extent of overfunding in our data set, and so did not pursue this.[17]

From the Census of Population and Housing we attempted to construct a measure of the median marginal personal income tax rate of residents in each community. The tape reports the median family income in each community. We then assigned to each family income the average marginal personal income tax rate observed for that income level in the NBER TAXSIM file for 1980.[18]

We did not have any data on average wealth or average property values of residents in each community, as an indicator of the tax capacity of the community. As a proxy, we used the total income of all residents in the community.

We also had no information on the percentage of the residents in a community who itemized. According to the theory, communities where the median voter itemizes will want to issue $1/(1 - t)$ times as much debt as communities where the median voter does not itemize. In most of the results reported on below, we made no attempt to control for differences across communities in the probability that the median voter itemizes. As we present the results, we will discuss what biases are likely to be present, given this omission.

Tables 3.1–3.4 present various summary characteristics of the financial policy of communities in our sample. In each table, we have divided our communities into six marginal tax-rate categories, with the average marginal tax rates of the categories ranging from 23.4% to 35.0%. Table 3.1 reports the average of the ratios within each category of the book value of outstanding municipal bonds divided by the total income of the community. It reports these figures for the entire sample, for large communities (population over 25,000), for small communities (population under 25,000), for relatively homogeneous communities, and for relatively heterogeneous communities.[19] Based on the tax arbitrage arguments of the previous section, we would expect the ratios to decline with the marginal tax rate and to decline more dramatically for large communities. Both of these expectations are borne out un-

Table 3.1	Municipal Debt as a Percentage of Municipal Income					
Sample	Range of marginal income tax rates					
	.210 – .245	.245 – .257	.257 – .275	.275 – .293	.293 – .325	.325 +
1. All	7.9	7.3	6.9	6.7	6.3	4.0
2. Large towns	10.7	8.7	6.8	7.2	3.7	3.1
3. Small towns	5.2	6.1	7.0	6.4	6.8	4.3
4. Homogeneous towns	4.5	7.8	6.9	6.4	7.0	5.4
5. Heterogeneous towns	10.2	6.6	7.0	7.4	4.8	3.0

ambiguously in the data. Higher tax rate communities do still borrow, but much less so relative to their aggregate income than do lower tax rate communities. In small communities, there is no clear pattern to the figures. The theory has no clear predictions about the differences between homogeneous and heterogeneous communities. Here we find that the ratios tend to decline in both cases.

The observed degree to which debt/income is lower in rich communities should underestimate the responsiveness of debt policy to tax incentives, since the median voter would be likely to itemize only in the richer communities. In such richer communities, we should observe $1/(1 - t)$ times as much debt as they would choose to accept if they did not itemize. Had we been able to control for the effects of itemization, the pattern observed in table 3.1 should have been much stronger.

Table 3.2 reports similar figures for several other measures of the financial position of these communities. The first and second lines report the average ratio of debt to municipal tax revenues for the total sample and for large communities. The theory suggested nothing directly about these ratios, though they do show a similar but weaker pattern than the figures in table 3.1. The next four lines describe the average ratio of federal and other securities held, excluding or including cash and deposits, divided by the total income of the community. If communities all prefer to borrow through the municipality rather than invest in a tax-free way, then these figures should all be a uniform fraction of the corresponding figures on the first two lines of table 3.1.

Table 3.2   **Alternative Measures of Financial Position**

Definition/Sample	Range of marginal income tax rates					
	.210 – .245	.245 – .257	.257 – .275	.275 – .293	.293 – .325	.325 +
Debt/Revenues						
1. All	71.4	74.1	73.5	74.1	69.8	48.3
2. Large towns	64.3	80.7	69.6	76.0	51.0	37.1
Securities/Income without deposits						
3. All	0.54	0.46	0.87	0.45	0.28	0.35
4. Large towns	0.88	0.96	1.07	0.41	0.26	0.41
with deposits						
5. All	2.8	2.5	2.8	1.9	2.3	2.0
6. Large towns	3.0	3.4	2.9	2.0	2.1	1.7
Securities/Debt with deposits						
7. All	65.8	60.6	49.1	40.7	54.2	64.7
8. Large	32.4	43.9	42.6	46.2	79.2	87.5

NOTE: All figures are reported as percentages rather than as fractions.

The average of the actual fractions, calculated using the cash-inclusive definition of federal securities, is reported on lines 7 and 8 for all and for large communities. For large communities, we do find that security holdings increase with marginal tax rate, as the theory forecasts.

Table 3.3 is designed to provide information about the size of the tax savings achieved through tax arbitrage within each marginal tax-rate category. The simplest form of arbitrage is to borrow at the municipal rate and invest at the taxable rate, gaining rt_m per year per dollar borrowed. The first line reports the average of $\min(D,S)/Y$ as a measure of how much of this arbitrage is occurring, where D represents debt, S represents security holdings, inclusive of cash and deposits, and Y represents total income of the community. The second form of arbitrage is to borrow and use the proceeds to lower taxes, saving residents $\max(t_m - t, 0)r$ per year.[20] In the second line of the table we report the average value of $\max(D - S, 0)/Y$, as a measure of the extent of this second arbitrage. Finally, communities might also raise property taxes and invest in securities tax free, saving rt per dollar invested. The third line of the table reports the average ratio of $\max(S - D, 0)/Y$ as a measure of this third form of arbitrage. By the theory, we would expect wealthier communities to favor this third form of arbitrage.

In order to approximate the average tax savings from municipal financial arbitrage within each marginal tax rate category, we require data on r and t_m. For r, we used .076, the average nominal rate on twenty-year government bonds in 1977.[21] There was no compelling reason for choosing this rate rather than many alternatives, and all figures would simply change proportionately if another rate were chosen. Choosing a value for t_m is more important. If we simply compare the interest rates on municipal and taxable bonds in 1977, we find an implicit tax rate of 32% comparing twenty-year prime municipals with twenty-year new issue AA industrials, and 51% comparing one-year

Table 3.3   **Extent of Various Forms of Tax Arbitrage**

Definition	Range of marginal income tax rates					
	.210 – .245	.245 – .257	.257 – .275	.275 – .293	.293 – .325	.325 +
1. min $(D, S)/Y$	2.7	2.3	2.3	1.8	2.2	1.7
2. max $(D - S, 0)/Y$	5.2	5.1	4.6	4.9	4.1	2.3
3. max $(S - D, 0)/Y$	0.14	0.26	0.48	0.12	0.08	0.27
Tax savings/Y						
4. $t_m = .225$	0.049	0.044	0.049	0.033	0.039	0.036
5. $t_m = .35$	0.120	0.105	0.101	0.075	0.074	0.052

NOTE: The definition of securities includes cash and deposits. All figures are reported as percentages rather than as fractions.

prime municipals with one-year governments. But none of these comparisons controls for risk, call provisions, etc. Gordon and Malkiel (1981) report a comparison of interest rates on taxable bonds and tax-exempt industrial revenue bonds issued simultaneously in 1978 by the same firm with similar provisions. In this sample, t_m is estimated to be only 22.5%. given this dispersion of estimates, we calculated the tax savings for each marginal tax category for both $t_m = .225$ and $t_m = .35$. These estimates equal:

$$r/Y[\max(t_m - t, 0) \cdot \max(D - S, 0) + t_m \cdot \min(D,S) + t \cdot \max(S - D,0)]$$

The resulting figures for $t_m = .225$ are reported on the fourth line and for $t_m = .35$ on the fifth line. Tax benefits are larger for poorer communities, particularly when $t_m = .35$: poor communities gain more from borrowing and do more of it than do rich communities, whereas rich communities do little to take advantage of the opportunity to invest tax free through their community. The reported figures represent the tax savings before taking account of itemization. Those communities where residents itemize, predominantly the richer communities, save only $(1 - t)$ times the reported figures given that the payments would have been tax deductible, so that the reported figures understate the degree to which poor communities gain relative to rich communities. For all communities, however, the tax savings are extremely small.

One question raised by the figures in the tables is whether communities do in practice borrow and establish substantial holdings of taxable securities, in spite of IRS rules attempting to limit it. In order to examine this, we calculated the distribution of S/D, and report this distribution in table 3.4, defining S to be either exclusive or inclusive of cash and deposits. Here we find that with the exclusive definition of S, over 10% of the communities hold taxable securities amounting to more than 20% of the book value of their debt, and six communities have invested more in taxable securities than they have borrowed. This evidence is not necessarily inconsistent with strict IRS enforcement of section 103(c)—these outlier communities could recently have had large issues of bonds, the proceeds from which had not yet been spent. However,

Table 3.4   Taxable Securities Held as a Percentage of Municipal Debt: Distribution across Communities

Definition Securities/Debt		Percentile Range					
	0	0–.1	.1–.2	.2–.3	.3–.4	.4–.5	>.5
1. Without deposits	60.9	23.6	4.7	2.2	0.4	2.9	5.4
2. With deposits	0.4	8.3	22.8	18.5	11.2	8.3	30.4

using the cash-inclusive definition of securities, most communities have far more securities than the IRS rules would seem to allow. This phenomenon is not restricted to the four states we focus on. In all municipalities in the United States, municipal security holdings were 37.5% of municipal debt.

3.3 Analysis of the Data

In the previous section, we compared the financial policies of communities with residents having different marginal income tax rates. In doing so, however, we made no attempt to control for other factors that also might affect financial policy. In this section, we construct measures of a few other factors that ought to influence financial policy, and then regress various measures of municipal financial policy against these factors as well as the marginal tax rate of the residents of the community, to see to what degree the association found above between a community's marginal tax rate and its financial policy might be caused by other factors.

In the discussion of tax incentives in section 3.1, we argued that if individuals itemize, if they itemize in some years but not in others, if they face different tax rates in any of the years in which they itemize, or if they intend to sell their house in the near future and the likely buyer faces a different tax rate or itemizes while the seller does not, then strong tax incentives exist to change municipal financial policy. No information is available that directly measures the frequency of occurrence of any of these circumstances. Instead, we picked a variety of indicators from the Census of Population and Housing.

The most direct indicator of the likelihood that the median voter of the community itemizes is the median income of residents. From the NBER TAXSIM file, we know the percentage of taxpayers who itemize (*PI*) at each income level. If communities segregate by itemization status as well as by income, then in this percentage of the communities of a given income level the median resident will itemize. If the median resident does itemize, then the community ought to be observed with $1/(1 - t)$ times as much debt, everything else being equal, or equivalently be observed with the fraction $t/(1 - t)$ more debt. Therefore, if communities do segregate by itemization status, then, everything else being equal, the expected debt/income ratio for a community would be changed by the factor $(1 + tPI/(1 - t))$ because of the effects of itemization.

The simplest indicator of changing itemization status over time is just the age distribution of the residents. Younger residents are more likely to itemize. Since they are less likely to be itemizing when they are older, they would wish to pay as much as they can in taxes while they are young when property tax payments are tax deductible. Older residents are less likely to itemize and more likely to expect to sell shortly. As a result, they may either want to borrow now, since a buyer will likely itemize to be able to deduct the payment, or avoid borrowing now, since the buyer might misperceive a high property tax as representing a fixed real rather than a fixed nominal burden. The particular summary measures of the age distribution that we chose were: (1) the percentage of the adult (over age twenty-five) population that was younger than age forty-five (% young) and (2) the percentage of the adult population over age sixty (% old).

The Census also contained several direct indicators of the past mobility of residents currently living in the town. High mobility among owners indicates that residents are more likely to be itemizing, having recently acquired a mortgage, so they prefer to pay for expenditures now while the tax payments are tax deductible. It also indicates that an existing resident will more likely sell his house in the near future, and prefer more debt if the buyer is itemizing and in a higher tax bracket. The particular indicators that we used were: (1) the percentage of housing units in which the current occupant moved in within the last five years (HMOVE), and (2) the percentage of residents who lived in a different county five years earlier (CMOVE).

In the first section, we also argued that renters would prefer debt finance if they are covered by rent control, but perhaps ought to prefer tax finance otherwise. The Census did report the percentage of housing units that were rented (% rent). Unfortunately, we knew nothing about whether rent control existed in any community.

If new housing units are being built in town, part of the burden of current expenditures can be pushed onto new housing units with debt finance, but not with tax finance. The particular measure of community growth we used was the percentage of existing housing units built within the last five years (HNEW).

Since state regulations can potentially limit (or at least influence) how much debt municipalities within the state do issue, we included separate constant terms in the regression for each state. Based on the severity of the state regulations reported in note 5, we would expect municipalities in Connecticut to have the most debt, and those in Rhode Island to have the least. However, the direction of causation may not be clear—the size of the state's limits may well just reflect common practice among the state's municipalities.

Finally, in some regressions reported below, we also included as a regressor the ratio of municipal expenditures to aggregate income (E/Y). Based on the arguments in the first section, there would be no reason to expect any causal relation between debt and expenditures. However, if the tax-exempt status of interest on municipal bonds is serving as a subsidy to municipal expenditures, then it must be true that communities that spend more are able as a result to borrow more. Finding an association between debt and expenditures in the data, after controlling for other factors, would at least suggest that spending more allows a community to borrow more, implying that the ability to issue tax-exempt bonds provides some subsidy to municipal expenditures. (Since it is commonly argued that this tax exemption specifically subsidizes capital expenditures, it would have been preferable to try as an additional variable the value of the municipal capital stock divided by income. No data were available on the municipal capital stock, however.)

Our basic measures of the financial position of a community were (1) total debt outstanding divided by total income, (D/Y), and (2) debt net of security holdings (measured inclusive of cash and deposits) divided by income $(D - S)/Y$. We tried a variety of regression specifications, reported in tables 3.5–3.7, in order to test the robustness of the association we found previously between a community's financial policy and the marginal income tax rate of its median resident. In the first, we simply regressed each of our two measures of a community's financial policy against the list of indicators described above (ignoring the itemization factor), and the marginal tax rate of the median resident of the community. Since the tax incentive to issue debt is proportional to $\max(t_m - t, 0)$, however, we expected that the effects of the marginal tax rate would be nonlinear, with variation in t mattering most when $t < t_m$. We therefore created two tax rate variables, $t_L = \min(t, .27)$ and $t_H = \max(t - .27, 0)$, thereby allowing the marginal effect of changes in t to differ depending on whether t is less than or greater than 0.27.[22] Our expectation was that the effect of each tax-rate variable on municipal debt holdings would be negative, but that t_H would be much less important.

These regression results are reported in tables 3.5 and 3.6, using either dependent variable, and estimated over either all communities or only large communities. In table 3.5, we omit (E/Y), while we include it in table 3.6.

In every case, the coefficients of the marginal tax rate variables have the signs and patterns forecast from the theory: forecasted gross and net debt declines with marginal tax rate, and more quickly when the tax rate is low than when it is high. The results show no clear difference in the degree to which communities invest in securities. If all communities invested in securities just up the allowed IRS limit, then the forecasted values of $(D - S)/Y$ should be proportional to those for D/Y, with a proportionality factor of about 0.80. The coefficients on the tax rate variables in table 3.5 do tend to be proportionately smaller, though only by about 12%, when $(D - S)/Y$ is the dependent variable. However, the tax coefficients in table 3.6 tend to be larger when $(D -$

Table 3.5   **Regression Results (Expenditures/Income Omitted)**

Independent variable	Dependent variable/sample			
	D/Y	$(D - S)/Y$	D/Y	$(D - S)/Y$
	All towns		Large towns	
1. Constant	0.43	0.42	0.84	0.87
	(0.13)	(0.13)	(0.20)	(0.25)
2. t_L	−0.93	−0.80	−2.32	−2.12
	(0.30)	(0.32)	(0.45)	(0.59)
3. t_H	−0.26	−0.23	−0.53	−0.45
	(0.14)	(0.15)	(0.27)	(0.36)
4. % young	−0.04	−0.12	−0.07	−0.21
	(0.13)	(0.14)	(0.23)	(0.31)
5. % old	−0.28	−0.35	−0.42	−0.56
	(0.13)	(0.14)	(0.22)	(0.29)
6. CMOVE	−0.07	−0.07	−0.02	−0.01
	(0.04)	(0.04)	(0.08)	(0.10)
7. HMOVE	−0.11	−0.05	−0.06	−0.03
	(0.10)	(0.11)	(0.19)	(0.25)
8. % rent	0.09	0.06	−0.02	−0.02
	(0.05)	(0.05)	(0.08)	(0.11)
9. HNEW	0.02	0.00	−0.04	−0.05
	(0.10)	(0.10)	(0.20)	(0.26)
10. Conn.	0.02	0.01	0.04	0.02
	(0.01)	(0.01)	(0.02)	(0.02)
11. Maine	−0.02	−0.02	−0.00	0.00
	(0.01)	(0.01)	(0.03)	(0.04)
12. Mass.	−0.00	−0.01	0.03	0.02
	(0.01)	(0.01)	(0.01)	(0.02)
Standard error of the regression	0.041	0.043	0.038	0.050
R^2	0.205	0.145	0.422	0.241

NOTE: Standard errors are in parentheses under the coefficients.

$S)/Y$ is the dependent variable, suggesting some tendency for wealthier communities to invest more in securities.

The estimated magnitude of the effects of the tax rate is substantial, particularly in table 3.5. For example, if we forecast using the estimated coefficients how much more debt relative to income a large community will have if its tax rate equals 0.35 rather than 0.234, the difference in tax rates between the highest and the lowest of the six groups examined previously, we forecast a difference in D/Y of 0.126 using the coefficients in table 3.5 and 0.069 using the coefficients in table 3.6. In comparison, when we estimated this difference previously in the second line of table 3.1, not controlling for anything else, we found a difference

Table 3.6   **Regression Results (Expenditures/Incomes Included)**

| Independent variable | Dependent variable/sample | | | |
	D/Y	$(D - S)/Y$	D/Y	$(D - S)/Y$
	All towns		Large towns	
1. Constant	0.18	0.24	0.38	0.56
	(0.12)	(0.13)	(0.19)	(0.27)
2. t_L	−0.35	−0.39	−0.86	−1.16
	(0.28)	(0.32)	(0.47)	(0.69)
3. t_H	−0.15	−0.15	−0.47	−0.41
	(0.13)	(0.15)	(0.24)	(0.35)
4. % young	0.02	−0.08	−0.05	−0.20
	(0.12)	(0.14)	(0.20)	(0.30)
5. % old	−0.15	−0.25	−0.33	−0.50
	(0.12)	(0.14)	(0.19)	(0.28)
6. CMOVE	−0.02	−0.03	0.03	0.03
	(0.04)	(0.04)	(0.07)	(0.10)
7. HMOVE	−0.17	−0.09	−0.17	−0.10
	(0.09)	(0.11)	(0.17)	(0.25)
8. % rent	0.08	0.06	0.03	0.07
	(0.04)	(0.05)	(0.07)	(0.11)
9. HNEW	0.12	0.08	0.15	0.07
	(0.09)	(0.10)	(0.17)	(0.26)
10. Conn.	0.02	0.01	0.03	0.01
	(0.09)	(0.01)	(0.01)	(0.02)
11. Maine	−0.01	−0.01	0.01	0.01
	(0.01)	(0.01)	(0.03)	(0.04)
12. Mass.	−0.02	−0.02	0.00	0.00
	(0.01)	(0.01)	(0.01)	(0.02)
13. E/Y	0.57	0.40	0.68	0.45
	(0.07)	(0.08)	(0.12)	(0.18)
Standard error of the regression	0.037	0.042	0.033	0.049
R^2	0.357	0.570	0.219	0.290

of 0.076. This implies that our previous results did not arise from a failure to control for other observable factors.

Comparing the results in tables 3.5 and 3.6, we find that including (E/Y) makes a large difference. It does appear that communities are able to borrow more if they spend more,[23] even though the theory in section 3.1 suggested no clear reason why additional spending should cause the community to incur additional debt. (In fact, one might argue that additional spending would make the community a less attractive risk to a lender, since the extra spending would be a competing demand on the tax base.)

If this observed association between spending and debt is interpreted as causal, then we conclude that spending is made cheaper because of a community's ability to issue tax-exempt debt. How large a subsidy to spending is implied by these estimates? The difficulty in answering this question is that in the data we are comparing the stock of debt with an annual flow of expenditures. In order to interpret the results, let us assume that half of new debt issues are short term (one year), and half are long term (twenty years), and let us assume that all debt is repaid when it matures.[24] Assume also that $d\%$ of expenditures each year are financed by debt, and assume expenditures have been growing in nominal terms at $g\%$ each year. Between 1957 and 1977, nominal state and local expenditures grew at 9.6% per year, so let us approximate g by .096. Then at any point in time, the stock of debt outstanding

would equal $.5(dE + \int_0^{20} dEe^{-gs}ds)$ where E equals the current level of

expenditures and s indexes years. Our regression coefficients imply that large communities that spend a dollar more have as a result \$0.68 more debt outstanding, so that the total current debt arising from past expenditures should equal $(0.68)E$. Equating the two expressions and solving for d, assuming $g = 0.096$, we find that $d = 0.1375$; that is, each extra dollar of spending allows a community to issue 0.1375 dollars of extra debt.

When a community issues a dollar of tax-exempt debt for twenty years, the cost of making payments on the debt, assuming that $t < t_m$,

equals $\int_0^{20} r_m e^{-r(1 - t)s}ds + e^{-20r(1 - t)}$. If $t = 0.234$ (the value for the

poorest of our six groups), if $t_m = 0.35$, and if $r = 0.076$, then this expression equals 0.90: the tax-exempt status lowers the cost of the long-term debt by 10%. Similarly, when debt is issued for one year, given the same procedure and parameter values, the debt is cheaper by 0.86% (approximately $r(1 - t) - r_m$) because of its tax-exempt status. Given our assumption that half of the debt issued is short term and half is long term, the average savings from issuing debt are 5.43% of the value of the debt issued. Since, by our calculations, a dollar of extra expenditures results in only 0.1375 dollars of extra debt, the cost of this dollar expenditure is reduced by only $0.0543 \cdot 0.1375 = 0.0075$ dollars as a result of the tax-exempt status of the debt, a trivial 0.75% subsidy rate for this low-income community. For wealthy communities, for whom $t > t_m$, there would be no reduction in the cost of extra expenditures. Our results therefore suggest that this tax exemption should have virtually no effect on the cost of municipal expenditures.

Among the other coefficients reported in tables 3.5 and 3.6, most tend to be small and insignificant. In many cases, the forecasts from the theory were also ambiguous. The coefficients do indicate the following: (1) Middle-aged communities tend to have the most debt, while younger communities have slightly less debt and older communities have much less debt. This pattern seems to be more consistent with the life-cycle pattern of spending on local public services, some fraction of which is debt financed, than with the tax arbitrage arguments of section 3.1. (2) Mobile communities tend to avoid debt, as expected. (3) Connecticut communities tend to have slightly more debt, as expected, though there are no clear differences among the other states.

The results reported in tables 3.5 and 3.6 suffer from the problem that the dependent variable is deflated by income, and in addition three independent variables, E/Y and the two tax-rate variables, are constructed using income information. If the reported income figures do not measure the correct theoretical concept without error, as is inevitable, then the previous coefficient estimates are somewhat biased.

We felt that the indirect correlation with the residual would be greatest for (E/Y), so we reran the previous regressions with instrumental variables, using as instruments all the independent variables except for (E/Y), plus $(E/\text{population})$, $(E/\text{population})^2$, and the fraction of the population of school age. The results were almost identical to those reported in tables 3.5 and 3.6.

Any bias that is due to correlation of the tax variables with the residuals should be slight—the tax variables are constructed using median family income, and the correlation of this with total income of the community should be small. To attempt to control for any bias, however, instrumental variables did not seem worthwhile—there seemed to be no good instruments for marginal tax rates. Instead, we tried deflating the dependent variable by tax revenues rather than income. Tax revenues are probably less highly correlated than is income with property values, the deflator argued for in section 3.1, but the correlation should still be high. In addition, with this specification we test whether communities simply rely proportionately on debt finance vs. tax finance when funding expenditures.

The resulting coefficient estimates are reported in table 3.7.[25] We have omitted (expenditures/revenues) from these regressions, as its variation reflects intergovernmental transfers as well as interest payments on existing debt, factors that are either irrelevant or endogenous. Since the mean value of the dependent variable is approximately ten times as large as that of D/Y, the coefficient estimates are also much larger. However, all previous patterns in the coefficients remain present, particularly for large communities. For example, the forecasted difference in the dependent variable between communities with $t = $

Table 3.7   **Debt/Revenue Regressions**

Independent variables	Dependent variable/sample			
	D/R	$(D - S)/R$	D/R	$(D - S)/R$
	All towns		Large towns	
1. Constant	2.6	2.9	4.5	5.9
	(1.6)	(1.5)	(1.7)	(2.5)
2. t_L	-1.2	-2.3	-8.1	-10.5
	(3.8)	(3.6)	(3.9)	(5.7)
3. t_H	-3.3	-2.8	-6.9	-6.3
	(1.8)	(1.7)	(2.3)	(3.4)
4. % young	-1.4	-1.7	-1.0	-2.2
	(1.7)	(1.6)	(2.0)	(3.0)
5. % old	-3.1	-3.5	-3.4	-4.7
	(1.7)	(1.6)	(1.9)	(2.8)
6. CMOVE	-0.4	-0.4	0.1	0.5
	(0.5)	(0.5)	(0.7)	(1.0)
7. HMOVE	-0.9	-0.5	-0.6	-0.7
	(1.3)	(1.2)	(1.6)	(2.4)
8. % rent	1.0	0.7	-0.4	-0.4
	(0.6)	(0.5)	(0.7)	(1.1)
9. HNEW	1.7	1.3	0.4	-0.0
	(1.2)	(1.1)	(1.7)	(2.5)
10. Conn.	0.2	0.1	0.3	0.1
	(0.2)	(0.1)	(0.1)	(0.2)
11. Maine	-0.2	-0.1	0.1	0.1
	(0.2)	(0.2)	(0.2)	(0.4)
12. Mass.	-0.2	-0.2	0.1	0.0
	(0.1)	(0.1)	(0.1)	(0.2)
Standard error of the regression	0.512	0.78	0.324	0.482
R^2	0.154	0.144	0.276	0.120

0.234 and $t = 0.350$ is 0.307, forecasting using the coefficients of the full sample, and 0.844, using the sample of large towns. In comparison, the differences reported in table 3.2 for these two cases were 0.231 and 0.272 respectively. While the statistical fit is somewhat poorer when D/R is the dependent variable, the qualitative results reported previously continue to be present—our previous findings do not seem to arise from a simple statistical bias.

Another bias caused by the multiple roles of income arises from the fact that residents in higher-income communities are more likely to itemize, and communities where residents itemize, by our theory, should have $1/1 - t)$ times as much debt. Since primarily rich communities itemize, had we controlled for the effects of itemization, the estimated effects of taxes should have been yet stronger. To estimate how sensitive our results are to the effects of itemization, we reran the previous regressions for large communities after multiplying all right-hand-side variables, including the constant, by the factor $(1 + tPI/(1 - t))$. As expected, the coefficients on the tax variables were larger, though not dramatically so. The other coefficient estimates were similar to those reported previously. Since our proxy for whether a community itemizes is far from perfect, these results should be interpreted with caution.

3.4 Conclusions

On theoretical grounds, we argued that poorer communities face much stronger incentives to issue municipal bonds than do wealthier communities, and our empirical work showed that poor communities do in fact borrow a great deal more. In contrast, wealthier communities should face an incentive to invest through their community and so avoid tax on income from savings, yet we found in the data only limited evidence of such a pattern. Apparently, municipal employees are not trusted as investment managers.

What then do we conclude about the distributional and efficiency effects of these tax incentives faced by municipalities? In section 3.2, we calculated the tax savings to residents resulting from municipal financial policy, and found that the poorest communities gained the most relative to their income, though for all communities the tax savings, as a percentage of income, were extremely small. Of course, the wealthy gain substantially as purchasers, rather than issuers, of municipal bonds, and this gain to the wealthy, as purchasers of tax-exempt bonds, should be the dominant distributional effect of the provision making these bonds tax exempt. Those in the middle of the income distribution are left with little gain from either side of the market.

Communities undertake only a limited amount of such tax arbitrage because there are some offsetting costs, owing perhaps to costs of risk bearing and agency and bankruptcy costs. These offsetting costs, which are real costs, are one component of the efficiency cost of the tax-exempt status of municipal bonds. At the margin, in equilibrium, these costs must be as large as any extra tax savings. In aggregate, these costs must be smaller, though, otherwise no arbitrage would occur. How much smaller is not clear. For a detailed simulation study of the efficiency and distributional effects of the tax-exempt status of interest on municipal bonds, see Gordon and Slemrod (1983).

One justification commonly given for the tax-exempt status of interest on municipal bonds is to subsidize municipal expenditures. Yet, according to our estimates, any reduction in the cost of municipal expenditures arising from the tax-exempt status of municipal bonds is trivial. The justification for tax-exempt bonds must be sought elsewhere.

Notes

We would like to thank Harvey Brazer for extensive comments on an earlier draft, and William Shobe for very able assistance with the empirical work. The work on this paper was begun while Gordon was employed at AT&T Bell Laboratories, and completed while Slemrod was a national fellow at the Hoover Institution of Stanford University. The opinions expressed in this paper are those of the authors, and not necessarily those of the NBER, AT&T Bell Laboratories, or the Hoover Institution.

1. We implicitly assume that individuals can borrow and lend freely at a before-tax interest rate of r, pay tax on any extra interest earnings (e.g., do not save at the margin in an IRA), and itemize if they borrow. If individuals face a higher opportunity cost of funds, owing, for example, to binding borrowing constraints, then the discussion in the text would need to be modified in a straightforward way.

2. See, for example, Poterba, chapter 2 of the present volume.

3. If the individual itemizes, then the accounting of cash flow is identical to that for an IRA. Given itemization, a property tax increase of $\$(1/(1 - t))$ costs the individual $1 net of income taxes. After a year, the community owns $\$(1 + r)/(1 - t)$ in assets. When it lowers property taxes by this amount, the individual saves $(1 + r)$ net of income taxes, given the deductibility of property tax payments. Since the dollar, if invested directly, would have been worth $(1 + r(1 - t))$, the net gain to investing a dollar in the community equals $(1 + r) - (1 + r(1 - t)) = rt$.

4. These incentives have also been described in Adams (1977) and Gordon and Slemrod (1983). If residents itemize, the story would be modified slightly, as in note 3. The community would borrow $\$(1/(1 - t))$, saving residents $1, given the deductibility of property taxes, which they can then invest at an interest rate $r(1 - t)$. When the municipal debt is repaid, the individual must pay $(1 + r_m)/(1 - t)$ extra in property taxes, but at a cost net of income taxes of $(1 + r_m)$. Arbitrage profits are still $r(1 - t) - r_m$, but now on municipal borrowing of $\$(1/(1 - t))$.

5. For example, in the states we examine below the limits are as follows. In Maine, each municipality may issue debt up to 7.5% of assessed value, school districts may borrow up to 12.5% of assessed value, and special districts and other government entities face their own debt ceilings. In Massachusetts, cities can borrow up to 2.5% of assessed value, towns up to 5%, and fire, water, light, and improvement districts up to 5%; however, the first two limits can be doubled with permission from the state. In Rhode Island, municipalities can borrow up to 3% of assessed value, but excluded from this limit are housing authority, public building authority, and various other bonds; the state can authorize towns to exceed these limits. Connecticut, in contrast, restricts general obligation debt to 2.25 times the latest tax receipts, though it makes certain types of debt exempt from these limits. The limits can also be increased for certain purposes, such as school building projects or urban renewal. For further discussion, see Starner (1961), or ACIR (1974).

6. The problem was that the reported figures for long-term debt issues in 1977 in our sample included a sizable amount of revenue bonds, used to finance such activities as utilities, pollution control, hospitals, single-family housing, industrial aid, etc. In aggregate in 1977, Peterson (1978) reports that total debt issues, including revenue bonds, equaled 118.7% of local capital outlays, and the figures in our sample were not much different. Revenue bonds, however, are with rare exception not legal liabilities of the municipality, and are repaid out of mortgage payments, rental income, or other user fees. The municipality, when issuing revenue bonds, is merely acting as a conduit for

funds for some other quasi-public or private organization, and not providing any tax arbitrage for residents. Unfortunately, we have no figures on issues of general obligation debt.

7. For an overview of these various factors, see Gordon (1982).

8. As in the discussion of corporate financial policy, further debt issues would raise the probability of default, leading to higher anticipated real expenditures by both lenders and the community when negotiating a settlement.

9. IRS rules do not allow interest on debt to be deducted if the funds are borrowed to buy tax-exempt securities. However, if an individual borrows for another purpose, interest is deductible even if municipal bonds are simultaneously held. In most case, an individual should be able to avoid this IRS rule. If the IRS rule is binding, however, then the risk-adjusted value of r_m would exceed $r(1 - t)$, and individuals in this situation would prefer to avoid municipal borrowing.

10. This could occur if the community has imposed tight zoning restrictions on new construction.

11. While the dates of the two censuses were three years apart, we felt that this gap was small enough to ignore.

12. With more time, we might have expanded the sample further to include New York (26%), New Hampshire (30%), and perhaps Wisconsin (40%).

13. Three towns were eliminated for which the reported figures were estimated by the Census rather than reported by the town.

14. Measurement error should be less, however, for growing communities, where debt would have been issued more recently.

15. This figure is the return on book value rather than market value, so its low value probably just reflects the fact that the bonds tend to be old.

16. For a description of these incentives, focusing on corporate plans, see Black (1980) and Tepper (1981).

17. Inman and Seidman (1980), however, find that local government pensions tend to be underfunded.

18. We would like to thank Daniel Feenberg for calculating these figures for us.

19. A community was defined to be homogeneous if at least 24% of its families had an income within 20% of the median income.

20. Residents do presumably bear some offsetting costs, however, such as risk and agency costs. Unless state restrictions on borrowing are binding, in equilibrium the marginal increase in these costs as more debt is issued would just equal the extra taxes saved. Average costs would be substantially less than average tax savings, however.

21. The interest rate data used in this paragraph come from the Salomon Brothers Center, *An Analytical Record of Yields and Yield Spreads*.

22. The break point of 0.27 was chosen because it provided a reasonable estimate of t_m, and because it divided the sample approximately in half.

23. Other explanations for the statistical association are possible, however. For example, communities with large amounts of commercial and industrial property can both spend more and find it attractive to borrow more—lenders would have the commercial and industrial tax base as additional collateral.

24. The results are very insensitive to these assumptions about the maturity structure of the debt.

25. Asefa, Adams, and Starleaf (1981) report similar regression results. Specifically, on a sample of 660 large towns taken from the 1972 and 1967 Censuses, they regressed (change in the book value of nominal debt between 1967 and 1972)/(estimated total expenditures) against median income, capital expenditures as a fraction of total expenditures, % old, HMOVE, percent growth rate in population, and a few other variables. They also found a negative effect of median income, and in addition found that a dollar of extra capital expenditure was associated with $0.314 of extra debt issues. However, changes in debt, the focus of their work, need have only a very weak connection with the equilibrium level of debt holdings, the focus of our paper. Communities may mostly finance large capital expenditures initially with debt in order to avoid large fluctuations in their property tax rates, but may differ substantially in how quickly they pay back the debt or the degree to which they build up reserves in anticipation of upcoming

expenditures. Their coefficient estimates also ought to be unstable across time periods, since the dependent variable, changes in nominal debt, is strongly affected by the inflation rate and the age distribution of the debt.

References

Adams, R. D. 1977. Individual preferences as supply determinants in the municipal and federal bond markets. *Public Finance Quarterly* 5: 175–202.

Advisory Commission on Intergovernmental Relations. 1974. *Federal-state-local finances: Significant features of fiscal federalism.* Washington, D.C.: Government Printing Office.

Asefa, S. A., R. D. Adams, and D. R. Starleaf. 1981. Municipal borrowing: Some empirical results. *Public Finance Quarterly* 9: 271–80.

Black, F. 1980. The tax consequences of long-run pension policy. *Financial Analysts Journal* 36: 25–31.

Gordon, R. H. "Interest Rates, Inflation, and Corporate Financial Policy." *Brookings Papers on Economic Activity* 2 (1982), 461–488.

Gordon, R. H., and B. G. Malkiel. 1981. Corporation finance. In H. J. Aaron and J. A. Pechman, eds., *How taxes affect economic behavior.* Washington, D.C.: Brookings Institution.

Gordon, R. H., and J. Slemrod. 1983. A general equilibrium simulation study of subsidies to municipal expenditures. *Journal of Finance* 38: 585–94.

Inman, R., and L. Seidman. 1980. Public employee pensions and U.S. aggregate savings behavior. NBER Conference Paper no. 57.

Peterson, G. 1978. Capital spending and capital obsolescence: The outlook for the cities. In R. Bahl, ed., *The fiscal outlook for cities: Implications of a national urban policy.* Syracuse: Syracuse University Press.

Peterson, J. 1981. The municipal bond market: Recent changes and future prospects. In N. Walzer and D. L. Chicoine, eds., *Financing state and local governments in the 1980's.* Cambridge: Oelgeschlager, Gunn, and Hain.

Poterba, J. M. Expected future tax policy and tax-exempt bond yields. Chapter 2 of the present volume.

Starner, F. J. 1961. *General obligation bond financing by local governments: A survey of state controls.* Berkeley: University of California Press.

Tepper, I. 1981. Taxation and corporate pension policy. *Journal of Finance* 36: 1–13.

Comment   Peter Mieszkowski

This paper on municipal financial policy is full of interesting ideas. It goes well beyond any paper I am familiar with in this area of research. The most thought-provoking result in that the reduction in the cost of municipal expenditures arising from the tax-exempt status of municipal bonds is very small, and that the justification for tax-exempt bonds must be sought elsewhere.

To understand this result better I distinguish between two interrelated issues. First, the effect of the existence of tax-exempt bonds on the choice between debt and taxes (equity) in the finance of municipal expenditures; second, the effect of tax-exempt bonds on the level of expenditures by local governments.

Following Gordon and Slemrod, I assume varying personal tax rates for the representative household in different communities. Also, I follow the authors and assume that the IRS severely limits the extent to which communities can engage in arbitrage by borrowing at the tax-exempt rate r_m and lending at the higher taxable rate, r, by holding taxable securities.

In a high-income, high-tax community, where the representative taxpayer is a net lender, itemizes deductions, and invests in tax-exempts, the existence of tax-exempts has no effect on the level of municipal expenditures for public consumption and on the choice between tax finance and bond finance.

In this community, by assumption, residents, at the margin, borrow and lend at a common rate r_m. It makes no difference whether the community finances a marginal project by levying taxes or by borrowing. If a tax levy is imposed, the taxpayer could sell some privately held municipal debt to finance the expenditure. The method of finance will have no effect on the net worth of the taxpayer. Also, as the lending and borrowing rates are both equal to r_m, the relative price of public and private goods is unchanged by the existence of tax-exempt securities.

If no constraints are imposed on municipalities to hold taxable securities, the public sector would not undertake real investments unless their yield was equal to or greater than r, the yield on taxable securities. But with restrictive IRS rules on their holdings of taxable financial securities, communities will undertake income-producing real investments that yield less than r but more than r_m. Thus, industrial-type public investment will expand as the result of tax-exempt securities.

In lower-income communities, where the representative taxpayer is a net borrower and does not itemize deductions under the income tax,

Peter Mieszkowski is professor of economics at Rice University and is a research associate of the National Bureau of Economic Research.

the private borrowing rate will be r, greater than the public borrowing rate r_m. These communities will have an incentive to borrow to finance public expenditures. Also, the lower cost of public borrowing does decrease the relative cost of public expenditures. And in the absence of borrowing constraints, industrial-type income generating investment will be profitable at a yield between r and r_m. However, the primary incentive will be for low-income communities to substitute debt for taxes. This objective, constrained by possible debt limitations, will restrict the expansion of public consumption and public income-generating investment.

Exactly the same rationale applies for communities dominated by corporate taxpayers. Businesses deduct taxes and interest under the corporate tax, and a $r > r_m$ will gain from the substitution of municipal debt for tax finance. Also, an incentive exists for the expansion of real income-generating investments financed by lower-cost municipal securities.

The empirical section of the paper, based on financial information for municipalities in four states, yields three basic results. First, that low-income communities with low marginal tax rates tend to borrow more relative to their incomes. This result is in accord with the theory developed by Gordon and Slemrod that we have discussed above. Second, there is no systematic evidence that wealthier communities hold relatively more taxable securities.

This second result is not in accord with the theoretical section, where the authors argue that communities might engage in arbitrage by raising property taxes now and investing the proceeds at the before-tax rate, r, and then lower the taxes in the future. When individuals invest through the community, residents gain rt each year in arbitrage profits. So the incentive to arbitrage is predicted to increase with the tax rate t (the level of income), but this prediction is not supported by the facts.

The third principal empirical finding is that the public expenditures per unit of income are positively related with the level of debt per unit of income. However, the authors calculate that an extra dollar of spending leads a community to issue fourteen cents of extra debt. The implied subsidy of additional public expenditures resulting from the lower cost of public borrowing is quite small, a result consistent with authors' conclusion that the tax exemption of municipal debt has little effect on the level of public expenditure.

The positive association between the level of public expenditures and the amount of debt does not negate the Gordon-Slemrod argument that lower-cost public debt may have a relatively small impact on the size of the municipal public sector. They are quite right in arguing that large, mature communities can anticipate lumpy capital expenditures and pay for them with tax finance. But the essential result of this paper is that, *given the level of public expenditures,* debt is either favored as a source of finance, or debt and tax finance are equivalent instruments. So it should not be surprising that the communities that have a relatively large public sector will issue relatively more debt. The empirical work is not a *direct* test of the proposition that the tax-exempt status of interest on municipal bonds has little impact on the size of public expenditures.

These minor reservations notwithstanding, this is a very valuable paper that will unquestionably stimulate further work on the relationships between tax-exempt municipal bonds and the level of local public expenditures. The "efficiency" of tax exemption for local debt has been called into question before, but never with arguments as devastating as those developed in this paper.

4   Property Taxes and Firm Location: Evidence from Proposition 13

Michelle J. White

4.1   Introduction

California's Proposition 13, passed by referendum in 1978, drastically changed the state's system of local property taxation. Until 1978, separate taxes were levied on real property by a variety of overlapping governmental units—counties, local governments, school districts, and other local authorities. Each tax rate reflected local voters' (or perhaps bureaucrats') preferences concerning the desired level of expenditure on local public goods. Assessed values reflected market values and were rising rapidly in the late 1970s as market values rose.

After Proposition 13, California localities essentially lost control of local property taxes. First, assessed values were set at 1975 market value, with all assessments subsequently readjusted upward at a rate of 2% per year. Reassessments now occur only when properties are sold, at which time they are set at market value. Second, a single overall property tax rate, arbitrarily set at 1%, replaced the menu of local property taxes levied by cities and towns, counties, school districts, and other local authorities.[1] This reduced the level of property tax collections in all localities, but by varying amounts. Emergency state aid to local governments offset some of the drop in property tax revenues, but at varying (and exogenously determined) levels.

Post–Proposition 13 California provides an excellent laboratory for studying the effects of taxes on firm location. This is because, first,

Michelle J. White is professor of economics at the University of Michigan and a research associate at the Urban Research Center, New York University. The author is grateful to Sharon Bernstein Megdal and Howard Chernick for very helpful comments. Partial funding for this project was provided by the Charles H. Revson Foundation under a grant to the Urban Research Center, New York University.

local property taxes changed from being determined by each locality to being uniform all over the state—thus the tax change was imposed from above and was independent of the levels of local public services provided to firms. Second, other attributes of the business climate in various parts of California presumably were unaffected by Proposition 13. Therefore the effect of the tax change on firm location patterns can be examined without having to correct for such factors as differential production or transportation costs in different California localities. These factors are assumed to remain unchanged.

In this paper we use data from pre- and post–Proposition 13 California to test whether the changes in local property taxes have affected firm location patterns. The paper is arranged as follows. Section 4.2 briefly reviews the literature on economic models of firm location. Section 4.3 develops various models of the effect of taxes on firm location. Section 4.4 describes the model to be tested and presents results.

4.2 Economic Models of Firm Location

There is a large literature dealing with models of firm location from many perspectives.

The classic approach is that of regional scientists, who have developed models of firm location that stress cost minimization or profit maximization when sources of inputs and markets for outputs are dispersed over space at exogenously determined locations and transportation costs for inputs or outputs are nonnegligible. Wages and the prices of land, capital, and output are assumed to be fixed. This type of model leads to results such as that production processes that reduce bulk should be located near input sources, while production processes that increase bulk should be located near product markets.[2]

Urban economists have examined firm location patterns within cities. Here the locations of markets and input sources are usually assumed to be fixed, as are output prices, but transportation costs, land prices, and wages are assumed to vary inversely with the firm's distance from the city center. Typical results in this literature suggest that firms' capital/land ratios fall with greater distance from the center and that firms in different industries segregate themselves in rings around the center of the city.[3]

Neither of these approaches considers taxes as a major factor in firm location. This is because the effect of spatial variation in input costs or in transportation costs is implicitly assumed to swamp the effect of tax changes over space. For most firms, total nonfederal taxes are a much smaller proportion of their expenditures than are wages or capital costs and usually are smaller than total profits. However, the absolute size of each cost item is potentially less important than its variability in determining location.

Those studies of firm location that take taxes specifically into account are quite divided on whether taxes are important or not. For example, Epping (1982) surveyed manufacturing firms that either moved to Arkansas or considered but did not move to Arkansas and asked managers of these firms to rank a set of factors in order of importance in the location decision. He found that taxes ranked second in importance in firms' location decisions, just behind labor costs but above all other factors. The tax factor here presumably included all state and local taxes, not just property taxes, but still the ranking seems extraordinarily high. On the other hand, in an earlier and much more detailed survey of manufacturing firms in Cincinnati and New England that expanded, moved, or opened branch plants, Schmenner (1978) found taxes to be an infrequently cited and relatively unimportant factor in the location decision. Schmenner's results suggest that purely technological considerations, such as the need to expand or modernize production facilities, to separate different product lines, or to provide better geographic coverage of the market are most important in determining whether plants move or not. Both taxes and labor cost considerations became important in his study only in the relatively rare situation when a relocation or a branch plant opening involved a move of more than a few miles. For most firms taxes were unimportant for the simple reason that the firm did not move far enough to allow any significant variation.

There have also been several econometric studies of firm location, which have produced equally conflicting results concerning the importance of taxes. Carlton (1979) used Dun and Bradstreet data to explain the pattern of new births of firms across SMSAs in three manufacturing industries that ship their output long distances and therefore are not tied to locations near particular output markets. The explanatory factors used included wage levels, average corporate and personal income tax and property tax levels, utility costs, and measures of agglomeration effects across SMSAs. The results indicated that neither income nor property taxes were a significant determinant of new births. More recently, Bartik (1984) used Dun and Bradstreet data to estimate a model of branch plant location behavior across the fifty states by the Fortune 500 companies. He found that state corporate income tax rates were a significant determinant of plant location behavior, but property taxes were not.

A variety of econometric studies have used data from cross-sectional samples of local jurisdictions, usually within a single metropolitan area, to test whether the existing pattern or changes in the pattern of firm locations are explained by tax differentials across jurisdictions and a variety of other variables. The latter include, in various studies, measures of transportation facilities; distance to the central city; level of spending on local public services; supply of sites; energy costs; wage costs; and measures of agglomeration economies. For example, Wasylenko (1981a) and Fox (1981) separately estimated a series of models in which they argue that supply conditions, such as whether particular communities zone out industrial uses, should be taken into account in explaining firm location. Fox found that tax variables were significant in explaining the amount of land occupied by firms in a sample of suburban jurisdictions in the Cleveland area when those communities that zone out industry completely were excluded from the sample. Wasylenko found that property taxes were significant in explaining location choice for a sample of manufacturing and wholesale trade firms that moved to suburban jurisdiction around Milwaukee. However, property taxes were not significant in explaining moving behavior in several other industrial categories.[4]

To the extent that these studies are consistent about anything, they suggest that firms are more likely to be tax sensitive in making relatively short-distance moves within a particular metropolitan area. In considering these moves, other factors, such as wages, are likely to be constant at all possible locations. But since most metropolitan areas contain many local jurisdictions, taxes may vary at different sites. On the contrary, when intercity long-distance moves are being considered, wages, transportation costs, and other factors are likely to vary widely, so that variations in tax liability—while present—are less likely to be important in firms' decision making.

A related literature (see Fischel 1975 and Ladd 1975) takes the approach of examining whether the presence of more firms in a community has the effect of lowering its property tax rate, correcting for factors that would otherwise cause residents to have high demand for public services and therefore a higher tax rate. Both authors use data from communities within a single SMSA. The results of both studies suggest that a higher proportion of nonresidential property has a downward effect on communities' tax rates. Ladd also argues that commercial property has a larger negative effect on the property tax rate than industrial property, suggesting that communities have more monopoly power over commercial than industrial firms. This seems reasonable since commercial firms' markets are smaller and more spatially sensitive.

Another study worthy of mention is by Grieson and his associates (1977). It examines the effect of a change in the form of the business tax in New York City from a gross receipts tax to a profits tax on the level of employment in the city. Since New York City taxes different industries at different rates, a cross-sectional study could be done within a single locality. Grieson and his coauthors found that manufacturing employment was significantly negatively related to the level of taxes, while nonmanufacturing employment was not. Thus only manufacturing firms were tax-sensitive in making their location decisions. Further, they argued that receipts from the business tax could be increased by lowering the rates applicable to manufacturing firms—i.e., New York's tax rates were too high.

Finally, a related literature deserves mention. In most European countries, "regional policies" are used to give firms financial incentives to locate or expand in depressed regions. The incentives may include tax abatements, subsidized provision of sites or buildings built by government authorities, and wage or training subsidies for employees. Sometimes the positive incentives for firms to move to depressed areas are accompanied by penalties or controls on firms moving to nondepressed areas. Moore and Rhodes (1976) is an example of a study of the effects of British regional policy instruments. Not surprisingly, they find that the British combined tax-plus-regulatory regional policy does have significant effects on firm location patterns.

In the United States, regional policies have never been explicitly adopted by the federal government, except for the Appalachia program of the 1960s. There has been active consideration recently of a federal regional policy that would favor depressed central cities. Generous investment tax credits were enacted by Congress in 1981 for renovation of buildings thirty or more years old and of buildings in historic districts. There has also been discussion (but no action) on a program of "urban enterprise zones," which would release firms located in specific depressed areas from federal minimum wage laws, the social security program, occupational safety and health regulation, and various taxes. However, states and localities have rushed in with their own policies to fill the federal void. They offer a wide variety of financial incentives for firms to move in, ranging from floating tax-exempt industrial revenue bonds to using federal community development funds in ways that benefit firms to abating firms' property taxes. What has emerged is in effect an uncoordinated, ad hoc regional policy in which states and cities compete for firms by offering, primarily, subsidies from the federal government attractively packaged by the states and, secondarily, state or local subsidies in the form of direct tax abatements. It would be of interest to compare the results of these state programs with those of the European regional policies, but thus far no one has even studied the various U.S. policies in a consistent way.

Thus the literature on whether taxes affect firm location patterns shows little sign of general agreement on whether taxes are important or not.

4.3 Theories

In this section I explore several theories of the effect of property taxes on location choice by firms.

4.3.1   The Pure Tax Approach

A rather simplistic view of the firm location problem starts with the assumption that property taxes (or any taxes) levied on firms are pure taxes, unrelated to the level of public goods or services provided by the governmental unit that levies the tax. This might be the case, for example, if the public goods provided by local governments benefit only households, but are financed by taxes on both households and firms. Alternatively, local public goods could benefit both firms and households, but the mix of residential versus business property may differ across communities. In either case, the taxes paid by firms would be unrelated to the level of services received by firms.

Assume also that localities do not (or cannot) engage in direct regulation of land use patterns, i.e., there is no zoning. And assume that production costs for firms in any industry are invariant over space. This means, first, that transport costs of inputs and outputs remain the same regardless of the firm's location, perhaps because its output is exported and it always hires local workers whose wages are constant everywhere. Second, it means that direct production costs are constant over space. Thus, for example, the firm cannot reduce its waste disposal costs by locating on a riverbank site, either because no river exists in the region or because there is a system of pollution charges equal to marginal benefit levied on users of the river.

Firms in this model have incentives to move to those communities having the lowest (equalized) property tax rates. The higher the community's tax rate, the greater the incentive firms have to move out.

Now consider the issue of capitalization: i.e., do differences in land prices across communities compensate for differences in the level of taxes paid by firms? In the simple model depicted here, the answer is probably that differences in land prices would compensate for at least part of the variation in tax liability faced by firms in different communities. This means that high taxes in a community should have less of a discouraging effect on firms locating there than would appear if land prices were assumed to be unaffected by fiscal variables. However, even with capitalization, taxes will still have some locational effects. First, if firms value the public services provided by local communities, then they would be attracted to communities having desirable service menus even if taxes were higher there. This would partially offset the capitalization of taxes. Second, capitalization may cause sites in particular communities to become unavailable or unattractive to firms, either because land values fall to zero without fully compensating firms for higher taxes in that community or because high taxes on firms allow residential or other users that are subject to lower taxes to outbid firms for land. Third, firms may adjust their demand for land in response to changes in land prices, by substituting capital for land if land values rise or by moving out entirely. The more elastic is firms' demand for land for any reason, the less capitalization can be expected to occur.

A final problem with the capitalization story is that firms have a long-time perspective in making location decisions. While capitalization may insulate them from existing tax differentials, it may not insulate them from future changes in taxes. Thus firms may avoid high tax areas if they feel that high taxes now increase the probability of high tax *increases* later. While some firms that are renters may be able to avoid paying future property tax increases, the usual lease arrangement is likely to allow a pass-through of property tax increases, leaving the renter firm paying a tax increase but getting no offsetting rent reduction. Owner firms are negatively affected by both higher tax payments and capital losses if property taxes rise.

Now suppose that a Proposition 13–type change occurs that reduces or eliminates the variance of property taxes across the state. Assume that the change was unanticipated and that the level of benefits provided to firms remains unrelated to taxes paid. With no capitalization, firms' location incentives would change: previously high tax localities would become relatively more attractive, since taxes have fallen, and previously low tax localities would become relatively less attractive, since taxes have fallen by less or have risen. In this model we expect that firms in all industries would react in the same way to tax changes.

Suppose now that transportation and/or production costs do vary over space, but that there is still no capitalization. In this case firms are attracted to low tax jurisdictions, but the attraction is now weighed against other cost factors such as higher-than-average transportation or land costs, if these apply. The effects of a Proposition 13–type change are the same in this context as in the simpler case just discussed, except that they are more discontinuous. For example, a tax decrease due to Proposition 13 that is not great enough to offset a locality's cost disadvantage because of high transportation costs will not cause firms to move there. But a tax decrease in a different locality having good transportation facilities may cause firms to move in.

Finally, what if capitalization is again introduced? If property values in different communities previously capitalized variations in tax levels, then Proposition 13 will wipe out these differentials, leaving only production and transportation cost differences determining land values. With capitalization, firms located in previously high-tax communities will pay lower taxes but higher rents, and firms located in previously low-tax communities will pay the same or lower taxes and rents. But if rents are fixed by long-term contracts while taxes vary, then previously high tax communities will still become more desirable locations relative to previously low-tax communities, as long as the existing leases remain in force.

4.3.2 A Tiebout Theory of Firm Location

The theory discussed above assumes that the level of property taxes in any jurisdiction is independent of the level of the public services provided. The opposite approach assumes that property taxes are levied by local governments providing public services and that local taxes are the sole or a major source of revenue used to finance public services. From the viewpoint of local residents, a change such as Proposition 13, which forces uniformity of property tax levels, will also force changes in the level of public services provided. This results merely from the arithmetic of balancing budgets for local governments. However, from the viewpoint of firms, whose contribution to the overall revenues and expenditures of local governments is likely to be small, simple considerations of arithmetic play a smaller role. However, competition across communities may nevertheless force local governments to change the levels of public service provided to firms when tax revenues change. The assumption of intercommunity competition providing a link between local taxes and expenditures stems from the work of Tiebout (1956).

Suppose community i contains n_i households and has average (equalized) assessed value per housing unit of $\bar{H}_i$. Suppose it also contains m_{ij} firms in industry j having average (equalized) assessed value per firm of $\bar{F}_{ij}$. Suppose the community's tax rate before Proposition 13 was t_i. Then total property tax revenues, T_i, equal to total expenditures on local public services are

$$(1) \qquad T_i = t_i[n_i\bar{H}_i + \sum_j m_{ij}\bar{F}_{ij}].$$

In this context, the immediate effect of Proposition 13 is to replace t_i with a fixed statewide property tax rate, $\bar{t}$, which is less than any t_i value. If n_i, $\bar{H}_i$, m_{ij}, and $\bar{F}_{ij}$ remain the same, then expenditures on public services increase or decrease by $(t_i - \bar{t})/t_i$ or by τ_i percent. But changes in expenditure levels may affect firms versus households in the same locality differently.

Local public services vary between those that are more or less Samuelsonian public goods and benefit all households and firms in a community (roads are an example), and those that are more or less private goods provided to individual households or firms (trash collection is an example). Services in the latter category may be provided only to households (education) or only to firms (special police protection). Thus an increase or decrease in the local tax rate of τ_i percent could cause services to firms to rise or fall by the same percentage as services to households—if, for example, all local public services were Samuelsonian or all were private but the share of expenditures devoted to services to firms remained unchanged. In either of these cases, offsetting changes in taxing and spending levels would tend to have little effect on the relative attractiveness of different localities, particularly if firms can offset changes in public service levels by increasing or decreasing their use of private services that substitute for publicly provided goods. An example of this might be firms using more private security guards if police protection is cut back.[5]

However, the share of expenditures devoted to services to firms versus households may change if tax rates change. One possibility is that changes in tax revenues—up or down—will mostly be absorbed by changes in the level of such services as education, parks, and recreation, which benefit households. Services such as roads, police, and fire protection, which benefit firms, are less likely to be cut if tax revenues fall or to be raised if revenues rise. In this case, if a change such as Proposition 13 causes a community's tax rate to fall by τ_i percent, then firms' tax payments will fall by τ_i percent but the value of services provided to them will fall by less. Thus the tax price of local public services in that community will fall and firms will have an incentive to move there. Conversely, if the change causes a community's tax rate to rise by τ_i percent, then firms' tax payments will rise by τ_i percent, but the value of services provided to them will rise by less. Thus the tax price of local services will rise and firms will have an incentive to move out. In this scenario, Proposition 13 will cause previously high-tax communities to become relatively more attractive to firms, while previously low-tax communities will become relatively less attractive to firms.

Other possibilities also exist. Communities might prefer to cut back services to firms rather than households, because the tax price to firms of substituting private for public goods is more favorable than that for households. For example, firms can deduct from taxable profits the cost of either paying higher property taxes to finance a larger police force or paying the salary of a private security guard if police protection is cut back. But households cannot deduct the cost of summer camp for their children if cutbacks in property taxes (which are deductible for households that itemize) cause summer public school classes to disappear. This suggests a tax incentive for communities to cut back services to firms if property tax revenues fall and not increase services to firms if property tax revenues rise. However some services are difficult to cut—either because they are Samuelsonian public goods or because there are no private services that can be substituted for public goods.

I have shown that a Proposition 13–type change in a Tiebout context is likely to cause offsetting changes in local tax and expenditure levels. If the changes offset each other completely, then firms will have little or no incentive to move. If they offset each other but not completely, then firms will have an incentive to move to communities having a more favorable tax price per unit of public services and away from communities whose tax price rises. In this case, however, location effects are of second-order importance and incentives for firms to move are likely to be quite muted.

4.3.3   A Tiebout Theory of Firm Location with Zoning

In actuality, local governments exert much more direct control over firms' location choice than by setting the tax price for public goods. Zoning is often used to set aside areas where firms can locate and zoning maps are often quite specific concerning which types of firms are allowed in which zones. Firms may be excluded completely if they generate excessive noise or traffic or emit pollutants above a fixed standard. Buffer strips or extensive landscaping may be required of firms permitted to enter. Communities wishing to exclude particular firms or all firms may refuse to grant sewer permits or may require bribes of various sorts in return for zoning variances. Certain types of firms may be excluded regardless of circumstances. Wealthy communities may exclude all types of firms, preferring a completely residential environment. Bargaining on a case by case basis is often the rule.

Fischel (1975) and White (1975a and 1975b) have developed models in which there is intercommunity competition for firms, similar to that for high-income households. Communities are willing to accept firms as long as the property taxes paid by a new firm equal the sum of (1) the marginal cost to the community of supplying local public services to the firm and (2) the value to residents of the loss in environmental amenities due to the firm locating there. Communities are assumed to be willing to allow firms to enter as long as their tax payments equal or exceed this level. Intercommunity competition should drive taxes down to equality with marginal public service plus amenity costs, except that communities having monopoly control of some scarce resource will receive taxes greater than this level. In this scenario, when communities admit firms, their residents are compensated for the negative environmental impact by enjoying a lower price per unit of local public goods.

There are two variants on this theme. In the first, property taxes are individually negotiated with each firm and bear no relation to the market value of property used by the firm. In the second, discussed in the next section below, property taxes are levied on the actual value of property used by the firm.

Suppose that a particular firm in industry j wishes to locate in community i. The value of its environmental or disamenity effect is E_{ij} per year. The marginal cost of public services provided to the firm is C_{ij}.

Then to allow the firm to enter, the community will demand a yearly tax payment of $T_{ij} \geq E_{ij} + C_{ij}$. If there is intercommunity competition for firms, T_{ij} will be driven down to equality with $E_{ij} + C_{ij}$.

In this context, each community's property tax rate is determined by the requirement of a balanced budget relating the community's property tax revenues to its overall expenditures. This tax rate, t_i, by assumption must be applied uniformly to both residential and business property. Therefore to raise tax revenues T_{ij} from firm j, the tax assessor in community i sets a taxable value on the firm's capital (building) plus land of F_{ij}, where

$$(2) \qquad F_{ij} = T_{ij}/t_i \geq (E_{ij} + C_{ij})/t_i.$$

F_{ij} will generally differ from the actual market value of capital and land used by the firm.

Under these assumptions, the property tax is actually a bribe in disguise, related only in a formal way to the firm's use of property. Here the form of the tax has no deterrent effect on any particular firm entering any particular community. However, the determination of E_{ij} and C_{ij} will depend on many factors, including the number of firms already in the community, the community's income level and its character, the amount of vacant land in the community, and what public services the community provides to the firm. For particular types of firms, E_{ij} will be higher for high-income communities and is likely to rise at an increasing rate as the number of firms in a community rises. But E_{ij} may be lower if the community has vacant land, so that firms can be buffered from nearby residents. Finally, note that E_{ij} may be zero (or even negative) for particular communities. An extreme example is provided by the Asarco plant in the state of Washington, where use of asbestos endangers the health of local residents, but the community nonetheless opposes closing down the plant because the jobs it provides are valued.

In this scenario, high-income communities will admit only nonpolluting firms, such as office or research facilities or perhaps shopping malls. Since E_{ij} is higher in general in high-income than in low-income communities, all firms (including nonpolluting firms) will tend to prefer to locate in low-income communities. Exceptions to this rule would occur only if particular firms had lower production costs or higher revenues in high-income communities. Examples might be stores selling luxury goods, which value proximity to high-income customers, or office or research operations that value short commuting trips for their high-income workers.

How would a Proposition 13 change location incentives in this type of model? If Proposition 13 only changed tax rates from t_i to a uniform $\bar{t}$, then communities could reestablish the previous level of tax payments merely by setting a new assessed value for each firm, F_{ij}', where

(3) $$F_{ij}' = T_{ij}/\bar{t} \geq (E_{ij} + C_{ij})/\bar{t}.$$

In this case the same tax revenues would be collected from firm j by community i, with a higher assessed value offsetting a lower tax rate.

However, Proposition 13 also mandated a system of market value assessment (actually 1975 market value rising at 2% per year or the most recent sale price) for all properties. This latter provision causes problems for communities. With assessed value now set equal to market value, F_{ij}^m, firm i in community j pays property taxes equal to $\bar{t}F_{ij}^m$. For particular firms, the new property tax payment will differ little if any across communities, since only differences in the value of land or the capital/land ratio can cause variation in tax liability.

The firm's new level of property taxes differs from the old payment, T_{ij}, by

(4) $$(\bar{t}F_{ij}^m - t_iF_{ij})/t_iF_{ij},$$

in percentage terms.

For particular firms, the new level of tax liability can be either higher or lower than the old. Under Proposition 13, the property tax rate fell for all counties, i.e., $\bar{t} < t_i$ for all i. (See the discussion below of table 4.1.) However, the relation between pre–Proposition 13 F_{ij} and post–Proposition 13 F_{ij}^m is more difficult to predict. F_{ij} would tend to be higher for firms with more adverse environmental effects, for firms receiving higher levels of public services, for firms in communities with lower property tax rates, or for firms using little land and/or capital. For firms in these situations, property tax payments fall after Proposition 13. For other firms, however, F_{ij}^m may exceed F_{ij}, in which case property tax payments could either rise or fall. Thus communities' tax revenues from firms could either rise or fall as a result of Proposition 13.

I have shown that Proposition 13 caused communities to incur windfalls on property tax receipts from firms. These windfalls could be positive or negative. Since the pre–Proposition 13 system of setting an artificial assessed value on different firms to generate the correct bribe cannot be reestablished, communities and firms in this case are thrown out of equilibrium by Proposition 13. They are likely, therefore, to engage in nonmarket means of persuasion to move toward a new equilibrium. Communities may apply pressure selectively to firms that are now paying taxes less than $E_{ij} + C_{ij}$ either to reduce their pollution levels or to move out. Firms paying taxes greater than $E_{ij} + C_{ij}$ may pressure communities to allow them to pollute more or to expand on site. As an alternative, they may threaten to move. Communities may impose new user fees on firms already there and development fees on firms seeking to move in. They may also use zoning variances, building code regulations, and building inspections more or less rigorously than before, depending on whether the community wants to encourage new firms to enter or existing firms to leave. Thus nonmarket mechanisms are likely to become more important as the firm location pattern moves toward its new post–Proposition 13 equilibrium.

4.3.4   A Tiebout Theory of Firm Location with Pollution and Market Value Assessment

Now change the assumptions concerning how property taxes paid by firms are determined. Suppose in particular that communities are forced to assess and tax firm property at market value. Then the value of firm j's property in community i, F_{ij}^m, is exogenously determined. In the pre-Proposition 13 world, the tax revenue received by community i is $t_i F_{ij}^m$. In this case, communities have an incentive to use their zoning power to select particular types of firms. Assume that communities compete for firms based on their marginal disamenity costs. Also assume that the marginal cost of local public goods supplied to firms is zero, i.e., $C_{ij} = 0$.

Firms are now assumed to use land (L_j), capital (K_j), and environment (E_j) to produce their output (Q_j). Rather than follow the usual approach of viewing, say, smoke emissions as a joint product with output of the firm's production process, I instead treat the environmental amenity level as an input in the production process. In other words, environment is used up at varying rates per unit of output by different types of firms.

Suppose each community levies a property tax on the firm which is intended to compensate residents for loss of environmental quality. Assume that each community sets a constant per unit price, $\emptyset_i$, as its opportunity cost of environmental quality loss per unit of the input E_j. $\emptyset_i$ will be higher for wealthier communities or those for which there is inelastic demand for land. The community wishes to raise property tax revenues from firm j equal to the opportunity cost of environmental quality loss due to the firm. Thus

(5) $t_i F_{ij}^m = T_{ij} = \emptyset_i E_j.$

If each community has a predetermined, fixed property tax rate, t_i, then it can only raise taxes equal to $\emptyset_i E_j$ from the firm if the community's tax rate t_i equals the value of the loss of environmental quality caused by the firm divided by the market value of the firm's land plus capital or

(6) $t_i = \emptyset_i E_j/(p_L L_j + p_K K_j),$

where p_L and p_K are (constant) prices per unit of land and capital.

This means that firms in a metropolitan area will tend to locate in different communities depending on the relationship between firms' use of the environment relative to other private inputs versus the community's tax rate. Firms making relatively intensive use of the environment will tend to locate in high-tax-rate communities, while firms having little or no polluting effect will locate in low-tax-rate communities. In this model, each community is predicted to contain firms in only one or a few industries. Further, firms having extremely high pollution levels may not be able to find any community willing to admit them unless they introduce pollution controls, while very clean firms may pay property taxes in excess of $\emptyset_i E_j$ even in the lowest-tax-rate community.

For the Cobb-Douglas production function, $Q_j = E^{\alpha j} L^{\beta j} K^{1-\alpha j-\beta j}$, the resulting stratification effect is quite straightforward. In this case, equation (6) becomes

(7) $t_i = \alpha_j/(1 - \alpha_j).$

Thus firms stratify across communities depending only on the community's tax rate and the firm's level of α_j. Firms in industries with higher α_j values locate in communities with higher tax rates. Here firm location can be predicted simply by ranking communities by their tax rates and firms by the α_j value pertaining to that industry.

Now suppose Proposition 13 again replaces the set of community tax rates t_i with a uniform tax rate $\bar{t}$. Communities have now lost both degrees of freedom in taxing firms—they can vary neither F_{ij}^m nor $\bar{t}$. All firms using property of market value F_{ij}^m must pay the same amount in property taxes regardless of where they locate. The change in tax revenues received by community i from firm j is (in percentage terms) $\tau_i = (\bar{t} - t_i)/t_i$. This differs from the change in tax revenues under the negotiated property tax system. Since $\bar{t}$ is less than t_i for all communities, property tax payments by all firms fall, although by varying amounts. Since high-income communities generally have lower property tax rates than low-income communities, the latter are likely to suffer larger losses of property tax revenues from firms as a result of the Proposition 13–mandated reduction in t_i.

The relocation incentives of firms in this situation are again difficult to predict. First, the stratification effect described above should gradually disappear, with firms in different industries no longer tending to segregate themselves in particular communities. Second, communities generally are likely to exert direct pressure on firms, by cutting services, by forcing them to reduce pollution, or by encouraging them to move out. Finally, low-income communities are likely to become relatively more attractive to firms, both because their property tax rates have fallen the most and because these communities have low $\emptyset_i$ values.

To summarize this section, we have postulated several theories that predict quite different firm location effects as a result of Proposition 13. First, the pure tax approach predicted that firms would react to the change by moving into communities whose tax rate decreased the most and out of communities whose tax rate rose or fell by relatively small amounts. In this model, the prediction is the same for firms in all industries.

Second, the Tiebout theory of firm location predicted that the location effects of Proposition 13 would be much weaker. Here tax reductions are likely to be offset by reductions in the level of public services provided. If these two effects offset each other, then firms have no incentive to move. If the tax reduction is larger or smaller than the value of the service reduction, then firms have incentives to move toward (away from) communities whose tax per unit of public service has fallen (risen) the most. However, relocation incentives are second order here and any effects are likely to be small.

Third, the Tiebout theory of firm location under zoning suggests that, after Proposition 13, communities will incur positive or negative windfalls vis-à-vis firms within their boundaries, since tax revenues will rise or fall relative to firms' environmental amenity and marginal public service cost. This means that communities will exert selective pressures on firms to move out and/or may encourage other firms to move in. The effects are likely to differ by industry, with the environmentally worst firms under the most pressure to relocate. Also, communities whose tax revenues from firms have fallen the most are likely to exert nonmarket pressures on all firms within their boundaries. But such pressures may be difficult to detect, since they could take the form either of firms moving out or of firms abating their adverse environmental effects. In general, the effects of Proposition 13 under the zoning model will differ by type of firm and type of community.

4.4 Estimation

The basic specification of the model to be tested is:

$$(8) \qquad \dot{A}_{ij} = \alpha + \beta\Delta t_i + \gamma\dot{A}_{US,j} + \delta\dot{E}_{i,t-1} + \psi T/R_i + \epsilon_{ij},$$

where $\dot{A}_{ij}$ is the percent change in a measure of the activity level of firms in the jth industry in the ith locality between 1977 and 1981 and Δt_i is the change in the property tax rate in locality i during the same period. ϵ_{ij} is the error term. (The other variables are discussed below.) β can thus be interpreted as the percent change in activity per one percentage point change in the tax rate. It is expected to have a negative sign. For example, if $\beta = -5$, then a reduction in the property tax rate from 2% before Proposition 13 to 1% after would be associated with a 5% increase in the level of firm activity, or from, say, 100 firms before to 105 firms after.

Because of the variety of theories posited above concerning communities' and firms' responses to changes in the property tax structure, the tax coefficient β in (8) is subject to a variety of interpretations. If capitalization is important, then β measures firms' response to tax changes net of capitalization. If zoning policies by communities are important, then the tax change is likely to be correlated with the strength of communities' zoning response. Then β will measure the combined effects of property tax changes under Proposition 13 and the resulting changes in communities' zoning policies. Finally, if public service levels provided to firms change as a result of Proposition 13, then β will measure the net effect on firm activity of tax and service level changes. (I attempt to correct for the latter by introducing a measure of fiscal sensitivity to property tax revenues directly—see below.)

The data used to measure firm activity A_{ij} are countywide and come from County Business Patterns (CBP).[6] For each SIC code, CBP data are available concerning the number of firms in the county, total number of employees, and total yearly payroll. Equation (8) is estimated separately for each of these three activity measures. CBP data have the advantage that they measure all sources of change in firm activity levels: expansions, contractions, relocations, and firm births and deaths are all included. Data from two-digit SIC codes (broad industrial classifications) are used, since the more disaggregated four-digit SIC codes contain many zero values for individual counties. The sample of SIC codes used contains manufacturing firms, firms in transportation and communications, firms providing financial services, firms in wholesale and retail trade, construction, and the service sectors. Primary industries (mining, farming) are excluded on the grounds that they are spatially tied. Also government industries such as the Postal Service and education and social services are excluded since public property is exempt from the property tax. The years used were 1977, the last year before Proposition 13 took effect, and 1981, the most recent year for which CBP data are available. Table 4.1 gives mean values for all variables and table 4.2 lists the set of SIC codes used.

Countywide average property tax rates and assessed value/market value ratios for 1977 were obtained from the State Board of Equalization, state of California, for thirty of California's fifty counties.[7] The resulting equalized property tax rates for each county are given in table 4.3 for 1977.[8] Since Proposition 13, the Board has not attempted to construct average assessed/market value ratios for counties. These can still vary across counties, either because of varying rates of capital

Table 4.1   **Means and Standard Deviations of Variables**

	Manufacturing		Retailing/Services	
	Mean	Standard deviation	Mean	Standard deviation
Proportional change in number of firms, 1977–81, California counties	.079	.258	.095	.284
Proportional change in number of employees, 1977–81, California counties	.355	.911	.359	.559
Proportional change in payroll, 1977–81, California counties	.817	1.19	.770	.878
Proportional changes in number of firms, 1977–81, U.S.	−.021	.073	.024	.116
Proportional change in number of employees, 1977–81, U.S.	.042	.074	.207	.164
Proportional change in payroll, 1977–81, U.S.	.427	.113	.588	.215
Proportional change in employed labor force, 1973–77, California counties	.226	.091	.229	.086
Property tax revenues/total revenues, 1977, California counties	.383	.058	.379	.056

appreciation or varying rates of turnover since 1978. However, from the point of view of a firm considering relocating to or within California, this omission does not seem to be a serious problem. If the firm purchases property, then the sale value will become the new assessed value, while if the firm rents property, then the rent level will capitalize any tax savings from a lower assessed value. In either case, the (perhaps implicit) property tax liability faced by a relocating firm should be constant anywhere in California.

The (uniform) tax rate used for 1981 was 1.144%.[9] Changes in tax rates for individual counties after Proposition 13 are also given in table 4.3. The sample thus consists of thirty counties times fifty-four SIC

Table 4.2   **SIC Codes Used in Regressions**

Manufacturing

2000	food and kindred products
2100	tobacco manufacturers
2200	textile mill products
2300	apparel and other textile products
2500	furniture and fixtures
2700	printing and publishing
2800	chemicals and allied products
2900	petroleum and coal products
3000	rubber and miscellaneous plastic products
3100	leather products
3200	stone, clay and glass products
3300	primary metal products
3400	fabricated metal products
3500	machinery, except electrical
3600	electric and electronic equipment
3700	transportation equipment
3800	instruments and related products
3900	miscellaneous manufacturing industries

Retail and wholesale trade, services, transportation, construction

4200	trucking and warehousing
4500	transportation by air
4700	transportation services
4800	communication
5000	wholesale trade—durable goods
5100	wholesale trade—nondurable goods
5200	building materials and garden supplies
5300	general merchandise stores
5400	food stores
5500	automotive dealers and service stations
5600	apparel and accessory stores
5700	furniture and home furnishings stores
5800	eating and drinking places
5900	miscellaneous retail
6000	banking
6100	credit agencies other than banks
6200	security, commodity brokers and services
6300	insurance carriers
6400	insurance agents, brokers, and service
6500	real estate
6600	combined real estate, insurance
6700	holding and other investment offices
7000	hotels and other lodging places
7200	personal services
7300	business services
7500	auto repair, services, and garages
7600	miscellaneous repair services

Table 4.2   (continued)

Retail and wholesale trade, services, transportation, construction

7800	motion pictures
7900	amusement and recreation services
8100	legal services
8900	miscellaneous services
1500	general building contractors
1600	heavy building contractors
1700	special trade contractors

codes. Eliminating observations for which the activity measure was zero or missing in either 1977 or 1981, the actual sample size used in the regressions is 1156 observations.

Several other variables were also used in the estimations. First, the period 1977–81 was one of recession in many industries. To correct for overall macroeconomic trends in each industry, I introduce the variable $\dot{A}_{US,j}$, the percent change in activity nationally in industry j. Activity nationally is measured by the same three variables over the same time period as are used in constructing $\dot{A}_{ij}$, except that the U.S. summary of the County Business Pattern data is used. (Thus when the percent change in number of firms in county i in industry j is being explained, the recession correction variable is the percent change in number of firms in the United States in industry j and similarly for the other two activity measures.) Note that if the coefficient of $\dot{A}_{US,j}$ equals one, then activity in county i in industry j has increased or decreased since 1977 at the same rate as it did nationally.

Second, to allow for differences in the rate of overall economic growth of different localities, which may be correlated over time, I introduce the variable $\dot{E}_{i,t-1}$, the rate of increase in the employed labor force in county i over the period before the adoption of Proposition 13. $\dot{E}_{i,t-1}$ is measured for the years 1973–77 and is also taken from County Business Patterns.

Finally, in an attempt to measure how the provision of local public services has been affected by the adoption of Proposition 13, we used as an additional variable the ratio of property tax revenues to total revenues in 1977. This variable, denoted T/R_i, was intended to measure the sensitivity of different areas' fiscal structure to reductions in property tax revenue. Higher values of this variable would indicate greater likelihood of extensive service reductions following Proposition 13. To the extent that firms are attracted to areas where better public services are provided (holding firms' own taxes constant), higher values of T/R_i would discourage firms from locating there. The data are taken from the 1977 Census of Governments and are listed in table 4.3.[10]

Table 4.3   Equalized Property Tax Rates in Thirty California Counties and
                   the Ratio of Property Tax Revenues to Total Government
                   Revenues

	1977 equalized tax rate	Percent change 1977–81	1977 property taxes/ total revenue
Alameda	.0257	−55%	.41
Butte	.0156	−27%	.40
Contra Costa	.0222	−48%	.50
Fresno	.0174	−34%	.33
Humboldt	.0129	−11%	.35
Kern	.0134	−15%	.39
Los Angeles	.0215	−47%	.40
Marin	.0188	−39%	.52
Mendocino	.0186	−38%	.38
Monterey	.0174	−34%	.38
Napa	.0160	−29%	.42
Orange	.0149	−23%	.43
Placer	.0180	−36%	.32
Riverside	.0194	−41%	.33
Sacramento	.0227	−50%	.30
San Bernadino	.0212	−46%	.34
San Diego	.0182	−37%	.36
San Francisco	.0199	−43%	.36
San Joaquin	.0207	−45%	.32
San Luis Obispo	.0137	−16%	.43
San Mateo	.0153	−25%	.45
Santa Barbara	.0153	−25%	.37
Santa Clara	.0197	−42%	.38
Santa Cruz	.0174	−42%	.44
Shasta	.0139	−18%	.38
Solano	.0187	−39%	.32
Sonoma	.0196	−42%	.35
Stañislaus	.0191	−40%	.32
Tulare	.0152	−25%	.27
Ventura	.0197	−42%	.40
Yolo	.0202	−43%	.45
Mean	.0181	−35%	.38

The relationship between the number of employees and the payroll measures of firm activity allows investigation of the issue of whether property tax changes cause offsetting changes in wage levels. Suppose we denote the first activity measure (number of firms) as $\dot{A}^1_{ij}$, the second activity measure (number of employees) as $\dot{A}^2_{ij}$, and the third activity measure (payroll) as $\dot{A}^3_{ij}$. Then we have

$$(9) \qquad \dot{A}^2 = \frac{N_2 - N_1}{N_1} \text{ and}$$

$$(10) \qquad \dot{A}^3 = \frac{w_2 N_2 - w_1 N_1}{w_1 N_1},$$

where N_2 and N_1 are number of employees in 1981 and 1977, respectively, and w_2 and w_1 are wage rates in 1981 and 1977, respectively. The i and j subscripts have been dropped temporarily. From (8), we have $\partial A^2/\partial \Delta t = \beta_2$ and $\partial A^3/\partial \Delta t = \beta_3$, where β_2 and β_3 are the coefficients of Δt in the equations explaining number of employees and payroll. We can differentiate (9) and (10), assuming that w_1, N_1, and t_1 are fixed and defining Δt as $t_2 - t_1$. Substituting, we get a relationship between the estimated effects of the property tax change on number of workers and payroll and the implied effect of the tax change on wage rates, or:

$$(12) \qquad \eta = \frac{w_1 N_1}{w_2 N_2} \beta_3 - \frac{N_1}{N_2} \beta_2,$$

where η is the percent change in w_2 (post–Proposition 13 wage rates) per percentage point change in the property tax rate. Thus by estimating equation (8) for the number of employees and payroll measures of activity, we can indirectly examine whether there were wage capitalization effects of Proposition 13.

The theories discussed above suggest that responsiveness to property tax changes might differ for firms in different types of industries. In particular, if zoning is an important factor in firms' location decisions, then firms in polluting industries may have very restricted options since they are excluded from many localities. These firms are less likely to react to the change in property taxes. Other firms will be more or less welcome in their pre–Proposition 13 locations after the change, depending on whether their new levels of property tax payments exceed or fall short of their disamenity plus local public service costs. Also, retailing firms and service firms face a different problem in moving from manufacturing firms, since their markets are spatially defined. If they move, they must develop a new customer base. On the other hand, these firms often have little invested capital, which makes moving easier for them than for firms with a more substantial capital investment.

To investigate these issues, the sample was subdivided into two groups: manufacturing firms and firms in retail trade and services. The latter group also includes firms in construction, transportation, and wholesale trade. (See table 4.2.) Equation (8) was estimated for the entire sample and for each subsample; in each case for all three activity measures. Chow tests on all three activity measures rejected the hypothesis of a common relationship; therefore only the separate results for the two subsamples are reported.

Tables 4.4 and 4.5 give the results. Examining the results for the property tax variable, Δt_i, its sign is consistently negative (except in the regression explaining changes in the number of manufacturing firms). It is significantly negative in all three regressions explaining service and retailing activity, but is never significant in the regressions explaining manufacturing activity. Thus the results provide support for

Table 4.4   **Regression Results Explaining Firm Activity Levels in California—Manufacturing Sectors**

	Activity measure ($\dot{A}_{ij}$)		
	Percent change in number of firms	Percent change in number of employees	Percent change in payroll
Constant	.224*	.132	−.317
	(.106)	(.399)	(.566)
Δt_i	1.38	−5.81	−15.5
	(4.89)	(18.4)	(23.7)
$\dot{A}_{US.j}$	1.06*	1.87*	1.70*
	(.186)	(.687)	(.578)
$\dot{E}_{i,t-1}$	.246	1.56*	2.12*
	(.165)	(.616)	(.798)
T/R_i	−.439	−.632	−.424
	(.237)	(.887)	(1.15)
R^2	.11	.04	.05
F	9.6	3.7	4.0
N	329	329	329
SSR	19.6	275.4	461.8

NOTE: Standard errors are in parentheses. Asterisks indicate significance at the 95% level.

the hypothesis that property taxes are a significant determinant of the level of firm activity for retailing and service firms, but not for manufacturing firms. In the retailing-services sector, a property tax decrease of one percentage point (which is close to the average impact of Proposition 13) causes an increase of about 6% in the number of firms, an increase of 6% in employment, and an increase of 15% in payroll. The results here thus do not support the usual presumption in the literature that manufacturing firms are more tax sensitive and footloose than retailing or service firms. While the coefficients of Δt_i are of similar magnitude in the regressions explaining the number of employees and payroll for manufacturing firms, they are never significant.

We can use these results and information in table 4.1 to calculate the wage capitalization effect described in equation (12) for the retailing-services sector. Substituting and using the values $N_1/N_2 = .74$ and $w_1N_1/w_2N_2 = .56$, we find that $\eta = -1.7$. Thus the same one-percentage-point decrease in the property tax rate implies an increase in wage rates of about 1.7%. Part of the benefit from the property tax reduction thus goes to workers in the form of higher wages.

The other variables have the expected signs and are generally significant. Both sets of regressions have elasticities of firm activity in California with respect to changes in activity nationally which are con-

Table 4.5   **Regression Results Explaining Firm Activity Levels in California—Service and Retail Sectors**

	Activity measure $(\dot{A}_{ij})$		
	Percent change in number of firms	Percent change in number of employees	Percent change in payroll
Constant	− 0.100*	.276*	− .883*
	(.0440)	(.105)	(.163)
Δt_i	− 6.14*	− 9.21*	− 15.05*
	(1.97)	(4.66)	(6.87)
$\dot{A}_{US,j}$	1.17*	.666*	1.32*
	(.0470)	(.0774)	(.0898)
$\dot{E}_{i,t-1}$	.436*	.715*	.869*
	(.0681)	(.161)	(.237)
T/R_i	.0460	.617*	1.43*
	(.0999)	(.236)	(.348)
R^2	.45	.11	.23
F	166.9	25.9	62.2
N	826	826	826
SSR	21.4	119.7	259.9

NOTE: Standard errors are in parentheses. Asterisks indicate significance at the 95% level.

sistently greater than unity. The lagged county employment variable is significant in all but one regression and is always positive. In the manufacturing regression it is generally greater than unity, while in the retailing-services sector regressions, it is always less than unity. The tax sensitivity variable has the expected negative sign in the manufacturing regressions, but is positive in the retailing-service sector regressions.

In conclusion, the empirical results provide support for the hypothesis that property taxes have a significant negative effect on firm activity levels in the services and retailing sector. A decrease of one percentage point in the property tax rate, about the change that occurred in California after Proposition 13, is associated with an increase of 6% in number of firms, 9% in number of employees, and 15% in payroll. The results suggest that the property tax drop also caused wages to rise slightly in these sectors, by about 1.5%. However, the study did not find any significant effect of property taxes on firm activity levels for manufacturing firms. It seems possible that these firms adjust to tax change only with a longer lag than the four years reflected in the data, perhaps because they have capital invested in their current locations that would decline substantially in value if moved. Retailing and service firms, in contrast, are more likely to be able to pick up their capital and take it with them.

Notes

1. Proposition 13 exempted school district debt service obligations contracted before 1978 from the 1% property tax levy. These amounts are added to the basic property tax.
2. See Isard (1956). A recent reference is Oster (1979).
3. See White (1976) and Moomaw (1980).
4. See Oakland (1978) and Wasylenko (1981b) for surveys of the empirical literature and further references.
5. See White (1979), which develops a theory of how governments respond to exogenously imposed tax cuts by reducing spending on various services depending on the substitutability of private for public inputs in producing "quasi-public goods."
6. These data are published annually by the Bureau of the Census.
7. I am grateful to Jeff Reynolds, Statistical Research and Consulting Division, California State Board of Equalization, and to Howard Chernick for providing data.
8. Before Proposition 13, state guidelines called for an assessed value/market ratio of .25, but many counties had lower ratios. The equalized property tax rates are the product of the assessed value/market value ratio and the statutory tax rate.
9. Obtained from the State Board of Equalization.
10. Several other fiscal variables were also tried, with similar results. These included the percent increase in total county expenditure over the period 1977–81 and the level of total government revenue per capita in 1977.

References

Bartik, T. J. 1984. Business location decisions in the United States: Estimates of the effects of unionization, taxes and other characteristics of states. Working paper no. 84–W05 Department of Economics, Vanderbilt University.

Carlton, D. W. 1979. Why new firms locate where they do: An econometric model. In W. C. Wheaton, ed., *Interregional movements and regional growth, COUPE papers on public economics 2*. Washington, D.C.: Urban Institute.

Dorf, R. J., and M. J. Emerson. 1978. Determinants of manufacturing plant location for nonmetropolitan communities in the west north central region of the U.S. *Journal of Regional Sciences* 18:1.

Epping, G. M. 1982. Important factors in plant location in 1980. *Growth and Change* 13:1.

Fischel, W. A. 1975. Fiscal and environmental considerations in the location of firms in suburban communities. In E. S. Mills and W. E. Oates, eds., *Fiscal zoning and land use controls*. Lexington, Mass.: Lexington Books.

Fox, W. 1981. Fiscal differentials and industrial location: Some empirical evidence. *Urban Studies* 18: 105–11.

Grieson, R. E., W. Hamovitch, A. M. Levenson, and R. D. Morgenstern. 1977. The effect of business taxation on the location of industry. *Journal of Urban Economics* 4: 170–85.

Isard, W. 1956. *Location and space-economy*. Cambridge: MIT Press.

Ladd, H. F. 1975. Local education expenditures, fiscal capacity, and the composition of the property tax base. *National Tax Journal* 28, no. 2: 145–58.

Moomaw, R. 1980. Urban firm location: Comparative statics and empirical evidence. *Southern Economic Journal* 47: 404–18.

Moore, B., and J. Rhodes. 1976. Regional employment policy and the movement of manufacturing firms to development areas. *Economica* 43: 17–31.

Oakland, W. H. 1978. Local taxes and intraurban industrial location: A study. In G. Break, ed., *Metropolitan financing and growth management policies*. Madison: University of Wisconsin Press.

Oster, S. 1979. Industrial search for new locations: An empirical analysis. *Review of Economics and Statistics* 61: 288–92.

Papke, L. E. 1984. The measurement and influence of interstate tax differentials on industrial activity. Mimeographed.

Schmenner, R. W. 1978. The manufacturing location decision: Evidence from Cincinnati and New England. Report to the U.S. Department of Commerce, Economic Development Administration.

Tiebout, C. 1956. A pure theory of local expenditures. *Journal of Political Economy* 64: 416–24.

Wasylenko, M. 1981a. Evidence on fiscal differentials and intrametropolitan firm location. *Land Economics* 56: 339–49.

———. 1981b. The location of firms: The role of taxes and fiscal incentives. In R. Bahl, ed., *Urban government finance: Emerging trends. Urban Affairs Annual Review*, 20.

Wheaton, W. C. 1983. Interstate differences in the level of business taxation. *National Tax Journal* 36: 83–94.

White, M. J. 1975a. Firm location in zoned metropolitan areas. In E. S. Mills and W. E. Oates, eds., *Fiscal zoning and land use controls*. Lexington, Mass.: Lexington Books.

———. 1975b. Fiscal zoning in fragmented metropolitan areas. In E. S. Mills and W. E. Oates, eds., *Fiscal zoning and land use controls*. Lexington Books.

———. 1976. "Firm Suburbanization and Urban Subcenters," *Journal of Urban Economics* 3:323–43.

———. 1979. Government response to spending limitations. *National Tax Journal* (supplement) 32: 201–10.

Comment   Sharon Bernstein Megdal

Michelle White examines the outcome of a natural experiment, California's implementation of Proposition 13, in her study of the effect of property taxes on firm location. The underlying premise is that firms' location decisions are influenced by a host of factors, including production and transportation costs and taxes. The distribution of business activity over a region will change as the relative costs of doing business change. If we are interested in studying changes in business activity relative to some base, as is White, we can do so without measuring those factors that remain constant over the period of interest. It is reasonable for White to assume that relative production and transportation costs within the state of California were not affected by implementation of Proposition 13. This assumption allows her to model intercounty variation in business activity without specifying a complete model of firm location behavior.

It is evident from White's literature survey that there is no set of consistent results regarding the effect of taxes on firm location. The studies suggest that taxes do not appear to be an important determinant of choice of location when a firm is deciding among different regions, but they may be of some importance when a firm selects a location within a region.

White's theoretical discussion, though lengthy, is rather peripheral to the empirical portion of the paper. I say this because she offers alternative theoretical models and predictions, only some of which are consistent with the central empirical hypothesis that activity growth rates will be higher where property tax decreases are greater. Given the sometimes similar and sometimes ambiguous predictions and the incongruity of some of the models, I would have liked some insight as to which model she thought most appropriately described the pre–Proposition 13 situation in California. She then could have discussed the empirical findings in the context of the predictions of the "preferred" theoretical model. A discussion of the relative advantages and disadvantages of the three measures of business activity used would also have been helpful. If the interest is in modeling the outcome of firm location choices, the first dependent variable (the number of establishments) would be preferred. If the interest is in modeling business activity in general, on the other hand, perhaps one of the other two measures better captures the relevant magnitudes.

Sharon Bernstein Megdal is serving as a commissioner on the Arizona Corporation Commission. She is on leave from her position as assistant professor of economics at the University of Arizona.

White's results are largely consistent with her hypotheses. Although her simple model does not explain a large proportion of the variation of the dependent variables, the results are quite reasonable both qualitatively and quantitatively. The paper represents a good first attempt at studying a complex issue; however, I would have liked more discussion and interpretation of the findings. The author presents a menu of theoretical models but does not select a model from that menu. She then presents several regression equations but offers the reader little in the way of interpretation of the results. Hence, the remainder of my comments are devoted to a discussion of her model and results, focusing on my reasons for finding the results quite reasonable but also pointing out why I find interpretation of them somewhat difficult.

What I would select from White's menu is a model with zoning, assessments not equal to fair markets values,[1] a weak relationship between property taxes paid and services received by firms, and partial capitalization of property tax differentials. According to the 1977 *Census of Governments,* which reports data for fiscal 1976–77, a year that would be expected to be indicative of the pre–Proposition 13 revenue structure, 48.1% of property taxes raised in California funded school expenditures, and 5.8% funded expenditures of special districts. County and municipal governments raised the remaining 32.1 and 14.0% respectively. Property tax revenues comprised 24% of municipal general revenue and 36% of county general revenue. The figures suggest that a substantial portion of property tax dollars paid by firms did not fund services received by firms and that services received by firms were funded to a significant extent by revenue sources other than the property tax. It is, therefore, difficult to predict the extent of service cutbacks experienced by firms as a consequence of Proposition 13.

Given these figures, the post–Proposition 13 distribution of state surplus funds, and the increased use of user charges and development fees,[2] I would predict little response of basic industry activity, such as manufacturing, to imposition of Proposition 13, which is exactly what White found. Predictions regarding the retail and service sectors, the other main grouping studied, depend upon predictions regarding basic and nonbasic employment and residential location activity. Examination of White's list of service and retail industries reveals industries whose activity levels largely depend on residential location activity, which in turn depends on the growth in and dispersion of the population. Population growth depends partly on employment growth, while the dispersion of the population depends on the relative attractiveness of alternative residential locations, as determined by numerous factors, including the proximity to employment, housing prices, the extent to which the property tax is a benefit tax, and perceptions regarding service levels. Before accurate predictions regarding nonbasic business activity can be made, a more complete model of business and residential activity must be specified. Although this endeavor is beyond the scope of this discussion, data for the thirty-one counties studied by White reveal some interesting patterns.

The following statistics are based on county level data (not broken down by industry) obtained from *County Business Patterns*. The average four-year growth rate in the number of establishments decreased from 16.1% for the 1973–77 period to 11.3% for the 1977–81 period, while the corresponding growth rate in number of employees increased over that same period from 19.8 to 25.7%. The correlation between the 1973–77 growth rate for establishments (employees) and the 1977 countywide average property tax listed in White's table 4.3 is − 0.27 (− 0.22). The simple correlation between the 1977–81 growth rate for establishments (employees) and the 1977 property tax rate is 0.20 (− 0.03). Finally, the correlation between the 1973–77 and 1977–81 growth rates for establishments (employees) is 0.56 (0.49). (I have not considered changes in payroll, the third of White's dependent variables, because of their heavy dependence on the salary mix of employees.) Whereas there is a positive relationship between growth in the number of establishments and the number of employees, the correlation is not perfect. The data indicate that the growth in the number of establishments may have slowed down, but employment figures suggest that larger-than-average firms opened up and/or existing establishments fared well during the 1977–81 period. Proposition 13 was implemented just before interest rates soared and just after rapid escalation of home prices in California. The high cost of living in California relative to that of other states, uncertainty surrounding the general tax and revenue situation,[3] and the general slowdown in the economy are likely responsible for a slowdown of business movement into California. Yet at the same time, the rate of employment growth increased. White's regression results indicate that employment increased more rapidly in pre–Proposition 13 high-tax counties, though the manufacturing sector coefficient is not significant. With increased employment comes increased demand for the goods and services of service and retail trade firms, which are likely to respond readily to increased demand by expansion or entry into local markets. However, the question to what extent property taxes influence the location decisions of firms is still largely unanswered. So much of the variation in the dependent variables remains unexplained. The model has not explained the variation in location activity of firms producing goods for nonlocal markets, nor has it established that taxes are an important determinant of location choices for retail and service firms. The results for the latter sectors could be reflecting residential location choices rather than firm response to tax differentials.

The problems in interpreting White's results are no different from those that arise whenever a simple structure is used to model complex phenomena. The results, for the most part, are consistent with her hypotheses. What is needed for more definitive conclusions is a more detailed model of growth and business activity in California.

I would like to discuss some other reasons, some of which have already been alluded to, for the rather poor performance of the empirical model in explaining variation in business activity. First, there are problems of data aggregation. The data are at the county level; consequently, intracounty variability in the data is masked. In addition, the dependent variable includes births, deaths, expansions and contractions, and relocations within, into, and out of the state. Some of these components would be expected to be more sensitive to relative property tax rates than others. Another problem is that the time since passage of Proposition 13 may not have been long enough for differences in manufacturing activity to be revealed. Manufacturing (re)locations are likely to involve substantial lead time. Some of the firm activity in the early part of the 1977–81 period may reflect decisions made prior to Proposition 13, while some decisions made in the period immediately following its passage may not have been realized until rather late in the 1977–81 period. Also, the uncertainty surrounding the fiscal future of California locales relative to each other and relative to those in other states may have led to postponement of relocation and/or expansion decisions. For example, increases in user and development fees and the distribution of state surplus revenues lessened the immediate impact of Proposition 13.

White's assertion that certain attributes of California's business climate could be assumed to be unchanged by Proposition 13 is reasonable; however, the business climate of California relative to the rest of the United States may have changed over this period. Thus, in addition to adjusting for the change in industry activity at the national level, controlling for the level of industry activity in California might be necessary. One way of incorporating such changes in a model explaining intrastate variation in business activity would be to redefine the dependent variable in terms of the share of state business activity. One could then examine the change in shares over time.

In summary, I think the question to what extent firm location decisions depend on property tax rates is still largely unanswered. White's model yields quite reasonable results, but further study is needed. I am not yet willing to accept or reject the hypothesis that Proposition 13's realignment of property tax rates has had an impact on firm location patterns. It may be a while before a new equilibrium is reached in California. A different data set, model, and/or patience will help shed further light on this important question.

Notes

1. See Oakland (1979, 396).
2. See Strauss, Mikels, and Hagman (1982).
3. For example, Proposition 4, which limits the growth in annual appropriations of state and local governments, was passed by initiative in November 1979, but did not take effect until July 1, 1980. Also, developers found that local jurisdictions could change development rules after commitment of funds for public improvements. (See Strauss, Mikels, and Hagman [1982].) There was also uncertainty as to the extent to which worldwide earnings of multinational corporations would be taxed under California's unitary tax. Although in *Container Corporation of America vs. Franchise Tax Board*, the United States Supreme Court recently ruled that the worldwide unitary method of taxation used by California is constitutional, it is likely that California and other states will change their methods of taxing multinational corporations because this particular tax does seem to affect location decisions of multinational firms.

References

Oakland, W. H. 1979. Proposition XIII—genesis and consequences. *National Tax Journal, supplement.*

Strauss, B., M. Mikels, and D. G. Hagman. 1982. Description of proposition 13 and 14. In J. G. Rose, ed., *Tax and expenditure limitations: How to implement and live within them.* Rutgers: Center for Urban Policy Research, the State University of New Jersey.

U.S. Department of Commerce, Bureau of the Census. *Census of Governments.* GC77(4)–2, 3, 4.

U.S. Department of Commerce, Bureau of the Census. *County Business Patterns.* CBP–74–6, CBP–77–6, CBP–81–6.

5

Welfare Effects of Marginal-Cost Taxation of Motor Freight Transportation: A Study of Infrastructure Pricing

Kenneth A. Small and Clifford Winston

5.1 Introduction

Recent physical failures in the United States highway system, resulting in vehicle damage and even catastrophic accidents, have lent urgency to a growing perception that our highway infrastructure is seriously degraded. Repair estimates run in the hundreds of billions of dollars.

While this problem is nationwide in extent, much of the financial burden rests squarely on state and local governments. In 1982, state and local tax revenues financed about three-fourths of all U.S. highway expenditures, consuming over 8% of all state and local own-source revenues.[1] Virtually every state has a list of defective bridges for which repairs await funding, and several have raised fuel taxes and license fees. Individual cities such as New York responded to fiscal pressure for many years by deferring highway maintenance; now they face a seemingly impossible catch-up task, made more difficult by recent congressional delays in appropriating interstate highway funds.

The most dramatic response has been the Surface Transportation Assistance Act of 1982, which increased federal fuel and truck-weight taxes in order to finance more federal highway assistance. Yet neither of these taxes bears a close relationship to the highway wear caused by various motor vehicles. Only the state weight-distance or ton-mile taxes vary with both weight and mileage, and only ten states have them.[2] Furthermore, gross weight is a poor proxy for the damage done to a highway. Highway wear depends critically on weight per axle,

Kenneth A. Small is an associate professor of economics at the University of California at Irvine. Clifford Winston is a research associate at the Brookings Institution.

hence it is not necessarily the heaviest vehicles that are most responsible for current conditions.

Thus, neither federal nor state policy seriously attempts to align motor vehicle taxes with the damage the vehicles inflict on highways, as would be required under a policy of marginal-cost pricing. The state weight-distance taxes come closest. They also use administrative mechanisms that could be adapted to such a policy, as recently proposed by staff members of the Oregon Department of Transportation.[3] At present, however, little is known about what impact such a policy would have.

The purpose of this paper is to estimate the welfare effects of instituting nationwide marginal-cost pricing for heavy highway vehicles, with marginal cost defined as the incremental contribution of a vehicle to repaving costs. We first describe such a tax, using existing evidence on the marginal costs of various vehicle movements. Next, we outline a procedure for estimating the tax's impact on the distribution of vehicle-miles traveled by different types of heavy trucks, and on shippers' modal choice between truck and other forms of freight transportation. We then show how to calculate net benefits and the distribution of costs and benefits among shippers, carriers, and the public treasury. These calculations are carried out using 1982 data. Even though we have attempted to be conservative throughout, we still find that such a tax could go a long way toward solving the physical and financial problems of maintaining a sound infrastructure.

5.2 The Size and Structure of Marginal Cost Highway Taxes

Conventional highway engineering practice defines a unit of road wear called the equivalent single axle load (ESAL), which refers to the amount of wear caused by a single axle bearing 18,000 pounds. A highway is designed to withstand a given number of ESAL applications, after which major repairs such as resurfacing become necessary.[4] This implicitly assumes that the passing of a given vehicle does the same pavement damage as the passing of a particular number of single axles each bearing 18,000 pounds. That number is called the load equivalent factor, or ESAL number of the vehicle, and it is a very sensitive function of the weights on each of its axles. As a rough approximation, the load equivalent factor of a truck (or tractor-trailer combination) is the sum for each of its axles of $(w/18)$ to the fourth power, where w is the weight on that axle in thousands of pounds. This relationship is based on a test-track experiment completed in the early 1960s,[5] and is further supported by mechanical models of pavement stress.[6] Corroborating evidence from actual highways is weaker but not entirely absent.[7]

Besides hastening the need for major repairs, pavement deterioration adversely affects user costs of all vehicles using the highway because of the lower average speeds and greater vehicle wear it entails. These costs are at present only very imprecisely known, and are not included here.

In an appendix to the recent Federal Highway Cost Allocation Study, the Federal Highway Administration (FHWA) included estimates of the properly discounted highway repair costs caused by an ESAL under various conditions (U.S. FHWA 1982a, p. E-28). These range from $.05 to $.50 per ESAL-mile. As a fairly conservative estimate, we use the average of rural interstate and rural arterial roads, which is $.09.

To avoid double-counting, we do not include any allocation of the extra construction costs required to build the original highway to heavy-duty specification. In future work, we intend to refine these estimates and possibly the ESAL unit itself as a measure of highway damage. There seems no doubt, however, about the basic premise: highway damage varies steeply with axle weight.

The Cost Allocation Study also provides estimates of the load equivalent factors for selected motor vehicle types and gross weights. We have adapted these to the vehicle types and weight classes chosen for our analysis,[8] then multiplied by the $.09 figure. Selected results are presented in table 5.1. Each vehicle type is identified by a code giving the basic configuration (SU for single unit, CS for conventional tractor and semitrailer, DS for tractor and double-trailer) followed by the number of axles. The vehicle types used in this study are displayed in figure 5.1.

Of the thirteen vehicle types distinguished in our data set, we have selected five as the starting points for what we think will be the most significant shifts, because of either high usage (e.g., the five-axle tractor-semitrailer combination designated CS5) or high load equivalent factor (e.g., the two-axle vans designated SU2 and registered above 33,000

Table 5.1   **Marginal Costs ($/vehicle mile)**

Vehicle type	Gross vehicle weight (thousands of pounds)				
	26	33	55	80	105
SU2	.066	.171	1.319		
SU3	.012	.031	.236	1.058	
CS4		.012	.090	.404	
CS5		.006	.046	.207	.614
CS6			.027	.120	.356
DS5			.080	.360	1.068
DS9			.007	.030	.090

KEY: SU = single unit truck
     CS = conventional tractor and semi-trailer
     DS = tractor and double-trailer
     The number following the letter code is the number of axles.

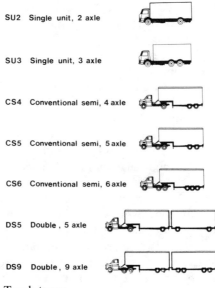

SU2   Single unit, 2 axle

SU3   Single unit, 3 axle

CS4   Conventional semi, 4 axle

CS5   Conventional semi, 5 axle

CS6   Conventional semi, 6 axle

DS5   Double , 5 axle

DS9   Double , 9 axle

Fig. 5.1   Truck types

pounds). In 1982 these five accounted for 90% of all vehicle-miles by vehicles larger than pickup trucks. Similarly, of all the possible vehicle types to which truckers initially using each of these five might shift, because of the new tax, our analysis is restricted to the one that is likely to be the most important. The resulting shifts are: from two-axle to three-axle single-unit trucks (SU2 to SU3); from SU3 to five-axle tractor-semitrailer combinations (CS5, also known as "eighteen-wheelers"); from four-axle to five-axle semitrailer combinations (CS4 to CS5); from CS5 to the relatively rare six-axle semitrailer combination (CS6); and from five-axle to nine-axle double-trailer combinations (DS5 to DS9).

The double-trailers are of greater interest than their small vehicle populations would suggest, because the 1982 federal legislation forced all states to legalize them. This raises a safety issue that is ignored here but that needs resolution before such a tax is adopted.

In order to translate the marginal costs into tax rates, we assume that each vehicle is taxed at 80% of its mileage. This is to account for the fact that between 10 and 25% of truck mileage is with no load, and that another 10% or so is with less than three-fourths of a load.[9] We also assume that each tax rate is an accurate reflection of the highway damage that vehicle produces. Finally, we assume that the tax replaces the existing (1982) federal and state mileage-related taxes, including fuel taxes, but not those taxes levied as an annual fee per vehicle. Our rationale is that annual fees are payments for services or externalities such as police, signaling, and congestion that are predominantly urban, and therefore not proportionally related to vehicle utilization.

A practical issue concerns implementation. As a first approximation, the tax could be collected on the basis of registered maximum gross weight, which is how we have modeled it and which accords with current taxing practice in those states that levy a weight- distance tax. A more fine-tuned tax could allow firms to document their actual load distributions and pay tax based on actual weight carried. A further refinement would be to vary the tax by road type, levying a higher rate for travel on noninterstates to reflect their greater vulnerability to wear from heavy loads. Each of these refinements requires greater record keeping, but if applied only to larger firms this does not seem an insurmountable burden. States with weight-distance taxes already require considerable record keeping and have extensive auditing capabilities (New York State Legislative Commission 1983).

5.3   Welfare Analysis Methodology

Instituting marginal-cost pricing for motor vehicles will have a number of effects, not all of which we can model here. Truckers themselves would potentially respond in at least three ways. They might redistribute the loads on existing vehicles more evenly in order to reduce their highest gross weights (since the tax rises more than proportionally with weight). They might expand their fleets so as to operate at lower average loads. Finally, they might shift their fleet composition toward vehicles with more axles, either by selling and buying vehicles or, where possible, by retrofitting existing vehicles. Based on conversations with industry experts, we believe the last to be the most likely, and model it under the heading of vehicle-type shifts.

Since in most cases the new tax would be higher than the one it replaces, trucking rates would rise (though not by as much as would be predicted ignoring vehicle-type shifts). Shippers would respond by shifting some traffic to other transportation modes, particularly rail. We also model this modal shift.

For each of these two shifts, we calculate the change in tax revenues and in road maintenance and repair expenditures, the difference between which measures the effect on governments' budget balance. From that is subtracted the loss of producers' and shippers' surplus to obtain the net welfare gain.

5.3.1   Vehicle-Type Shifts

We analyze shifts within the five vehicle-type pairs described previously by assuming that exactly the same payloads will be carried in the new vehicles.[10] We originally planned to model vehicle-type choice as one of simply using the vehicle type with lowest cost including tax.

In reality, however, firms have greatly varying needs that may make them favor some vehicles over others for reasons other than relative costs. To approximate this, we assume that shifts between vehicle types are proportional to the change in their relative costs. We accomplish this by postulating a fixed elasticity of substitution. By doing this we implicitly assume that the shift is also proportional to the extent to which the new vehicle type is in use initially; this recognizes that it will take a long time to alter habits, vehicle stocks, and truck manufacturing capacity.

Each shift is measured as the change in vehicle-miles traveled by the new vehicle type. For the given vehicle-type pair and weight class under consideration, let $i = 0,1$ denote the initial and new vehicle type, respectively, let q_i be the corresponding number of vehicle-miles, and let p_i be the average cost per vehicle-mile including taxes. Let t^f_i be the fuel and weight-distance tax per mile, which we estimate from U.S. FHWA 1982b, and which is to be replaced by the new marginal-cost tax of t_i. Letting Δ denote a change, the changes in the two tax rates are $\Delta t_i \equiv t_i - t^f_i$, $i=0,1$; and the vehicle-type shift as defined above is $\Delta q_1 = -\Delta q_0$.

The elasticity of substitution σ between vehicle types 0 and 1 is defined (so as to be positive) by:

$$(1) \qquad d(\log q_1) - d(\log q_0) = \sigma[d(\log p_0) - d(\log p_1)],$$

where d denotes a differential and log the natural logarithm. Since taxes are the only part of costs that change, we can write the approximation of this for discrete changes as:

$$(2) \qquad (\Delta q_1/q_1) - (\Delta q_0/q_0) = \sigma[(\Delta t_0/p_0) - (\Delta t_1/p_1)].$$

The vehicle-type shifts will tend to come from firms that are nearly indifferent between the two vehicle types in the initial equilibrium. We represent this by the approximation $p_1 = p_0$. Setting $\Delta q_1 = -\Delta q_0$ and rearranging terms, we therefore have:

$$(3) \qquad \Delta q_1 = -\Delta q_0 = \sigma[q_0 q_1/(q_0 + q_1)](\Delta t_0 - \Delta t_1)/p_0.$$

Since we have chosen our vehicle types so that type 0 has a larger tax rise than type 1, expression (3) is positive.

All welfare effects refer to those shipments originally using type 0 vehicles. These represent q_0 vehicle-miles of travel, both before and after the shift. To avoid double-counting, no welfare effects are measured for shipments originally using type 1 vehicles, since in most cases those vehicles are also treated as type 0 vehicles in another pair. Tax revenues from these shipments were originally $q_0 t^f_0$ and become $(q_0 - \Delta q_1)t_0 + (\Delta q_1)t_1$. Using the above definitions, this change in revenues can be written:

(4) $$\Delta R = q_0 \Delta t_0 - \Delta q_1 (t_0 - t_1).$$

Note that $(t_0 - t_1)$ is positive since the new tax rewards carrying a given load in a vehicle with more axles.

Because t_0 and t_1 reflect highway maintenance and rehabilitation expenditures caused by the respective shipments, the shift causes those expenditures to change by

(5) $$\Delta M = \Delta q_1 (t_0 - t_1).$$

This quantity will usually be negative, reflecting a cost saving. The change in the government budget balance is

(6) $$\Delta B = \Delta R - \Delta M = q_0 \Delta t_0.$$

Expression (6) is independent of the amount of shifting because the new tax is assumed exactly equal to the maintenance cost caused by the vehicle paying it.

The marginal cost tax will generally lead to higher trucking costs, some or all of which will be passed on in higher shipping charges and, ultimately, in higher consumer prices. This will cause a loss in producers' and consumers' surplus that can be computed in the usual way using the simultaneous demand for services of the two vehicle types as a function of prices p_0 and p_1. Because of the absence of income effects in our model, it is independent of the particular path by which the prices are assumed to change. We use the path shown in figure 5.2. First we simultaneously raise p_0 and p_1 by an amount Δt_1; since this does not change q_0, it causes a change in surplus of $-q_0 \Delta t_1$. Next, holding p_1 constant, we raise p_0 by an amount $(\Delta t_0 - \Delta t_1)$, causing the shift Δq_0 and consequent change in surplus $-(q_0 + \Delta q_0/2)(\Delta t_0 - \Delta t_1)$. Thus we can write the total change in surplus as

(7) $$\Delta S = -q_0 \Delta t_0 + (1/2)\Delta q_1 (\Delta t_0 - \Delta t_1).$$

The first term in (7) represents a näive calculation of the loss to truckers and shippers; the second term is an offset representing ability to reduce

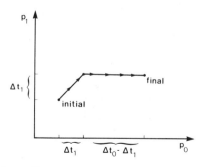

Fig. 5.2   Price path

the tax burden through vehicle-type shifting. Noting that ΔS is negative, it is useful to restate (7) as

$$(8) \qquad \Delta p \equiv -\Delta S/q_0 = \Delta t_0 - (1/2) (\Delta q_1 / q_0) (\Delta t_0 - \Delta t_1).$$

If truckers earn no economic profits, this is the cost increase per vehicle-mile passed on to shippers through higher rates. It is used in the next subsection as the basis for computing shippers' response through modal shifts.

Combining equations (6) and (7), we obtain a net welfare gain from the vehicle-type shifts of

$$(9) \qquad \Delta W = \Delta B + \Delta S = (1/2)\Delta q_1 (\Delta t_0 - \Delta t_1).$$

This equation should be recognized as an example of the "rule of a half" for measuring the welfare effects of simultaneous changes in tax rates on several goods (Harberger 1964, 40).

5.3.2   Modal Shifts

With the higher trucking rates expressed in equation (8), some shippers will shift to other modes of freight transportation such as railroads. Use of trucks will therefore be reduced still further. Assuming an own-price elasticity of demand for trucking of $-e_m$ from this effect, the resulting change in vehicle-miles is $\Delta q_m = -q_0 e_m \Delta p/p_0$. Using (8), this can be written as:

$$(10) \qquad \Delta q_m = -e_m q_0 \Delta t_0/p_0 + (1/2)e_m \Delta q_1 (\Delta t_0 - \Delta t_1)/p_0.$$

Note the loss in tax revenue from this shift, $t_0 \Delta q_m$, just cancels the reduction in highway maintenance and rehabilitation expenditures. Hence there is no net effect on the budget balance: $\Delta B_m = 0$. However, the existence of the rail option does offset the loss of producers' and consumers' surplus calculated above. Analytically, allowing for this shift is equivalent to adding a new transportation option at the old price, which is Δp below the new price. Shippers and consumers therefore realize an increase in surplus of one-half the demand for the option $(-\Delta q_m)$ times the price reduction (Δp):

$$(11) \qquad \Delta S_m = -(1/2)\Delta q_m \Delta p = (1/2)e_m(q_0/p_0) (\Delta p)^2.$$

Finally, we note that net welfare gain from modal shifting is

$$(12) \qquad \Delta W_m = \Delta B_m + \Delta S_m = \Delta S_m.$$

To summarize, equations (9) plus (12) capture the net welfare gain from instituting a marginal cost taxation policy for trucks, accounting for vehicle-type and modal shifts. In the next section, we calculate this welfare gain and the other quantities defined above using data on U.S. highway transportation for 1982.

5.4   Data

Our basic traffic and cost data were compiled by the U.S. Department of Transportation's Transportation Systems Center for use in a large computer model of highway operations.[11] The data are for 1982, reflecting the situation before implementation of the Surface Transportation Act of that year. Data on numbers and usage of vehicles were derived from the U.S. Census Bureau's 1977 Truck Inventory and Use Survey, and were updated using the Federal Highway Administration's Revenue Forecasting Model. Since the weight classes used in that survey were too broad for our purposes, we allocated the totals for each class to finer categories within that class in proportion to that vehicle type's registrations as reported in the FHWA's Truck Weight Study of 1979–82. The cost information is based on 1977 figures derived by the Transportation Systems Center as part of the Highway Cost Allocation Study and the Truck Size and Weight Study, updated using truck cost indices published by Data Resources, Inc. The initial fixed and variable taxes reflect the actual 1982 situation.

For reasons of data availability, we use registered weights as proxies for actual weights. This raises the question of whether this procedure systematically over- or underestimates the gains to be reaped from marginal-cost taxation. While legally operated vehicles will often weigh less than they are registered for, there is also widespread overloading (U.S. General Accounting Office 1979). On balance we suspect average highway damage from vehicles in a given registered gross weight class exceeds the damage that would done if, as we assume, every vehicle traveled 80% of its mileage loaded to exactly its registered weight. Thus if anything this procedure probably underestimates benefits from the tax.

There is no direct empirical measurement of the elasticity of substitution among vehicle types, σ. However, Friedlaender and Spady (1981, 271) did estimate trucking firms' elasticity of substitution between capital and "purchased transportation," which means expenditures on rail, air, water, and hired-out trucking services. This elasticity, which they found to be roughly 1.25, provides an indication of the degree to which trucking firms respond to changing vehicle costs by substituting other carriers' services for their own vehicles. The substitutability among firms' own vehicles ought to be much higher than this, particularly if there are low-cost possibilities for retrofitting existing vehicles with more axles.[12] Hence we have assumed a value of 5.0. We discuss later the sensitivity of our results with respect to this parameter.

For the modal diversion elasticity, e_m, there is considerable empirical evidence (see Winston 1985) suggesting a figure of about 1.0. Although it is known that this elasticity varies considerably with commodity shipped, we are not able to disaggregate our analysis by commodity.

5.5 Results

The results of our calculations are summarized in table 5.2. For each of the five initial vehicle types, the figures shown are the totals for between seven and fourteen distinct weight categories.

The welfare gain is substantial, roughly $1.2 billion per year. This represents real resources saved: the savings in highway maintenance and repair expenditures less the increase in real resources used in shipping. Keeping in mind that we have tried to make this estimate a conservative one, it seems large enough at least to arouse interest.

The policy contributes significantly to solving the "infrastructure problem." Not only does it raise $10 billion of additional tax revenues annually, it also reduces annual highway maintenance and repair expenditures by nearly $3 billion, or about 17% of total expenditures incurred because of these five truck types.

Accompanying these gains is a very sizable redistribution from truckers, shippers, and consumers to the public treasury. The nearly $12 billion reduction in producers' and consumers' surplus is, in effect, collected through the trucking industry, which can be relied upon to resist strenuously. However, the total rise in after-tax trucking costs is less than 4%, and much of this will be passed on to the public at large—which is also the beneficiary of the redistribution. Furthermore, there seems to be a growing public awareness that the current excess of highway damage costs of heavy vehicles over the taxes they pay, which averages about $3,000 per vehicle annually from our figures, can be regarded as an unjustified subsidy. Thus we do not think the policy should be ruled out immediately as politically infeasible, especially if the possibilities for reducing its initial impact through vehicle-type shifting are adequately publicized.

Another possible distributional effect is a one-time capital loss on trucking firms' vehicle stock. Marginal-cost taxation might render certain vehicles economically obsolete and thereby lower their resale value, so that their owners would incur a disproportionate share of the tax burden. In other words, some of the loss of surplus could be capitalized into lower asset values for certain vehicles. (This represents a redistribution of costs we have already accounted for, not an additional cost.) Given the possibilities of retrofitting and an international resale market, we doubt that capital losses would be very important. But if they are, one way to mitigate them is for the government to purchase obsolete vehicles for domestic use (but with smaller loads!) or for resale abroad. To ensure that government vehicles themselves do not obstruct the policy, the tax should also apply to them.

Table 5.2   Welfare Calculations

		Vehicle type					
		SU2	SU3	CS4	CS5	DS5	Total
Initial values:							
Vehicles	v	4226.20	749.01	328.30	625.63	40.51	5969.65
Vehicle-miles traveled	q_0	56.40	14.70	10.97	36.39	2.58	121.03
Maint. & repair expend.	M	4.88	3.30	1.31	4.95	0.65	15.09
Total trucking costs	C	111.76	39.04	29.45	76.06	7.63	263.95
Changes from vehicle shifts:							
Vehicle-miles traveled	Δq	-1.60	-2.39	-0.50	-0.22	-0.09	-4.80
Revenue	ΔR	3.61	2.01	1.08	4.13	0.56	11.38
Maint. & repair expend.	ΔM	-0.43	-1.02	-0.04	-0.02	-0.03	-1.54
Budget balance	ΔB	4.03	3.03	1.11	4.15	0.59	12.92
Producer & consumer surplus	ΔS	-3.82	-2.52	-1.09	-4.14	-0.58	-12.14
Net welfare gain	ΔW	0.22	0.52	0.02	0.01	0.02	0.78
Changes from modal diversion:							
Vehicle-miles traveled	Δq	-1.78	-0.79	-0.43	-2.05	-0.24	-5.29
Revenue	ΔR	-0.23	-0.30	-0.08	-0.35	-0.08	-1.05
Maint. & repair expend.	ΔM	-0.23	-0.30	-0.08	-0.35	-0.08	-1.05
Budget balance	ΔB	0.00	0.00	0.00	0.00	0.00	0.00
Producer & consumer surplus	ΔS	0.10	0.11	0.04	0.15	0.04	0.44
Net welfare gain	ΔW	0.10	0.11	0.04	0.15	0.04	0.44
Total changes:							
Vehicle-miles traveled	Δq	-3.38	-3.18	-0.93	-2.27	-0.32	-10.09
Revenue	ΔR	3.37	1.71	0.99	3.78	0.48	10.33
Maint. & repair expend.	ΔM	-0.66	-1.32	-0.12	-0.37	-0.11	-2.59
Budget balance	ΔB	4.03	3.03	1.11	4.15	0.59	12.92
Producer & consumer surplus	ΔS	-3.72	-2.41	-1.06	-3.99	-0.54	-11.71
Net welfare gain	ΔW	0.31	0.63	0.06	0.16	0.05	1.22

NOTE: All figures are in billions of vehicle-miles or billions of dollars, except v, which is in thousands of vehicles. Notation is explained in text.

Table 5.2 shows a $15 billion estimate of total highway expenditures caused by these five truck types. This is based on our marginal cost estimates and on the assumed linear relationship between total ESAL applications and highway expenditures.[13] One check on our assumptions would be to compare this estimate with actual highway expenditures in 1982, which were $41 billion.[14] The latter figure includes new construction as well as maintenance and repair. Furthermore, our estimate is of the annual expenditures needed over a period of many years to maintain the infrastructure at a constant level of service, whereas current expenditures may be either lower (allowing the level of service to deteriorate) or higher (compensating for past neglect). Nevertheless, it is reassuring that our numbers are of the right order of magnitude.

Two other interesting points emerge from a close look at table 5.2. First, more than one-third of the net benefits are attributable to modal diversion. This suggests that if highways were priced as we recommend, any private or public actions that were to improve railroad pricing and service quality would generate additional benefits heretofore overlooked.

Second, in contrast to conventional thought,[15] we find that the smaller vehicles, the single-unit trucks, are the largest potential source of welfare improvement. Perhaps too much attention has been focused on the heaviest trucks as the cause of our infrastructure problem. Indeed, highway maintenance officials often cite cement mixers and garbage trucks as the worst culprits. The latter are often municipally owned: again, it is better that the tax apply to the public as well as the private sector.

The most uncertain of our numerical assumptions is the elasticity of substitution between vehicle types, σ. If there is more substitutability than our figure of 5.0 suggests, overall benefits would be larger and the loss to the truckers and shippers smaller. Table 5.3 shows that the main

Table 5.3   Sensitivity of Selected Results

	Elasticity of substitution		
	2.5	5.0	10.0
Modal shift:			
Δq_m	−5.54	−5.29	−4.87
Total changes:			
ΔM	−2.04	−2.59	−3.01
ΔS	−11.99	−11.71	−11.47
ΔW	0.94	1.22	1.45

NOTE: All figures are in billions of vehicle-miles or billions of dollars, and are totals for the five vehicle types shown in table 5.2. Except for Δq_m, they include the effects of both vehicle type and modal shifts.

results change by at most 25% from their baseline values as the elasticity of substitution varies between 2.5 and 10.0.

5.6   Qualifications and Suggestions for Future Work

There are several factors omitted from our analysis that may be important. We discuss three below. The first two would cause us to underestimate the benefits of marginal cost taxation, while the third would cause an overestimate.

First, there is a reason to believe that prices exceed marginal costs in many rail markets (Keeler 1983). If so, there are additional benefits from modal diversion in the form of producers' surplus to railroad firms. We note in passing that, from a second-best perspective, uncorrectable distortions in rail prices would call for compensating distortions in motor carrier markets; however, the latter should be done through shipping rates, not infrastructure taxes.

Second, we would expect some net improvement in highway safety to result from these taxes. The major reason is simply the reduction in number of trucks and perhaps, though we have not modeled it, a reduction in average payloads. In addition, improved pavement quality should have some positive effect on safety. Offsetting these somewhat is the relative increase in larger vehicles, including double-trailer combinations.

Third, our calculation assumes that truckers' earnings reflect their opportunity costs in other occupations. This is not the case if displaced drivers or other trucking employees are unable to secure comparable employment elsewhere.

Regardless of how precise our numerical results prove to be, one point stands out: the current basis for taxing trucks is the wrong one. Neither gross weight, fuel consumed, nor number of axles (the sole basis for Ohio's distance-related tax and for many turnpike tolls) is a suitable proxy for contribution to highway costs. Although we have argued for a tax that is higher and more complex than current taxes, even a less thoroughgoing reform might be worthwhile. Switching to *any* distance-related tax based on a schedule increasing sharply with weight per axle would very likely bring substantial benefits, even if it were no more complex than current taxes and brought in the same revenues. In this respect, the recent congressional directive to study the feasibility of a nationwide weight-distance tax threatens to lock us into an unsatisfactory solution for many years. Attention should instead be focused on an axle-weight-distance tax.

We have not discussed the related question of choosing axle weight limits. Given that most states already have such limits, adjusting them is an alternative to the tax policy analyzed here. Indeed, Weitzman

(1974) identifies certain conditions when such quantity controls are superior to corrective taxes. However it is doubtful that the trucking industry, with its large number of firms with independently varying marginal costs, would meet those conditions.

Methodologically, at least three extensions to our work are worth pursuing. First, the assumption that the distribution of payload weights carried would be unchanged should be replaced by an optimization model of vehicle loading. Second, our knowledge of the kinds and magnitudes of vehicle substitutions that would take place could be greatly improved by developing and estimating an empirical model of motor vehicle type choice.

Finally, it would be worthwhile to analyze the welfare effects of an optimal highway maintenance policy that corresponds to our optimal pricing policy. It seems likely that some of the enormously expensive one-time highway rehabilitation being considered would be done differently, or not at all, if marginal-cost pricing were in effect. Furthermore, ongoing maintenance policies, often based on long-standing rules of thumb developed in an era of more or less unrestricted truck traffic, probably would need revision. Indeed, this might reduce the magnitude of the marginal-cost taxes through the adoption of maintenance procedures better suited to the altered vehicle mix. This in turn would soften the impacts of the tax change on the trucking industry, while adding to the net welfare gains.

Despite these qualifications, our results suggest that significant benefits can be realized through a realistic and operationally feasible policy of marginal-cost taxation of truck transportation. Such a policy has the appealing feature of providing significant new public revenues while correcting, rather than aggravating, economic distortions. Over a longer period, it promises to help solve the problem of how to maintain the very large and important portion of the nation's capital stock represented by its highway system.

Notes

This work was partially supported by the Institute of Transportation Studies, University of California.

1. Advisory Commission on Intergovernmental Relations 1984, 6, 20.
2. See Merriss and Henion 1983, 4, 6. Recently the U.S. Congress has ordered the secretary of transportation to evaluate the feasibility of nationwide weight-distance taxes.
3. See Merriss and Krukar 1982.
4. Peattie 1978; U.S. Federal Highway Administration 1982a, pp. IV-42 to IV-43.
5. See American Association of State Highway and Transportation Officials 1981.
6. See U.S. Federal Highway Administration 1982a, appendix D, pp. D-12 to D-22.
7. Elliott 1981.
8. The CS4 and CS6 were not included in the FHWA figures; their ESAL numbers are derived from those of the CS5 assuming that weight on each axle is inversely pro-

portional to number of axles and that each axle's contribution to ESAL is proportional to the fourth power of its weight. Similarly, we use the fourth-power law to adapt the FHWA figure for a given vehicle type at a given gross weight to each of the gross weights considered.

9. U.S. Interstate Commerce Commission, 1977, 9, 11.

10. This means the gross weight (which includes the vehicle itself) is slightly higher after the shift. Based on data in U.S. FHWA 1982b, 12–13, it appears that each of the shifts we are considering is to a vehicle that is about 5,000 pounds heavier (8,000 in the case of DS5 to DS9). The tax rates for the new vehicles are adjusted accordingly, using the fourth-power law discussed in the text and in note 8. The increase in gross weight will slightly lower fuel efficiency and hence increase truckers' costs. This small effect is excluded here.

11. We are grateful to Mike Nienhaus and Mark Hollyer of the Transportation Systems Center for providing these data, and for many helpful discussions of how best to use them for our purposes.

12. We are grateful to Paul Courant for suggesting the possibility of retrofitting.

13. Specifically, total initial maintenance and repair expenditures are taken to be the sum over all truck types of $M_0 = q_0 t_0$. This implied linearity assumption is consistent with the methodology used by FHWA to estimate the marginal costs, though there is no direct evidence for or against it.

14. U.S. FHWA 1983, 40, table HF-10.

15. See, for example, U.S. FHWA 1982a and the written testimony of Alice M. Rivlin, director of the Congressional Budget Office, before the U.S. Senate Committee on Environment and Public Works, 18 August 1982.

References

Advisory Commission on Intergovernmental Relations. 1984. *Significant features of fiscal federalism, 1982–83 edition.* Washington, D.C.: Advisory Commission on Intergovernmental Relations.

American Association of State Highway and Transportation Officials. 1981. *AASHTO interim guide for design of pavement structures 1972: Chapter III revised.* Washington, D.C.

Elliott, R. P. 1981. Rehabilitated AASH(T)O road test. *Pavng Forum* (Summer): 3–9.

Friedlaender, A. F., and R. Spady. 1981. *Freight transport regulation.* Cambridge, Mass.: MIT Press.

Harberger, A. 1964. Taxation, resource allocation and welfare. In J. Due, ed., *The role of direct and indirect taxes in the federal revenue system.* Washington, D.C.: The Brookings Institution.

Keeler, T. E. 1983. *Railroads, freight, and public policy.* Washington, D.C.: The Brookings Institution.

Merriss, J., and L. Henion. 1983. Oregon's weight-distance tax: Theory and practice. Paper submitted for presentation at the Transportation Research Forum, Washington, D.C., November 3–5.

Merriss, J., and M. Krukar. 1982. A proposal for an axle weight-distance road user charge. *Transportation Research Forum Proceedings* 23:405–11.

New York State Legislative Commission on the Modernization and Simplification of Tax Administration and the Tax Law. 1983. Transportation taxes in New York State. Staff working paper, May 17.

Peattie, K. R. 1978. Flexible pavement design. In P. Pell, ed., *Developments in highway engineering—1*. Essex, U.K.: Applied Science Publishers.

U.S. Federal Highway Administration. 1982a. *Final report on the federal highway cost allocation study*. Washington, D.C.

———. 1982b. *Road User and Property Taxes On Selected Motor Vehicles*. Washington, D.C.

U.S. Federal Highway Administration. 1983. *Highway statistics 1982*. Washington, D.C.

U.S. General Accounting Office 1979. *Excessive truck weight: An expensive burden we can no longer support*. Report to the Congress. Washington, D.C.

U.S. Interstate Commerce Commission. 1977. Empty/loaded truck miles on interstate highways during 1976. Bureau of Economics. Washington, D.C.

Weitzman, M. L. 1974. Prices vs. quantities. *Review of Economic Studies* 41:477–91.

Winston, C. 1985. Conceptual developments in the economics of transportation: An interpretive survey. *Journal of Economic Literature* 23:57–94.

Comment   Paul N. Courant

It is always a pleasure to be called upon to discuss a topic that one knows nothing about, and it is a double pleasure to be introduced to a whole new family of acronyms in the process. In just the first few pages of this paper, we are introduced to RGW, kips, ESAL, VMT SU2, SU3, CS4, CS5, CS6, DS5, and the terrifying DS9, also known as the "rocky mountain double." I certainly can't say that I didn't learn anything reading this paper.

The new acronyms were the least of what I learned. Far more important, the authors make a convincing case that marginal-cost pricing of the road wear imposed by trucks could lead to substantial welfare improvement and also relieve a good deal of the fiscal burden imposed by the "infrastructure problem" facing the U.S. highway system. I find the case convincing in spite of the fact that the authors fail to

Paul N. Courant is professor of economics and public policy and director of the Institute of Public Policy Studies at the University of Michigan.

consider a number of plausible changes in trucker and shipper behavior that might occur in response to the imposition of marginal-cost taxes, and in spite of the fact that I have a few quibbles with their particular implementation of the adjustments that they did consider. Before going into a summary and criticism of the paper, I note that the authors are to be commended on their frankness regarding the limitations of the data and assumptions they employed. They do not make overblown claims for their work, and, indeed, the issues that I raise below tend to strengthen their case rather than weaken it.

Summary of the Paper

The paper begins by noting that there is a widely perceived fiscal problem associated with the nation's roads and bridges, and that current "user fees" on trucking bear little relationship to the costs actually imposed by the vehicles. (Note that costs here are limited to resurfacing and rebuilding costs. Safety, environment, and other issues are absent from both the paper and this discussion.) It turns out that the actual costs imposed by trucks depend critically on axle loadings, and that there is a standard measure, called an ESAL (equivalent single-axle load) that can be used to calculate the costs imposed, per vehicle-mile, by a truck. Moreover, there is tremendous variation in the ESAL numbers of different types of trucks currently in service, leading to tremendous variation in estimated costs per vehicle-mile. (In table 5.1, the range of these costs for the types of vehicles considered is from .012 dollars to 1.068 dollars.) If ever there were a potential role for marginal-cost pricing, this looks like it, and authors devote the bulk of the paper to estimating and evaluating the effects of replacing current fuel taxes with taxes equal to the marginal road repair and maintenance costs that trucks impose.

The authors consider two types of responses to the imposition of such taxes. First, truckers will shift to vehicles with more axles carrying the same load, thus reducing their ESAL numbers and their tax. Second, shippers will shift to other modes of transportation, specifically rail. Regarding the first type of adjustment, the authors consider such shifts for five initial truck types and numerous vehicle weights, each holding payload constant in each case. They then calculate Harberger triangles for each of the shifts and add them up.

The procedure employed is straightforward and the resulting welfare measures are as accurate as the Harberger triangle procedure and the estimates of marginal costs themselves.[1] Three important assumptions are made in implementing the procedure: (1) The elasticity of substitution between each pair of truck types is assumed to be 5.0. (2) The only form of trucker adjustment that takes place is switching between truck types. (3) The magnitude of the shipments shifted to the lower-

ESAL truck types in each of the pairs considered is proportional to the number of vehicle mile tons currently provided by those truck types. (This last is an artifact of the constant elasticity of substitution.) The authors themselves do some sensitivity testing regarding the elasticity of substitution, and show that the overall results are not much affected over much of the relevant range. I comment further on the latter two assumptions below.

The second adjustment, that toward rail, is also handled via the Harberger triangle approach, and again depends on an assumed elasticity, namely the own-price elasticity of demand for shipments by truck. The authors provide some justification for their assumption that unity is the right value.

To get their overall welfare measure, the authors add the intra-trucking welfare estimates to the modal shift estimates, and the numbers that emerge from this exercise are striking. The authors calculate the overall welfare gain from imposition of the marginal-cost tax (making allowances for the fact that not all trucks operate at full load all of the time) would be on the order of $1.22 billion annually. Tax revenues would rise by about $10 billion, road wear would decline by $2.6 billion,[2] and producers' and consumers' surplus would decline by $11.7 billion. Moreover, the authors calculate that the current net subsidy to the five truck types from which their model shifts is about $3,200 per vehicle per year. Imposition of the marginal-cost tax would eliminate the subsidy. Further, there are good reasons to believe that the positive effects of imposing the new tax are understated. The truck types considered do not exhaust the fleet (although the authors do not tell us what fraction of vehicle ton miles they account for), and the estimate of maintenance and repair costs per ESAL mile that the authors use in the paper is by their own admission a conservative one. Finally, there are lots of other types of adjustment that might take place, both in the short and long run,[3] that would tend to attenuate the politically difficult transfers implicit in the new taxing system, and that would also increase the net benefits.

Other Adjustments

Not knowing anything about the trucking industry, my first response to reading the Small and Winston paper was to turn to that tried and true method of empirical research, introspection. Suppose I were a trucker, cheerfully running an SU2 (two-axle van) rated at 55 kips (55,000 pounds), and were suddenly faced with a tax of $1.32 per mile. Would I, as Small and Winston argue implicitly, be limited to switching to an SU3 (24 cents tax per mile for the same load), switching to rail, or eating the tax increase, or might there be other things I could do? A number of other things came into mind. (1) I would downrate my truck to something less than 55 kips. This looks especially promising in light of the fact that the tax rate is strictly convex in kips, while revenues are at worst linear, and may be concave under some circumstances. (2) I could switch to some truck other than an SU3, reducing my taxes still further. (3) I could, using my knowledge of the industry, respond optimally to the changed circumstances.

Downrating the vehicle weight and adhering to the downrating will be profitable if the marginal revenue lost from reduced loads is less than the marginal tax reduction, both evaluated at the initial registered rate. It seems plausible that this condition would hold given the extremely steep marginal tax function that obtains for high ESAL values under the Small-Winston scheme, but I do not know enough about trucking rates (nor have any of the experts I have talked to been willing to give simple enough answers to my questions) for me to be sure.

What is important here is to recognize that there are many types of adjustment that neither Small and Winston nor I consider. In order to model them properly, and derive detailed estimates of welfare gains and losses and the distributional consequences of imposing marginal cost taxes, a detailed model of trucker behavior would be required, with the full range of long-, medium-, and short-term technologies available well specified. Small and Winston recognize this in their paper, and quite properly leave the job to someone else. However, it is important to recognize the true ratio of welfare gains to changes in producers' and consumers' surplus could be very different from the ones shown here in the paper, and that the policy implications of the paper depend crucially on this ratio.

In a way, the key policy implication in the paper derives directly from the large misallocation of resources that is implicit in table 5.1. To the extent that much truck traffic imposes costs that are widely at variance with what is paid by the truckers, then there is clearly great scope for efficiency gains through the imposition of marginal-cost taxation. Small and Winston have made an estimate of these gains under a particular set of assumptions about how the industry would respond. Allowing a broader range of responses (assuming that fraud is not one of them—this is to be considered below) can only increase the scope for welfare gains and for the ratio of welfare gains to transfers.

Politics and Policy

Political Acceptability

In arguing for the political feasibility of their scheme, Small and Winston note that the tax should not be viewed as an increased source of revenue from the trucking industry, but rather as a removal of a large subsidy to that industry. Additionally, they note that to the extent that the industry is competitive, the burden of the tax will be borne by the public at large (the end users of shipping services). Since the public at large is a net winner in welfare terms, it is implied that if the proposal is marketed honestly, it should be politically feasible for it to be adopted. I have some fear that the "should" in the last sentence may have more normative than positive content. It is a commonplace of political life that well-organized interest groups can set much of the political agenda in domains that affect their direct interests, and in this case I would imagine that truckers and shippers would have considerable influence. Moreover, the industry will be able to correctly tell the general public that a consequence of the tax will be higher prices for goods. The fact that lower road use taxes imposed on individuals (or at least better roads enjoyed by individuals) will also be a consequence may be harder to sell. To the extent that the case can be made that the ratio of transfer elements to net social benefits is small, however, it should be easier to implement the policy. Here the existence of adjustments other than those considered by Small and Winston becomes more than an academic issue. Their paper establishes that the net benefits of the marginal cost tax warrant its adoption. Unfortunately, they also estimate a large increase in tax revenues, because the adjustments available to the industry are fairly expensive. If there are easier ways to adjust, the net benefits remain, but the direct costs perceived by truckers and shippers are smaller, and thus the political difficulty of implementing the policy may be reduced. In short, convincing economists that something is a good idea is hardly sufficient for its adoption, and it may well be worth the considerable research effort involved in finding out if this particular good idea places smaller direct burdens on the parties who will see themselves as most directly affected, and who will make their perception known in the political arena.

Interstate Competition

To this point, we have framed the issue as if we were considering a uniform national tax. In fact, the bulk of the relevant taxes are imposed by states, and only a few states currently have the apparatus necessary to impose a tax of the kind proposed. It is interesting to speculate on what might happen if (say) Kansas imposed the marginal cost tax and Nebraska did not.[4] Clearly, traffic would be diverted from Kansas to Nebraska, and Kansas would gain less revenue than it would under a uniform tax system but it would also have reduced wear and tear on its highways. Traffic that stayed in Kansas after the change would clearly do so only if there was considerable rent involved, and Kansas would be able to tax some of the rent. Traffic that was diverted to Nebraska would not pay taxes, but would not impose costs of the same magnitude. Without having worked out a model, it would seem that the states that imposed the tax would be better off than those that did not, and that the process of interstate competition in this dimension would tend to lead to everyone imposing the tax. (There is one potential interest group that might get in the way—truck-stop owners.)

Enforcement Problems

Successful imposition of the marginal-cost tax would require that truckers pay what will in some cases be large taxes based on their mileage and their registered gross vehicle weight. The incentives to dissemble regarding both of these variables would be considerable. Indeed, even under current laws, where much smaller taxes are imposed on vehicle weight, popular wisdom has it that there is a considerable amount of traffic above the rated weights, and that there is an effective CB network among truckers to assist each other in avoiding those weigh stations that happen to be open. I have no great insights about how to resolve the enforcement problem, but I suspect that successful monitoring of truck traffic is not a trivial exercise, and that before the Small-Winston proposal can be considered as a viable policy option, a careful analysis of the enforcement mechanisms available, and their costs, must be undertaken.

Accounting for Different Costs in Different Places

The tax schedule proposed by Small and Winston is based on estimates of the costs imposed on rural highways. The estimated cost for urban roads is over seven times higher. While it seems unlikely that there is much opportunity for urban/rural substitution in transportation, there is certainly an opportunity for mode shifting, and there is no compelling reason why urban residents should be transferring large sums of money to the trucking industry. Thus, the ideal form of the Small-Winston scheme would have much higher tax rates applied to urban miles driven. This would clearly complicate administration of the scheme, but an estimate of the potential gains would be worth undertaking in order to find out if they would be worth the costs.

Conclusion

One of the most popular papers to assign in urban economics courses is William Vickrey's old analysis of marginal congestion cost pricing of urban roadways. The idea behind that paper is similar to the idea behind this one, and the paper's conclusions are beloved by economists and opaque to the policy community. The Small-Winston tax has a number of advantages relative to the Vickrey proposal. Politically, it can be attached to the infrastructure issue, which is a fairly hot topic, and the tax provides the hope of real resources to deal with that problem. Moreover, while the problems of administration and enforcement are by no means trivial, and need much more study, at least they do not seem to require adoption of an as yet untried technology. In any event, Small and Winston have made a convincing case for their proposal. We can hope that their paper is the beginning of a policy, rather than something that we will merely enjoy assigning to our classes in the years to come.

Notes

1. Small and Winston's discussion leaves this issue open to some doubt. Before a tax scheme of the kind proposed here were implemented, one would have to do very careful engineering studies of the marginal cost imposed by truck traffic.

2. Another quibble: throughout the paper, the authors call what is plainly road wear "repair and maintenance expenditures" and term the difference between new revenue raised and this value "budget surplus." This terminology implies that current maintenance and repair policy exactly maintains the current capacity of the highway system. Such an assumption seems implausible at best.

3. In the long run we should see a change in the mix of vehicles manufactured, and perhaps in road construction and maintenance policy to adjust to the new load mix. In the shorter run, truckers will make adjustments other than the vehicle-type shifts considered in the paper, easing their transition and reducing the lost shippers' and truckers' surplus.

4. I am grateful to Roger Gordon for suggesting that I think about this.

6 State Personal Income and Sales Taxes, 1977–1983

Daniel R. Feenberg and Harvey S. Rosen

6.1 Introduction

State governments account for a large growing level of tax collection in the United States. In 1960, states' tax receipts were $20.2 billion, about 16% of taxes raised by all levels of government. By 1982, the figure was up to $178 billion, about 20% of all taxes.[1] The relative importance of various tax instruments in state revenue structures has changed over time. As table 6.1 indicates, over the last several decades, state reliance upon individual income taxation has increased dramatically, while property taxes have waned in relative importance. In broad terms, the two main workhorses of state revenue systems are general

Table 6.1   Percentage of State Tax Revenues From Each Type of Tax[a]

Source	1960	1970	1982
Property	3.4	2.3	1.9
General sales	23.8	29.6	31.0
Other sales[b]	36.4	26.8	14.3
Individual income	12.2	19.1	28.1
Corporation	6.5	7.8	8.6
Other[c]	17.7	14.4	16.1

a. Computed from Tax Foundation, Inc. 1983, 251.
b. Sum of taxes on sales of motor vehicles fuels, tobacco products, alcoholic beverages, and motor vehicle licenses.
c. Includes death and gift, severance, and other taxes.

Daniel R. Feenberg is a postdoctoral research economist at the National Bureau of Economic Research. Harvey S. Rosen is professor of economics at Princeton University, and a research associate of the National Bureau of Economic Research. The research in this paper has been supported by NSF Grant no. SES-8419238, and the NBER's Project on State and Local Public Finance.

Table 6.2 Percentage of State Taxes Raised from Various Sources[a] (Fiscal Year 1982)

State	General sales	Selective sales	Personal income	Corporate income	Property	Other[b]
Alabama	28.7	32.4	21.9	5.6	2.1	9.3
Alaska		2.6	.1	27.7	5.6	64.0
Arizona	43.2	12.7	23.7	6.2	7.0	7.3
Arkansas	33.2	20.6	28.0	7.3	.4	10.5
California	35.4	8.9	34.2	12.1	3.2	6.1
Colorado	36.3	15.4	32.5	5.4	.3	10.1
Connecticut	42.9	27.5	5.9	14.9		8.8
Delaware		14.6	48.1	6.1		31.2
Florida	50.1	25.3		6.9	2.0	15.7
Georgia	33.2	18.6	36.0	8.2	.4	3.7
Hawaii	54.1	13.1	26.5	4.1		2.2
Idaho	25.3	16.1	38.0	7.9		12.6
Illinois	31.4	18.8	29.9	9.6	1.8	8.5
Indiana	49.3	15.1	24.4	4.1	.9	6.2
Iowa	26.2	16.5	36.1	7.4		13.8
Kansas	32.6	15.6	31.9	8.5	1.7	9.7
Kentucky	27.4	18.1	24.1	6.7	7.9	15.8
Louisiana	29.3	15.8	7.0	9.3		38.5
Maine	34.1	19.9	28.7	4.9	2.0	10.4
Maryland	25.0	19.0	42.4	4.7	3.5	5.5
Massachusetts	19.1	14.3	48.4	12.5		5.7
Michigan	29.2	12.3	33.7	15.1	2.5	7.2
Minnesota	23.0	17.2	40.8	8.6	.1	10.3
Mississippi	52.5	14.6	11.5	4.9	.4	16.2

State						
Missouri	36.3	15.1	32.9	5.3	.2	10.1
Montana		19.4	27.2	8.4	6.4	38.5
Nebraska	33.5	23.5	26.3	5.6	.4	10.6
Nevada	50.4	35.1			3.2	11.3
New Hampshire	24.7	46.9	4.6	24.5	2.3	21.7
New Jersey	43.5	26.6	23.4	13.0	1.0	11.2
New Mexico	20.7	13.4	1.3	4.9	.9	36.0
New York		13.2	52.0	8.7		5.4
North Carolina	20.6	23.6	38.2	7.3	1.5	8.8
North Dakota	27.6	13.6	6.7	7.1	.4	44.7
Ohio	31.3	25.6	21.4	9.4	2.7	9.6
Oklahoma	17.8	15.7	23.6	5.1		37.8
Oregon		12.3	62.4	8.0		17.3
Pennsylvania	27.2	22.4	24.3	10.6	1.3	14.1
Rhode Island	29.6	24.6	31.9	7.8	1.1	5.1
South Carolina	33.0	21.8	32.8	6.7	.4	5.4
South Dakota	54.3	31.7		.3		13.6
Tennessee	52.1	23.9	2.1	9.6		12.3
Texas	38.8	24.4				37.4
Utah	40.8	13.2	34.8	4.3		6.9
Vermont	14.6	30.9	33.9	7.5	.1	13.1
Virginia	20.7	21.2	44.7	5.5	1.1	6.8
Washington	53.6	18.5			17.5	10.4
West Virginia	53.2	15.8	20.8	2.3	.1	6.7
Wisconsin	24.4	15.2	42.7	8.2	2.6	6.8
Wyoming	29.9	5.9			4.7	58.5

a. Based on Tax Foundation, Inc. (1983, pp. 254–55)

b. Includes death and gift taxes, severance taxes, license fees, and other taxes. Excludes unemployment tax collections.

sales taxes and individual income taxes, and these will be the main focus of this paper.[2]

The aggregate figures of table 6.1 mask the very substantial differences across states in the methods used to raise revenue. Table 6.2 shows how some states, such as Delaware, Massachusetts, and Oregon, rely very heavily on personal income taxation. Others—Florida, Nevada, South Dakota, Texas, and Wyoming—levy no income tax at all. Moreover, states differ considerably in how they structure the various taxes. This is the most striking in the case of personal income taxes. Nebraska's income tax is simply an excise tax on residents' federal liability. Illinois has a linear tax on federally defined adjusted gross income. On the other hand, some states rival the federal tax in complexity. Interestingly, a number of long-considered changes in federal law are already in place in some state tax codes, including inflation indexing, optional separate filing for married couples, vanishing exemptions, full taxation (or complete exemption) of realized capital gains, and the complete elimination of personal deductions.

The main purpose of this paper is to develop and implement a coherent methodology for characterizing the structures of state tax systems. The measures thus generated are used to show how the various systems differ and how they evolved over the seven-year period 1977–83. We believe that the availability of such measures will be of use to investigators studying a wide array of questions. A few of these are:

1. How sensitive are state tax revenue yields to changes in income?
2. How does state tax structure influence business location?
3. Do state taxes affect individuals' migration decisions?
4. How do economic and demographic characteristics of a state's inhabitants affect the tax structure?
5. Do states take into account the tax structures of "competing" states when modifying their own systems?
6. How does inflation affect the state tax structure?
7. Does the structure of the tax system exert an independent effect on the size of the government sector?

Of course, many writers have understood the importance of state tax structures in these and other contexts. (See, for example, Oates 1975, DiLorento 1982, Greytak and Thursby 1979, Bradbury et al. 1982, Maxwell and Aronson 1979, and Advisory Commission on Intergovernmental Relations 1979.) However, previous investigators have used (admittedly) inadequate indicators of tax structure. For example, Oates (1975) characterizes each state's tax system by the proportion of revenue raised by the income tax.[3] For this procedure to be meaningful requires, *inter alia,* that each state income tax be more or less the same in structure. As we indicate below, this appears not to be the case.

Investigators have been forced to use such measures because, as Gold indicates, "unfortunately, no recent estimates of elasticities are available on a consistent basis for all states" (1983, 15).

We remedy this situation using the individual income and deduction data from a stratified random sample of 25,000 actual federal income tax returns. The data include the state of each taxpayer for most returns. We have programmed the major income and sales tax rules for every state for the period 1977–83. For each taxpaying unit, then, we can estimate tax liabilities. With this information in hand, any desired summary measure of each state's tax structure can be computed. Several different measures are presented. We do not have comparable data on state corporation income taxes; hence, our study must ignore them. However, as the discussion surrounding table 6.1 indicated, corporate taxes represent a rather small portion of state revenues.

Sections 6.2 and 6.3 of this paper discuss the personal income and sales taxes, respectively. Section 6.4 aggregates the results to allow characterization of the tax structures as a whole. This section also discusses the interaction of the state tax systems with the federal income tax—i.e., how does the deductibility of state taxes (for itemizers) affect the real burden of state taxation? Section 6.5 presents some conclusions and suggestions for future research.

6.2 Personal Income Taxes

6.2.1 General Description

Although state personal income taxes differ significantly from state to state, they share the basic general structure of the federal tax. That is, deductions and exemptions are subtracted from adjusted gross income to obtain taxable income. A schedule converts taxable income to income tax before credits, from which a variety of credits (sometimes refundable) are subtracted. Even so, the state taxes are not generally clones of the federal tax. As of 1983, fifteen states allowed a deduction for federal income taxes paid (seven limit the deductions), while all but four states disallowed the federal deduction for state income taxes paid. Seventeen states allow income splitting (as the federal law did before 1969) while fifteen have separate schedules for couples and individuals (only New Mexico does both). Child-care credits, rent credits, minimum and maximum taxes, among other possible features, each have found expression in at least one state. The most ubiquitous provision in state laws that have no correspondence to the federal law are the property-tax credits included in thirteen states and the rent credits and deductions found in thirteen (mostly overlapping) states.

We coded the tax laws for 1977–83 using information obtained from the tax forms distributed by states to their residents and from summaries such as those published by Commerce Clearing House, the Advisory Commission on Intergovernmental Relations, and the Tax Foundation. We have attempted to code every aspect of the systems which our data would allow.

6.2.2   Methodological Problems in Characterizing a Tax Structure

State personal income tax systems, like their federal counterpart, are nonproportional and nonlinear as well. It is well known that in the presence of nonproportionality, it is generally impossible to summarize completely the characteristics of a tax structure in a single number.[4] Therefore, rather than constrain ourselves to one measure, we have constructed several. Certain measures will be more useful than others depending on the particular context. We compute: (a) the elasticity of tax revenues with respect to before-tax income; (b) the average tax rates faced by "high-," "middle-," and "low-" income taxpaying units; and (c) the corresponding marginal tax rates. For our purposes, the annual incomes of high- , middle-, and low-income units are $40,000, $20,000, and $10,000, respectively, measured in 1979 dollars.

6.2.3   Procedure

Because of the complexity of the tax laws, any given summary measure for a state will depend upon the income distribution in that particular state. To facilitate comparisons across states, we create a synthetic data base reflecting the distribution of income in the United States rather than in any particular state. The records in the synthetic data base are not actual tax returns. They are obtained by sorting the original 25,000 returns by filing status (single, joint, or head of household) itemization status (itemizer or nonitemizer), and age (over sixty-five or not). There are thus twelve (= 3 × 2 × 2) categories. Within each category the returns were ordered by adjusted gross income and divided into blocks representing approximately one million returns each. Each of the ninety-six blocks of demographically similar returns is then averaged to form a single return with the average income, deductions, and exemptions of its cohort.

With this data base and the state tax laws we can calculate summary measures for each state dependent on the law of the state, but independent of the income distribution in that state. The average tax rate is calculated as revenue divided by reported income.[5] The marginal tax rate is obtained by adding 1,000 dollars to wage income on every return and finding the implied increase in tax liability. In this calculation, the change in federal tax liability associated with the income change is included in the calculation; this effect can be important in those states that allow deductibility of federal taxes. The elasticity of revenue with respect to income is found by increasing each dollar amount on the tax return (including deductions, but not exemptions) by one percent, and finding the implied percentage increase in tax liability.

Note that there is some asymmetry in the methods used to compute marginal tax rates and elasticities. The marginal tax rate calculations assume that no deductions other than federal income tax change with income, while the elasticity calculations assume that most dollar amounts also change. The reason for the difference is the fact that the two sets of numbers are likely to be put to different uses. The marginal tax rate data show the wedge between before- and after-tax earnings in each state; there is no reason to take into account how other deductions change at the same time. On the other hand, the elasticity calculations indicate how revenues would change when nominal income increases by a given percentage; it therefore makes sense to try to incorporate the impact of income-induced deductions upon revenues. Of course, the assumption that other deductions and income would increase at the same percentage rate is only an approximation, but it is probably not too far wide of the mark. In every case where federal tax liability affects (next year's) state tax liability, this effect is applied to the current year.

Data limitations forced us to impute several variables that have an impact on tax liabilities: (1) Federal tax returns provide no data on household rent payments, but rent credits are an important component of state tax systems. We assumed that families with few or no property tax deductions were renters, and estimated their rent by a linear equation based on consumer expenditure data.[6] (2) Social security benefits for most households are not reported. We imputed to the income of each aged individual a benefit equal to the average benefit level in 1979. (3) In some states separate filing is allowed, but federal tax returns do not list husbands' and wives' incomes separately. We assumed that one-third of total family income could be attributed to the wife.

For some other missing variables we could not arrive at a satisfactory imputation scheme. Certain aspects of state tax systems were therefore ignored. The most important of these are: (1) Tax-exempt interest. Because federal tax returns do not include interest from municipal securities, we cannot compute the state tax liability generated by such interest. (2) Interest from federal securities. We do not know what proportion of each household's interest income is generated by federal securities; such income is not taxable by the states. (3) Property tax credits. Some states allow credits against local property taxes paid. For nonitemizers, we have no estimates of property tax liability. While we do not believe that these omissions have a major impact on our substantive results, it would obviously be desirable to redo the calculations if and when more complete data become available.

6.2.4   Basic Results

The income tax elasticity results are reported in table 6.3. The most striking feature of table 6.3 is the substantial variation across states in the elasticities for a given year. In 1983, they ranged from 1.02 for Pennsylvania to 2.50 for New Mexico. (We exclude Connecticut, New Hampshire, and Tennessee from all comparisons because they have only a small tax base limited to some property income.) The reason for New Mexico's extraordinarily high elasticity is the fact that it has a system of very generous income-related credits—so many that *net* revenues are very small and very sensitive to income. The mean elasticity (conditional on having an income tax) in 1983 is 1.54, with a standard deviation of 0.39. (In table 6.3 and all succeeding tables, means are weighted by the 1979 population of the states.) The substantial heterogeneity present in the table suggests that considerable care must be taken in generalizing about the forms of state income taxes. Similar heterogeneity is exhibited in each of the preceding years.

On average, the elasticity of state income tax systems declined between 1977 and 1983, with an average value of 1.66 in the former year, and 1.54 in the latter. However, a glance at table 6.3 indicates substantial variations in the pattern of changes over time.

When we turn to the figures on the average and marginal tax rate faced by individuals in various positions in the income distribution (tables 6.4a, 6.4b, 6.4c), the following story emerges.[7] From table 6.4a, the mean marginal tax rate for high-income individuals in 1977 was 5.55%, with a standard deviation of 3.53. By 1983, the figure was 5.93% (s.d. = 3.14). The mean average tax rate for this group was lower and also rose during this period, with a value of 3.23% (s.d. = 1.70) in 1977 and 3.78% (s.d. = 1.75) in 1983. Similar trends are apparent for rates on the middle- and low-income taxpaying units. From table 6.4b, the mean marginal tax rate for the middle-income taxpayer rose from 4.44% (s.d. = 2.50) to 5.62% (s.d. = 3.53) over our sample period, while the average rate rose from 2.27% (s.d. = 1.17) to 2.89% (s.d. = 1.36). From table 6.4c, for low-income taxpayers, the mean marginal tax rate increased from 3.27% (s.d. = 1.66) to 4.19% (s.d. = 2.44) from 1977 to 1983, and the average rate from 1.54% (s.d. = 0.91) to 1.98% (s.d. = 1.19). The presence of some negative average tax rates in table 6.4c is due to the presence of refundable tax credits.

A comparison of tables 6.4a, 6.4b, and 6.4c indicates that in some states, the marginal tax rate declines with income. In 1983, for example, in Alabama, the marginal tax rates on the low-, middle-, and high-income taxpaying units were 3.66%, 3.74%, and 3.19% respectively. One reason for this phenomenon is that some states allow a deduction for taxes paid to the federal government, and such deductions increase

Table 6.3   **Elasticity of Personal Income Tax Liability with Respect to Income**

State	1977	1978	1979	1980	1981	1982	1983
Alabama	1.33	1.29	1.25	1.21	1.18	1.18	1.18
Alaska	1.54	1.94	.	.	.	.	.
Arizona	1.48	1.44	1.50	1.90	2.02	2.09	2.00
Arkansas	1.60	1.57	1.57	1.54	1.51	1.49	1.47
California	2.14	2.10	2.09	2.34	2.29	2.29	2.24
Colorado	1.59	1.56	1.57	1.21	1.44	1.47	1.34
Connecticut	1.10	1.12	1.12	1.11	1.18	1.09	1.09
Delaware	1.70	1.65	1.65	1.37	1.57	1.55	1.44
District of Columbia	1.71	1.69	1.65	1.39	1.60	1.57	1.45
Florida	.	.	.	.	.	.	.
Georgia	1.73	1.69	1.64	1.43	1.54	1.44	1.47
Hawaii	1.55	1.53	1.57	1.20	1.79	1.56	1.27
Idaho	1.72	1.68	1.62	1.63	1.57	1.53	1.50
Illinois	1.22	1.20	1.18	1.17	1.15	1.14	1.13
Indiana	1.18	1.16	1.15	1.24	1.23	1.21	1.20
Iowa	1.67	1.46	1.44	1.29	1.41	1.43	1.44
Kansas	1.53	1.53	1.54	1.30	1.58	1.52	1.38
Kentucky	1.45	1.42	1.37	0.94	1.29	1.28	1.16
Louisiana	2.51	2.22	1.88	1.84	3.07	2.72	2.24
Maine	2.08	2.11	2.01	1.96	1.93	1.87	1.86
Maryland	1.34	1.32	1.30	1.11	1.27	1.24	1.09
Massachusetts	1.29	1.27	1.25	1.24	1.35	1.31	1.33
Michigan	1.47	1.35	1.39	1.49	1.46	1.41	1.35
Minnesota	1.95	2.15	2.19	1.47	2.46	1.89	2.07
Mississippi	2.11	2.04	1.94	1.60	1.96	1.89	1.91
Missouri	1.73	1.71	1.64	1.44	1.55	1.54	1.52
Montana	1.44	1.40	1.50	1.21	1.42	1.48	1.37
Nebraska	2.08	2.07	2.05	2.14	2.05	1.97	1.88
Nevada	.	.	.	.	.	.	.
New Hampshire	1.45	1.41	1.40	1.39	1.40	1.37	1.35
New Jersey	1.56	1.54	1.50	1.50	1.47	1.45	1.41
New Mexico	4.19	3.69	3.47	3.05	3.60	2.78	2.50
New York	1.73	1.72	1.71	1.57	1.60	1.62	1.57
N. Carolina	1.48	1.46	1.44	1.43	1.42	1.40	1.38
N. Dakota	1.79	1.76	1.59	1.52	2.10	1.79	1.65
Ohio	1.75	1.74	1.70	1.65	1.63	1.65	1.73
Oklahoma	2.04	1.98	1.93	1.70	1.81	1.86	1.73
Oregon	2.21	2.13	2.18	2.15	2.02	1.95	1.83
Pennsylvania	1.20	1.15	1.11	1.05	1.04	1.01	1.02
Rhode Island	1.76	1.77	1.81	1.78	1.75	1.72	1.72
S. Carolina	1.68	1.63	1.61	1.59	1.55	1.52	1.51
S. Dakota	.	.	.	.	.	.	.
Tennessee	1.00	1.00	1.00	1.00	1.00	1.00	1.00
Texas	.	.	.	.	.	.	.
Utah	1.40	1.35	1.31	1.06	1.21	1.21	1.11
Vermont	1.71	1.75	1.77	1.75	1.72	1.69	1.68
Virginia	1.65	1.62	1.60	1.43	1.49	1.45	1.40
Washington	.	.	.	.	.	.	.
W. Virginia	1.52	1.52	1.52	1.30	1.52	1.54	1.61
Wisconsin	2.10	2.00	2.33	1.98	2.05	2.03	1.72
Wyoming	.	.	.	.	.	.	.
Federal	1.78	1.79	1.84	1.80	1.78	1.73	1.72
Mean	1.66	1.62	1.60	1.54	1.63	1.59	1.54
Standard deviation	0.40	0.38	0.38	0.41	0.47	0.42	0.39

Table 6.4a State Personal Income Tax Rates at $40,000 (1979 Dollars) AGI

State	Marginal rate							Average rate						
	1977	1978	1979	1980	1981	1982	1983	1977	1978	1979	1980	1981	1982	1983
Alabama	3.32	3.24	3.20	3.06	2.99	3.09	3.19	2.84	2.89	2.96	2.96	2.97	2.94	3.03
Alaska	5.28	5.39						3.55	3.09	.				.
Arizona	4.84	4.72	4.64	4.44	4.24	4.47	4.66	3.19	3.28	3.06	2.71	2.49	2.49	2.69
Arkansas	6.87	6.87	7.03	7.03	7.04	7.05	7.05	4.14	4.28	4.46	4.64	4.78	4.87	4.90
California	9.57	9.76	10.19	9.55	9.58	9.43	9.61	3.97	4.10	4.22	3.78	3.82	3.68	3.90
Colorado	4.87	4.74	4.16	3.97	3.62	4.59	4.82	3.00	3.00	2.61	2.63	2.42	2.97	3.16
Connecticut	0.00	0.00	0.00	0.00	0.00	0.00	0.00	0.23	0.21	0.21	0.21	0.21	0.21	0.21
Delaware	8.34	8.35	8.69	8.68	8.79	9.03	9.26	4.53	4.70	5.00	5.05	5.23	5.35	5.44
District of Columbia	8.76	8.93	9.10	9.53	9.78	9.97	10.06	4.75	4.93	5.16	5.41	5.61	5.76	5.87
Florida								.	.	.	.	.	.	.
Georgia	6.03	6.03	6.03	6.03	6.04	6.04	6.05	3.49	3.59	3.72	3.85	3.95	4.05	4.05
Hawaii	8.51	8.68	8.84	8.90	8.97	9.07	9.19	5.32	5.44	5.61	5.60	5.75	5.69	5.91
Idaho	7.54	7.54	7.54	7.54	7.54	7.55	7.56	4.57	4.69	4.83	4.82	4.93	5.01	5.07
Illinois	2.50	2.50	2.50	2.50	2.50	2.50	3.00	2.28	2.31	2.33	2.35	2.37	2.38	2.81
Indiana	2.00	2.00	1.70	1.90	1.90	1.90	3.00	1.82	1.83	1.57	1.72	1.73	1.74	2.76
Iowa	4.60	4.64	4.61	4.62	4.75	5.16	5.47	2.96	3.05	3.11	3.19	3.26	3.48	3.67
Kansas	4.42	4.36	4.54	4.35	4.26	4.53	4.73	2.39	2.42	2.58	2.54	2.58	2.77	2.95
Kentucky	3.83	3.77	3.80	3.63	3.59	3.80	3.97	2.65	2.71	2.84	2.88	2.91	3.05	3.18
Louisiana	1.33	1.30	1.78	2.06	1.20	1.47	2.23	0.74	0.77	0.87	0.93	0.53	0.60	0.86
Maine	7.87	7.87	8.51	8.85	9.05	9.06	9.07	3.19	3.19	3.60	3.95	4.23	4.42	4.54
Maryland	5.00	5.00	5.00	5.00	5.00	5.00	5.00	3.53	3.56	3.57	3.63	3.67	3.70	3.71
Massachusetts	5.32	5.32	5.32	5.32	5.31	5.29	5.25	5.48	5.54	5.56	5.51	5.21	5.24	5.20
Michigan	4.60	4.60	4.60	4.60	4.60	5.10	6.35	3.84	3.89	3.95	4.01	4.06	4.53	5.66
Minnesota	9.84	9.60	9.48	9.05	8.88	9.71	10.10	7.46	7.43	7.27	7.16	7.00	7.78	8.18
Mississippi	3.76	3.81	3.87	3.87	3.87	3.87	4.65	1.87	1.97	2.09	2.22	2.15	2.22	2.48
Missouri	3.55	3.51	3.52	3.44	3.42	3.64	3.80	2.02	2.09	2.21	2.29	2.31	2.45	2.59

State														
Montana	5.50	5.55	5.51	5.40	4.84	5.13	5.44	3.48	3.59	3.48	3.46	3.35	3.44	3.60
Nebraska	5.45	5.72	6.58	5.91	6.11	6.73	6.93	2.44	2.52	2.85	2.48	2.63	2.97	3.07
Nevada	.	.	.	.	.	.	.	.	.	.	.	.	.	.
New Hampshire	0.00	0.00	0.00	0.00	0.00	0.00	0.00	0.47	0.48	0.49	0.50	0.51	0.52	0.52
New Jersey	2.52	2.52	2.52	2.52	2.52	2.52	2.52	1.81	1.86	1.92	1.97	2.02	2.05	2.08
New Mexico	4.80	5.02	5.28	5.70	4.43	6.18	8.33	1.36	1.52	1.63	1.88	1.34	2.10	3.00
New York	12.40	12.46	12.63	11.93	10.97	10.86	10.83	6.23	6.46	6.77	6.91	6.88	6.89	6.98
N. Carolina	6.78	6.89	6.92	7.00	7.02	7.02	7.06	4.42	4.54	4.68	4.78	4.87	4.95	5.01
N. Dakota	5.50	5.61	2.84	2.78	2.76	3.55	3.75	2.70	2.86	1.62	1.67	1.45	2.12	2.48
Ohio	2.85	2.93	2.93	3.01	3.19	4.08	6.09	1.74	1.81	1.90	2.00	2.08	2.68	3.87
Oklahoma	5.38	5.28	5.50	5.40	5.49	5.88	5.83	2.28	2.45	2.76	2.95	3.11	3.22	3.39
Oregon	7.64	8.19	7.09	8.16	8.53	9.20	9.10	1.64	1.78	1.51	1.70	1.87	2.51	2.82
Pennsylvania	2.00	2.20	2.20	2.20	2.20	2.20	2.45	2.03	2.24	2.24	2.24	2.24	2.24	2.49
Rhode Island	6.47	6.79	6.94	7.48	7.33	8.18	9.27	3.08	3.17	3.14	3.38	3.59	3.81	4.25
S. Carolina	6.48	6.52	6.66	6.84	6.39	6.90	6.94	3.31	3.45	3.63	3.82	3.97	4.07	4.14
S. Dakota	.	.	.	.	.	.	.	.	.	.	.	.	.	.
Tennessee	0.00	0.00	0.00	0.00	0.00	0.00	0.00	0.85	0.85	0.85	0.85	0.85	0.85	0.85
Texas	.	.	.	.	.	.	.	.	.	.	.	.	.	.
Utah	4.94	4.82	4.86	4.64	4.57	4.91	5.12	3.38	3.42	3.55	3.57	3.59	3.74	3.90
Vermont	8.52	8.93	8.41	9.06	9.36	8.97	9.01	4.20	4.31	3.92	4.21	4.40	4.28	4.23
Virginia	5.33	5.33	5.43	5.46	5.64	5.67	5.71	2.71	2.80	2.91	3.03	3.13	3.19	3.23
Washington	0.00	0.00	0.00	0.00	0.00	0.00	0.00	0.00	0.00	0.00	0.00	0.00	0.00	0.00
W. Virginia	4.42	4.64	4.84	5.15	5.45	5.54	7.98	2.34	2.43	2.56	2.71	2.84	2.93	3.54
Wisconsin	10.60	8.94	7.59	8.63	8.64	8.64	9.64	5.96	5.48	4.68	4.12	4.13	4.11	5.05
Wyoming	.	.	.	.	.	.	.	.	.	.	.	.	.	.
Federal	34.07	35.72	36.55	39.38	40.71	37.38	34.64	16.59	17.01	16.83	18.08	18.91	17.61	16.06
Mean	5.55	5.56	5.59	5.49	5.40	5.54	5.93	3.23	3.31	3.36	3.35	3.36	3.47	3.78
Standard deviation	3.53	3.51	3.58	3.38	3.25	3.19	3.14	1.70	1.71	1.75	1.73	1.73	1.74	1.75

Table 6.4b   State Personal Income Tax Rates at $20,000 (1979 Dollars) AGI

State	Marginal rate							Average rate						
	1977	1978	1979	1980	1981	1982	1983	1977	1978	1979	1980	1981	1982	1983
Alabama	3.86	3.82	3.86	3.80	3.75	3.63	3.74	2.45	2.59	2.72	2.80	2.87	2.77	2.87
Alaska	4.44	4.58	.	.	.	.	.	3.00	2.09	.	.	.	.	.
Arizona	4.73	4.84	4.46	4.17	3.85	3.87	4.11	2.44	2.60	2.28	1.87	1.67	1.65	1.78
Arkansas	5.31	5.44	5.89	6.10	6.28	6.38	6.43	2.75	2.92	3.11	3.35	3.53	3.68	3.76
California	6.06	6.19	6.32	5.95	5.98	5.74	6.04	2.17	2.27	2.35	1.96	2.01	1.93	2.09
Colorado	4.56	4.81	3.92	3.86	3.54	4.35	4.60	2.36	2.39	1.97	2.07	1.92	2.35	2.49
Connecticut	0.00	0.00	0.00	0.00	0.01	0.00	0.00	0.15	0.13	0.13	0.14	0.14	0.14	0.14
Delaware	6.99	7.12	7.78	7.67	7.97	7.99	8.04	3.28	3.47	3.68	3.84	4.07	4.25	4.36
District of Columbia	7.51	7.66	7.82	8.19	8.25	8.39	8.48	3.30	3.46	3.72	4.17	4.40	4.58	4.69
Florida	.	.	.	.	.	.	.	.	.	.	.	.	.	.
Georgia	5.64	5.87	5.97	6.03	6.09	6.04	6.04	2.27	2.45	2.66	2.90	3.09	3.47	3.27
Hawaii	8.56	8.26	8.58	8.72	9.05	8.21	8.27	4.36	4.60	4.75	4.74	4.93	4.81	5.18
Idaho	7.37	7.47	7.50	7.56	7.61	7.55	7.55	3.10	3.33	3.57	3.57	3.81	3.99	4.09
Illinois	2.50	2.50	2.50	2.51	2.52	2.50	3.00	2.08	2.13	2.17	2.20	2.23	2.25	2.67
Indiana	2.00	2.00	1.70	1.91	1.92	1.90	3.00	1.70	1.72	1.48	1.60	1.62	1.63	2.60
Iowa	4.61	4.71	4.59	4.74	4.75	5.01	5.27	2.38	2.54	2.46	2.60	2.72	2.89	3.03
Kansas	3.23	3.33	3.64	3.76	3.75	4.03	4.43	1.77	1.79	1.89	1.84	1.94	2.11	2.25
Kentucky	4.09	4.16	4.27	4.32	4.28	4.35	4.51	2.25	2.38	2.50	2.62	2.73	2.88	2.99
Louisiana	1.53	1.51	1.64	1.71	1.40	1.57	1.79	0.39	0.46	0.63	0.71	0.14	0.23	0.53
Maine	4.67	4.72	5.42	6.71	6.95	7.33	7.69	1.63	1.58	1.89	2.20	2.50	2.72	2.86
Maryland	5.00	5.00	4.80	4.89	4.95	4.97	5.00	3.16	3.24	3.12	3.22	3.30	3.37	3.40
Massachusetts	5.17	5.16	5.06	5.15	5.07	5.02	5.02	4.36	4.48	4.56	4.52	4.15	4.22	4.16
Michigan	4.60	4.60	4.60	4.62	4.64	5.10	6.35	3.27	3.36	3.46	3.57	3.65	4.11	5.16
Minnesota	11.33	11.02	10.82	10.54	10.08	10.98	11.48	5.82	6.11	5.50	5.74	5.81	6.44	6.85
Mississippi	3.24	3.25	3.38	3.52	3.51	3.57	3.91	0.96	1.12	1.27	1.45	1.26	1.38	1.49
Missouri	3.04	3.17	3.36	3.54	3.55	3.78	3.99	1.33	1.44	1.58	1.71	1.81	1.96	2.09

Montana	5.15	5.26	5.30	5.48	4.97	5.51	5.74	3.05	3.20	2.89	2.87	2.96	2.97	3.05
Nebraska	3.76	3.89	4.24	3.80	3.99	4.42	4.46	1.45	1.47	1.71	1.42	1.54	1.79	1.92
Nevada														
New Hampshire	0.00	0.00	0.00	0.00	0.00	0.00	0.00	0.18	0.20	0.20	0.21	0.22	0.22	0.23
New Jersey	2.02	2.05	2.09	2.21	2.30	2.36	2.43	1.24	1.30	1.37	1.38	1.45	1.50	1.58
New Mexico	2.92	3.17	3.32	3.77	2.93	4.07	5.50	0.18	0.33	0.40	0.63	0.34	0.84	1.40
New York	8.35	9.18	10.04	11.90	13.72	14.11	14.52	3.51	3.67	3.91	4.20	4.47	4.49	4.64
N. Carolina	5.95	6.11	6.32	6.47	6.68	6.66	6.71	3.44	3.60	3.78	3.89	4.02	4.15	4.23
N. Dakota	3.46	4.11	2.28	2.41	2.61	3.49	3.66	1.44	1.60	1.08	1.14	0.72	1.42	1.95
Ohio	2.13	2.29	2.43	2.60	2.80	3.56	5.27	0.95	1.02	1.13	1.26	1.36	1.81	2.50
Oklahoma	3.17	3.70	4.19	4.71	5.18	5.43	5.82	1.10	1.25	1.46	1.69	1.90	1.95	2.16
Oregon	5.68	5.95	5.60	5.60	5.78	6.56	6.76	1.23	1.41	1.30	1.48	1.62	2.22	2.65
Pennsylvania	2.00	2.20	2.20	2.20	2.20	2.20	2.45	2.09	2.31	2.31	2.31	2.31	2.30	2.56
Rhode Island	4.46	4.62	4.48	4.81	5.11	5.38	5.97	2.17	2.16	2.15	2.32	2.46	2.61	2.92
S. Carolina	5.10	5.26	5.69	5.95	6.14	6.23	6.31	2.31	2.45	2.64	2.87	3.05	3.19	3.28
S. Dakota														
Tennessee	0.00	0.00	0.00	0.00	0.00	0.00	0.00	0.44	0.46	0.46	0.46	0.46	0.46	0.46
Texas														
Utah	5.57	5.49	5.57	5.49	5.41	5.55	5.78	3.00	3.18	3.36	3.51	3.62	3.81	3.95
Vermont	5.87	6.08	5.42	5.82	6.11	5.90	5.80	2.97	2.96	2.71	2.91	3.04	2.97	2.95
Virginia	4.61	4.71	4.90	5.14	5.38	5.41	5.49	2.23	2.36	2.49	2.66	2.84	2.95	3.02
Washington	0.00	0.00	0.00	0.00	0.00	0.00	0.00	0.00	0.00	0.00	0.00	0.00	0.00	0.00
W. Virginia	3.34	3.44	3.62	3.78	3.97	4.16	5.16	1.91	1.98	2.04	2.15	2.25	2.32	2.56
Wisconsin	8.55	7.69	6.37	7.38	7.44	7.40	8.43	4.18	4.23	3.53	2.88	2.92	2.95	3.78
Wyoming														
Federal	23.47	24.34	23.57	25.32	26.56	24.58	22.31	11.42	11.38	11.31	12.19	12.77	11.93	10.91
Mean	4.44	4.57	4.65	4.87	5.06	5.21	5.62	2.27	2.38	2.42	2.45	2.51	2.63	2.89
Standard deviation	2.50	2.57	2.69	3.03	3.42	3.49	3.53	1.17	1.21	1.18	1.22	1.28	1.32	1.36

Table 6.4c State Personal Income Tax Rates at $10,000 (1979 Dollars) AGI

State	Marginal rate							Average rate						
	1977	1978	1979	1980	1981	1982	1983	1977	1978	1979	1980	1981	1982	1983
Alabama	3.23	3.49	3.44	3.69	3.80	3.59	3.66	1.71	1.82	2.01	2.15	2.26	2.28	2.38
Alaska	4.03	3.38						2.35	0.98					
Arizona	4.27	4.49	3.81	3.64	3.24	3.08	3.37	2.27	2.40	2.07	1.05	0.72	0.64	0.77
Arkansas	3.28	3.53	3.74	4.14	4.44	4.54	4.56	1.45	1.56	1.72	1.90	2.05	2.17	2.25
California	3.88	3.97	4.07	4.04	3.83	3.67	3.89	0.84	0.93	1.01	0.44	0.52	0.48	0.62
Colorado	3.59	3.66	3.23	2.98	2.81	3.41	3.64	1.93	1.94	1.63	1.80	1.66	2.00	2.09
Connecticut	0.00	0.00	0.00	0.00	0.00	0.00	0.00	0.00	0.00	0.00	0.00	0.00	0.00	0.00
Delaware	5.30	5.63	5.93	6.36	6.65	6.84	6.99	2.45	2.63	2.80	2.96	3.21	3.39	3.51
District of Columbia	5.66	5.91	6.16	7.35	6.79	7.00	7.18	2.36	2.51	2.72	2.95	3.23	3.38	3.49
Florida														
Georgia	3.69	3.89	3.98	4.39	4.65	5.53	4.97	1.33	1.48	1.67	1.88	2.05	2.91	2.15
Hawaii	7.01	7.17	7.42	7.83	8.29	7.92	7.92	3.42	3.64	3.91	3.88	3.71	3.83	4.29
Idaho	5.74	5.99	6.21	6.24	6.41	6.54	6.61	1.76	2.04	2.27	2.37	2.64	2.83	2.96
Illinois	2.50	2.50	2.50	2.50	2.50	2.50	3.00	1.95	1.99	2.03	2.07	2.10	2.13	2.56
Indiana	2.00	2.00	1.70	1.90	1.90	1.90	3.00	1.60	1.63	1.41	1.36	1.39	1.41	2.27
Iowa	3.25	3.43	3.93	4.20	4.41	4.43	4.64	1.76	1.86	1.79	1.93	2.06	2.22	2.34
Kansas	2.85	2.95	3.21	3.26	3.38	3.89	3.76	1.42	1.42	1.58	1.55	1.67	1.77	1.91
Kentucky	3.47	3.66	3.75	4.00	4.12	4.26	4.36	1.83	1.94	2.12	2.27	2.39	2.55	2.66
Louisiana	1.17	1.23	1.46	1.59	0.85	0.86	1.25	0.12	0.20	0.40	0.49	0.05	0.10	0.30
Maine	3.25	3.28	3.69	4.14	4.29	4.48	4.61	0.92	0.91	1.15	1.38	1.58	1.70	1.80
Maryland	4.83	4.86	4.42	4.55	4.63	4.69	4.71	2.80	2.88	2.74	2.88	2.98	3.05	3.10
Massachusetts	5.06	5.05	5.05	5.05	5.02	5.01	5.01	3.21	3.34	3.49	3.62	2.71	2.84	2.80
Michigan	4.60	4.60	4.60	4.60	4.60	5.10	6.35	3.06	3.16	3.28	3.40	3.49	3.93	4.95
Minnesota	8.19	7.38	12.02	10.26	15.33	15.78	16.38	2.13	1.47	1.52	1.91	2.29	3.63	4.03
Mississippi	1.68	1.94	2.06	2.32	2.12	2.39	2.43	0.29	0.39	0.51	0.66	0.44	0.52	0.59

Missouri	2.20	2.36	2.51	2.79	3.02	3.25	3.50	0.78	0.87	1.03	1.16	1.25	1.39	1.49
Montana	4.74	4.92	4.86	5.02	4.81	4.83	5.03	2.86	2.98	2.76	2.64	2.74	2.59	2.64
Nebraska	3.30	3.07	4.11	3.23	3.08	3.46	3.54	0.76	0.87	0.99	0.86	1.01	1.20	1.38
Nevada														
New Hampshire	0.00	0.00	0.00	0.00	0.00	0.00	0.00	0.11	0.13	0.14	0.15	0.17	0.17	0.18
New Jersey	2.00	2.00	2.00	2.00	2.00	2.00	2.00	0.77	0.85	0.94	1.03	1.10	1.15	1.19
New Mexico	1.36	1.53	1.66	1.97	1.54	2.25	3.14	-0.51	-0.37	-0.31	-0.12	-0.27	0.01	0.31
New York	4.61	4.79	4.90	5.23	5.56	5.86	6.15	2.11	2.21	2.36	2.53	2.69	2.40	2.48
N. Carolina	5.04	5.17	5.38	5.64	5.78	5.90	5.97	2.76	2.90	3.07	3.16	3.31	3.44	3.52
N. Dakota	1.86	2.06	1.45	1.52	1.33	2.39	3.07	1.09	1.14	0.85	0.88	0.10	0.59	1.43
Ohio	0.87	0.94	1.15	1.37	1.57	2.23	3.35	0.47	0.50	0.53	0.59	0.65	0.87	1.06
Oklahoma	2.11	2.27	2.55	2.85	3.18	3.36	3.60	0.76	0.84	0.98	1.12	1.24	1.25	1.37
Oregon	2.55	2.57	2.64	2.88	3.41	4.66	5.12	0.17	0.23	0.19	0.27	0.34	0.71	1.00
Pennsylvania	2.17	2.20	2.20	2.20	2.20	2.20	2.45	1.88	2.09	2.09	2.09	2.10	2.10	2.34
Rhode Island	3.91	3.65	4.34	4.10	3.94	4.21	4.73	1.41	1.52	1.43	1.68	1.85	1.96	2.24
S. Carolina	3.93	4.17	4.44	5.03	5.31	5.54	5.63	2.04	2.16	2.33	2.52	2.70	2.82	2.92
S. Dakota														
Tennessee	0.00	0.00	0.00	0.00	0.00	0.00	0.00	0.41	0.41	0.41	0.41	0.42	0.42	0.42
Texas														
Utah	4.74	4.69	4.55	4.58	4.84	5.11	5.33	2.46	2.60	2.79	2.92	3.03	3.28	3.40
Vermont	5.15	4.80	5.25	4.96	4.71	4.61	4.60	1.86	2.00	1.74	2.04	2.22	2.16	2.19
Virginia	3.56	3.83	4.09	4.21	3.94	4.10	4.24	1.40	1.53	1.71	1.92	2.25	2.33	2.39
Washington	0.00	0.00	0.00	0.00	0.00	0.00	0.00	0.00	0.00	0.00	0.00	0.00	0.00	0.00
W. Virginia	2.58	2.74	2.86	3.11	3.30	3.49	4.22	1.72	1.77	1.84	1.92	2.00	2.06	2.15
Wisconsin	5.74	5.55	4.70	5.03	5.02	4.99	5.76	2.90	3.06	2.66	0.62	0.63	0.62	1.52
Wyoming														
Federal	20.61	19.19	22.84	21.57	20.49	19.21	17.70	7.43	7.97	7.52	8.86	9.63	8.97	8.39
Mean	3.27	3.33	3.47	3.56	3.65	3.86	4.19	1.54	1.62	1.68	1.64	1.68	1.78	1.98
Standard deviation	1.66	1.63	1.95	1.84	2.34	2.40	2.44	0.91	0.93	0.93	1.03	1.04	1.11	1.19

with income. Another reason is the existence of income-related credits, which could induce a high marginal tax rate for a low-income household.

To summarize: all the measures we have computed suggest substantial interstate variability in personal income tax structure in a given year, as well as differences in how the systems have evolved over time. On average, however, there has been a tendency for the systems to become less revenue elastic and for the marginal tax rates to increase over time. Why have the two measures tended to move in opposite directions? Most of the systems are not indexed for inflation. Over time, inflation has tended to push people into high tax brackets. But once in the highest bracket, the elasticity tends to decrease, in some cases going down to unity.

6.2.5   Results Holding the Tax Law Constant

Year-to-year variations in our tax structure measures come from a combination of two sources: change in nominal incomes and changes in the tax statutes. At the federal level, considerable attention has been focused on the phenomenon of "bracket creep"—how real tax liabilities change merely as a consequence of changes in nominal income, without any statutory changes.[8] (See, e.g., Congressional Budget Office 1980.) Is a similar phenomenon operative at the state level? To what extent are intertemporal changes in tax structure due to nominal income changes and to what extent to changes in the laws? To investigate these questions, we computed individuals' tax liabilities for every year from 1977 to 1983 assuming that the tax law stayed in its 1977 incarnation. Hence, any changes in year-to-year summary measures are due only to nominal income changes.

The results for elasticities are reported in table 6.5; for marginal and average tax rates on various representative individuals in tables 6.6a, 6.6b, and 6.6c. A comparison of tables 6.3 and 6.5 suggests that, on average, changes in the statutes made during our sample period tended to make state tax systems more revenue elastic than otherwise would have been the case. If the 1977 tax law had been in effect the entire period (*ceteris paribus*), the average revenue elasticity would have fallen from 1.66 to 1.44, but, as noted above, the actual change was from 1.66 to 1.54. Similarly, tables 6.4a and 6.6a indicate that statute changes during the period tended to make the systems more progressive with respect to marginal tax rates. In the absence of any changes, the marginal tax rate for the high-income group would have grown from 5.55% to 5.82%, while in fact the increase was from 5.64% to 5.93%. Tables 6.4b and 6.6b indicate a somewhat different story for marginal tax rates on middle-income taxpaying units; changes in the statutes have tended to make their marginal rates slightly lower than would otherwise have been the case. Similarly, 6.4c and 6.6c suggest that

Table 6.5   **Elasticity of State Personal Income Tax Liability with Respect to Income (1977 Law Applies to All Years)**

State	1977	1978	1979	1980	1981	1982	1983
Alabama	1.33	1.29	1.26	1.21	1.18	1.16	1.14
Alaska	1.54	1.53	1.53	1.53	1.52	1.51	1.52
Arizona	1.48	1.44	1.41	1.35	1.30	1.28	1.26
Arkansas	1.60	1.57	1.56	1.53	1.51	1.49	1.47
California	2.14	2.08	2.02	1.96	1.88	1.85	1.82
Colorado	1.59	1.60	1.49	1.43	1.39	1.21	1.35
Connecticut	1.10	1.10	1.10	1.09	1.15	1.08	1.08
Delaware	1.70	1.65	1.61	1.58	1.56	1.46	1.53
District of Columbia	1.71	1.68	1.63	1.59	1.61	1.44	1.58
Florida	.	.	.	.	.	.	.
Georgia	1.73	1.69	1.64	1.57	1.52	1.45	1.47
Hawaii	1.55	1.53	1.47	1.47	1.50	1.24	1.38
Idaho	1.72	1.68	1.61	1.54	1.50	1.47	1.45
Illinois	1.22	1.20	1.18	1.16	1.15	1.14	1.13
Indiana	1.18	1.16	1.28	1.13	1.12	1.11	1.11
Iowa	1.67	1.46	1.60	1.38	1.35	1.45	1.47
Kansas	1.53	1.51	1.51	1.52	1.45	1.29	1.44
Kentucky	1.45	1.42	1.38	1.32	1.28	1.13	1.24
Louisiana	2.51	2.25	2.10	1.99	1.94	1.84	1.86
Maine	2.08	2.04	1.96	1.92	1.86	1.81	1.80
Maryland	1.34	1.32	1.29	1.26	1.24	1.06	1.22
Massachusetts	1.29	1.27	1.25	1.22	1.21	1.20	1.19
Michigan	1.47	1.43	1.38	1.33	1.29	1.27	1.25
Minnesota	1.95	1.83	1.89	1.46	1.55	1.42	1.45
Mississippi	2.11	2.05	1.94	1.82	1.75	1.72	1.70
Missouri	1.73	1.70	1.65	1.58	1.52	1.50	1.47
Montana	1.44	1.40	1.39	1.35	1.34	1.15	1.30
Nebraska	2.08	2.02	1.92	1.89	1.85	1.81	1.79
Nevada	.	.	.	.	.	.	.
New Hampshire	1.45	1.41	1.40	1.39	1.40	1.37	1.35
New Jersey	1.56	1.54	1.50	1.47	1.45	1.42	1.41
New Mexico	4.19	3.65	3.17	2.83	2.63	2.51	2.43
New York	1.73	1.71	1.67	1.65	1.62	1.56	1.58
North Carolina	1.48	1.46	1.44	1.41	1.38	1.37	1.36
North Dakota	1.79	1.75	1.71	1.68	1.64	1.51	1.56
Ohio	1.75	1.74	1.69	1.64	1.63	1.61	1.61
Oklahoma	2.04	1.97	1.94	1.86	1.81	1.70	1.74
Oregon	2.21	2.18	2.21	2.10	2.01	1.93	1.96
Pennsylvania	1.20	1.15	1.11	1.05	1.04	1.01	1.02
Rhode Island	1.76	1.74	1.69	1.70	1.68	1.66	1.66
South Carolina	1.68	1.63	1.61	1.57	1.55	1.52	1.50
South Dakota	.	.	.	.	.	.	.
Tennessee	1.00	1.00	1.00	1.00	1.00	1.00	1.00
Texas	.	.	.	.	.	.	.
Utah	1.40	1.35	1.31	1.24	1.20	1.09	1.16
Vermont	1.71	1.72	1.65	1.66	1.81	1.64	1.64
Virginia	1.65	1.62	1.59	1.54	1.51	1.49	1.47
Washington	.	.	.	.	.	.	.
West Virginia	1.52	1.52	1.52	1.52	1.52	1.42	1.53
Wisconsin	2.10	2.01	2.70	1.76	1.69	1.58	1.60
Wyoming	.	.	.	.	.	.	.
Federal	1.78	1.76	1.71	1.70	1.68	1.66	1.66
Mean	1.66	1.61	1.60	1.51	1.48	1.43	1.44
Standard deviation	0.40	0.36	0.37	0.31	0.29	0.28	0.27

Table 6.6a State Personal Income Tax Rates at $40,000 (1979 Dollars) AGI (1977 Law Applies to All Years)

State	Marginal rate							Average rate						
	1977	1978	1979	1980	1981	1982	1983	1977	1978	1979	1980	1981	1982	1983
Alabama	3.32	3.24	3.14	2.99	2.88	2.81	2.76	2.84	2.85	2.86	2.87	2.86	2.85	2.84
Alaska	5.28	5.39	.	.	.	.	.	3.55	3.67	.	.	.	.	.
Arizona	4.84	4.73	4.57	4.36	4.19	4.07	3.99	3.19	3.26	3.33	3.39	3.42	3.44	3.45
Arkansas	6.87	6.87	7.03	7.03	7.04	7.05	7.05	4.14	4.28	4.45	4.63	4.77	4.86	4.92
California	9.57	10.24	10.73	10.91	11.09	11.10	11.11	3.97	4.28	4.67	5.11	5.45	5.68	5.84
Colorado	4.87	4.80	4.70	4.55	4.46	4.37	4.30	3.00	3.09	3.18	3.27	3.34	3.37	3.39
Connecticut	0.00	0.00	0.00	0.00	0.00	0.00	0.00	0.23	0.24	0.24	0.24	0.24	0.24	0.24
Delaware	8.34	8.35	8.47	8.61	8.85	9.24	9.45	4.53	4.70	4.90	5.12	5.29	5.42	5.51
District of Columbia	8.76	8.92	9.10	9.49	9.78	9.97	10.06	4.75	4.93	5.16	5.41	5.62	5.77	5.87
Florida	.	.	.	.	.	.	.	.	.	.	.	.	.	.
Georgia	6.03	6.03	6.03	6.03	6.03	6.04	6.05	3.49	3.60	3.72	3.85	3.95	4.01	4.06
Hawaii	8.51	8.68	8.84	8.93	8.96	9.14	9.20	5.32	5.44	5.61	5.79	5.93	6.02	6.09
Idaho	7.54	7.54	7.54	7.54	7.54	7.55	7.56	4.57	4.69	4.83	4.98	5.09	5.16	5.21
Illinois	2.50	2.50	2.50	2.50	2.50	2.50	2.50	2.28	2.30	2.32	2.34	2.36	2.37	2.38
Indiana	2.00	2.00	2.00	2.00	2.00	2.00	2.00	1.82	1.83	1.85	1.86	1.87	1.88	1.89
Iowa	4.60	4.64	4.55	4.58	4.56	4.53	4.49	2.96	3.03	3.11	3.18	3.24	3.28	3.31
Kansas	4.42	4.49	4.48	4.27	4.14	4.16	4.08	2.39	2.48	2.59	2.70	2.77	2.81	2.83
Kentucky	3.83	3.78	3.72	3.56	3.43	3.37	3.31	2.65	2.70	2.74	2.78	2.80	2.81	2.82
Louisiana	1.33	1.30	1.56	1.83	2.09	2.04	2.00	0.74	0.76	0.78	0.84	0.90	0.94	0.97
Maine	7.87	7.96	8.38	8.71	8.88	8.89	8.90	3.19	3.42	3.70	4.03	4.30	4.48	4.59
Maryland	5.00	5.00	5.00	5.00	5.00	5.00	5.00	3.53	3.57	3.62	3.67	3.71	3.74	3.75
Massachusetts	5.32	5.32	5.32	5.32	5.33	5.37	5.37	5.48	5.53	5.59	5.65	5.69	5.72	5.74
Michigan	4.60	4.60	4.60	4.60	4.60	4.60	4.60	3.84	3.89	3.95	4.01	4.06	4.08	4.10
Minnesota	9.84	9.62	9.41	8.98	8.65	8.42	8.27	7.46	7.53	7.59	7.63	7.64	7.63	7.62

Mississippi	3.76	3.81	3.87	3.87	3.87	3.87	3.87	1.87	1.96	2.08	2.20	2.29	2.35	2.39
Missouri	3.55	3.51	3.45	3.37	3.30	3.30	3.25	2.02	2.09	2.17	2.24	2.29	2.33	2.35
Montana	5.50	5.55	5.53	5.34	5.44	5.30	5.32	3.48	3.56	3.66	3.77	3.84	3.88	3.91
Nebraska	5.45	5.70	6.04	6.50	6.87	7.12	7.30	2.44	2.58	2.76	2.99	3.17	3.31	3.41
Nevada	.	.	.	.	.	.	.	.	.	.	.	.	.	.
New Hampshire	0.00	0.00	0.00	0.00	0.00	0.00	0.00	0.47	0.48	0.49	0.50	0.51	0.52	0.52
New Jersey	2.52	2.52	2.52	2.52	2.52	2.52	2.52	1.81	1.86	1.92	1.98	2.03	2.06	2.08
New Mexico	4.80	5.00	5.34	5.79	6.17	6.43	6.56	1.36	1.53	1.75	2.00	2.22	2.37	2.48
New York	12.40	12.48	12.67	12.75	12.60	12.46	12.46	6.23	6.52	6.87	7.24	7.52	7.70	7.81
N. Carolina	6.78	6.89	6.92	7.00	7.04	7.06	7.06	4.42	4.53	4.67	4.82	4.94	5.02	5.07
N. Dakota	5.50	5.58	5.68	5.71	5.68	5.53	5.43	2.70	2.83	3.01	3.19	3.32	3.41	3.47
Ohio	2.85	2.93	2.93	3.01	3.19	3.26	3.32	1.74	1.81	1.91	2.00	2.08	2.14	2.18
Oklahoma	5.38	5.29	5.39	5.26	5.18	5.20	5.10	2.28	2.43	2.61	2.80	2.94	3.03	3.09
Oregon	7.64	8.50	9.39	9.42	9.43	9.44	9.45	1.64	1.82	2.07	2.38	2.61	2.77	2.87
Pennsylvania	2.00	2.00	2.00	2.00	2.00	2.00	2.00	2.03	2.03	2.03	2.03	2.03	2.03	2.03
Rhode Island	6.47	6.76	7.17	7.72	8.16	8.46	8.67	3.08	3.23	3.44	3.69	3.90	4.05	4.16
S. Carolina	6.48	6.53	6.66	6.84	6.39	6.90	6.94	3.31	3.45	3.63	3.82	3.98	4.07	4.14
S. Dakota	.	.	.	.	.	.	.	.	.	.	.	.	.	.
Tennessee	0.00	0.00	0.00	0.00	0.00	0.00	0.00	0.85	0.85	0.85	0.85	0.85	0.85	0.85
Texas	.	.	.	.	.	.	.	.	.	.	.	.	.	.
Utah	4.94	4.82	4.71	4.52	4.37	4.25	4.18	3.38	3.41	3.43	3.45	3.45	3.44	3.44
Vermont	8.52	8.90	9.44	10.16	10.73	11.13	11.41	4.20	4.40	4.66	4.98	5.25	5.45	5.60
Virginia	5.33	5.33	5.42	5.45	5.64	5.67	5.71	2.71	2.80	2.91	3.03	3.12	3.18	3.23
Washington	0.00	0.00	0.00	0.00	0.00	0.00	0.00	0.00	0.00	0.00	0.00	0.00	0.00	0.00
W. Virginia	4.42	4.65	4.83	5.15	5.45	5.55	5.67	2.34	2.43	2.56	2.71	2.84	2.93	3.00
Wisconsin	10.60	10.69	10.88	11.07	11.24	11.31	11.37	5.96	6.18	6.45	6.73	6.96	7.11	7.22
Wyoming	.	.	.	.	.	.	.	.	.	.	.	.	.	.
Federal	34.07	35.61	37.77	40.65	42.93	44.54	45.63	16.59	17.38	18.43	19.69	20.78	21.59	22.16
Mean	5.55	5.65	5.76	5.80	5.83	5.82	5.82	3.23	3.35	3.49	3.64	3.76	3.84	3.89
Standard deviation	3.53	3.65	3.77	3.82	3.82	3.81	3.82	1.70	1.77	1.86	1.96	2.03	2.09	2.12

Table 6.6b   State Personal Income Tax Rates at $20,000 (1979 Dollars) AGI (1977 Law Applies to All Years)

State	Marginal rate							Average rate						
	1977	1978	1979	1980	1981	1982	1983	1977	1978	1979	1980	1981	1982	1983
Alabama	3.86	3.81	3.75	3.67	3.61	3.57	3.49	2.45	2.53	2.61	2.69	2.75	2.78	2.80
Alaska	4.44	4.56	.	.	.	.	.	3.00	3.10	.	.	.	.	.
Arizona	4.73	4.78	5.01	5.10	5.14	5.11	5.00	2.44	2.55	2.70	2.87	3.00	3.08	3.14
Arkansas	5.31	5.44	5.89	6.07	6.22	6.37	6.43	2.75	2.90	3.10	3.33	3.52	3.65	3.74
California	6.06	6.43	6.94	7.49	7.95	8.34	8.51	2.17	2.39	2.68	3.03	3.33	3.54	3.69
Colorado	4.56	4.96	4.78	4.86	5.00	5.01	4.98	2.36	2.47	2.59	2.75	2.88	2.97	3.03
Connecticut	0.00	0.00	0.00	0.00	0.01	0.00	0.00	0.15	0.15	0.15	0.16	0.16	0.16	0.16
Delaware	6.99	7.12	7.46	7.55	7.86	7.89	7.96	3.28	3.48	3.68	3.95	4.17	4.33	4.43
District of Columbia	7.51	7.64	10.23	8.11	8.22	8.38	8.48	3.30	3.50	3.77	4.17	4.41	4.57	4.68
Florida	.	.	.	.	.	.	.	.	.	.	.	.	.	.
Georgia	5.64	5.87	5.97	6.00	6.04	6.04	6.04	2.27	2.45	2.66	2.91	3.10	3.22	3.30
Hawaii	8.56	8.26	8.97	8.44	8.50	8.30	8.38	4.36	4.61	4.76	5.05	5.23	5.36	5.44
Idaho	7.37	7.47	7.50	7.55	7.55	7.55	7.55	3.10	3.33	3.61	3.89	4.10	4.24	4.34
Illinois	2.50	2.50	2.50	2.50	2.50	2.50	2.50	2.08	2.11	2.15	2.19	2.22	2.23	2.24
Indiana	2.00	2.00	2.00	2.00	2.00	2.00	2.00	1.70	1.72	1.74	1.77	1.78	1.79	1.80
Iowa	4.61	4.70	4.76	4.74	4.75	4.75	4.69	2.38	2.50	2.60	2.75	2.87	2.94	2.99
Kansas	3.23	3.48	3.72	3.87	4.02	4.12	4.18	1.77	1.85	1.92	2.05	2.15	2.23	2.28
Kentucky	4.09	4.16	4.15	4.15	4.12	4.07	3.99	2.25	2.34	2.41	2.54	2.62	2.68	2.72
Louisiana	1.53	1.51	1.59	1.64	1.69	1.69	1.65	0.39	0.45	0.52	0.60	0.65	0.70	0.72
Maine	4.67	5.36	5.75	6.67	6.96	7.23	7.59	1.63	1.80	2.05	2.37	2.65	2.85	2.98
Maryland	5.00	5.00	5.00	5.00	5.00	5.00	5.00	3.16	3.25	3.30	3.40	3.48	3.53	3.56
Massachusetts	5.17	5.22	5.29	5.31	5.34	5.34	5.34	4.36	4.45	4.55	4.67	4.75	4.81	4.85
Michigan	4.60	4.60	4.60	4.60	4.60	4.60	4.60	3.27	3.36	3.47	3.57	3.65	3.70	3.74
Minnesota	11.33	11.17	11.07	10.81	10.66	10.52	10.31	5.82	6.10	6.33	6.64	6.87	7.01	7.10
Mississippi	3.24	3.24	3.37	3.50	3.65	3.66	3.67	0.96	1.10	1.25	1.43	1.57	1.66	1.73

Missouri	3.04	3.17	3.36	3.50	3.61	3.68	3.65	1.33	1.42	1.53	1.67	1.78	1.86	1.91
Montana	5.15	5.18	5.36	5.53	5.62	5.63	5.60	3.05	3.15	3.22	3.37	3.49	3.58	3.63
Nebraska	3.76	3.93	4.10	4.38	4.54	4.70	4.94	1.45	1.58	1.74	1.92	2.07	2.17	2.25
Nevada	.	.	.	.	.	.	.	.	.	.	.	.	.	.
New Hampshire	0.00	0.00	0.00	0.00	0.00	0.00	0.00	0.18	0.19	0.19	0.20	0.20	0.21	0.21
New Jersey	2.02	2.05	2.09	2.21	2.30	2.36	2.43	1.24	1.30	1.36	1.44	1.50	1.55	1.58
New Mexico	2.92	3.19	3.51	3.92	4.26	4.45	4.68	0.18	0.33	0.54	0.78	0.99	1.13	1.24
New York	8.35	9.26	10.28	11.46	12.44	13.20	13.53	3.51	3.75	4.06	4.46	4.82	5.08	5.27
N. Carolina	5.95	6.11	6.32	6.49	6.64	6.67	6.75	3.44	3.58	3.77	3.97	4.13	4.24	4.32
N. Dakota	3.46	4.13	4.62	5.20	5.46	5.48	5.39	1.44	1.56	1.74	1.99	2.19	2.34	2.44
Ohio	2.13	2.29	2.43	2.59	2.78	2.86	2.88	0.95	1.03	1.13	1.26	1.36	1.44	1.49
Oklahoma	3.17	3.61	3.91	4.42	4.87	5.07	5.19	1.10	1.22	1.38	1.59	1.78	1.92	2.02
Oregon	5.68	5.93	5.51	5.76	5.70	6.21	6.38	1.23	1.40	1.59	1.79	1.94	2.03	2.12
Pennsylvania	2.00	2.00	2.00	2.00	2.03	2.00	2.00	2.09	2.09	2.09	2.09	2.09	2.09	2.09
Rhode Island	4.46	4.66	4.87	5.20	5.39	5.58	5.86	2.17	2.29	2.44	2.62	2.78	2.88	2.96
S. Carolina	5.10	5.25	5.70	5.90	6.10	6.22	6.30	2.31	2.46	2.64	2.87	3.05	3.18	3.26
S. Dakota	.	.	.	.	.	.	.	.	.	.	.	.	.	.
Tennessee	0.00	0.00	0.00	0.00	0.00	0.00	0.00	0.44	0.44	0.44	0.44	0.44	0.44	0.44
Texas	.	.	.	.	.	.	.	.	.	.	.	.	.	.
Utah	5.57	5.55	5.51	5.41	5.34	5.27	5.16	3.00	3.13	3.24	3.38	3.48	3.54	3.58
Vermont	5.87	6.14	6.40	6.84	7.09	7.34	7.71	2.97	3.13	3.33	3.57	3.77	3.91	4.01
Virginia	4.61	4.71	4.94	5.09	5.34	5.36	5.47	2.23	2.36	2.49	2.67	2.81	2.92	2.98
Washington	0.00	0.00	0.00	0.00	0.00	0.00	0.00	0.00	0.00	0.00	0.00	0.00	0.00	0.00
W. Virginia	3.34	3.44	3.63	3.75	3.97	4.16	4.21	1.91	1.98	2.04	2.16	2.25	2.32	2.37
Wisconsin	8.55	8.92	9.28	9.70	10.05	10.24	10.35	4.18	4.43	4.72	5.08	5.38	5.59	5.73
Wyoming	.	.	.	.	.	.	.	.	.	.	.	.	.	.
Federal	23.47	24.54	25.62	27.35	28.36	29.35	30.85	11.42	12.05	12.87	13.80	14.62	15.19	15.59
Mean	4.44	4.64	4.86	5.10	5.30	5.44	5.51	2.27	2.39	2.53	2.71	2.86	2.96	3.03
Standard deviation	2.50	2.66	2.89	3.12	3.34	3.53	3.61	1.17	1.22	1.28	1.36	1.43	1.49	1.53

Table 6.6c   State Personal Income Tax Rates at $10,000 (1979 Dollars) AGI (1977 Law Applies to All Years)

State	Marginal rate							Average rate						
	1977	1978	1979	1980	1981	1982	1983	1977	1978	1979	1980	1981	1982	1983
Alabama	3.23	3.48	3.58	3.70	3.73	3.72	3.73	1.71	1.81	1.94	2.09	2.21	2.30	2.35
Alaska	4.03	4.20	.	.	.	.	.	2.35	2.46	.	.	.	.	.
Arizona	4.27	4.48	4.69	4.68	4.73	4.79	4.81	2.27	2.39	2.55	2.75	2.89	2.98	3.04
Arkansas	3.28	3.53	3.74	4.14	4.47	4.54	4.56	1.45	1.56	1.72	1.90	2.06	2.18	2.26
California	3.88	4.18	4.78	5.49	5.70	6.06	6.36	0.84	1.03	1.28	1.59	1.88	2.07	2.21
Colorado	3.59	3.87	4.40	4.44	4.65	4.85	5.02	1.93	2.02	2.16	2.35	2.50	2.60	2.67
Connecticut	0.00	0.00	0.00	0.00	0.00	0.00	0.00	0.00	0.00	0.00	0.00	0.00	0.00	0.00
Delaware	5.30	5.63	5.98	6.47	6.66	6.78	6.86	2.45	2.62	2.86	3.14	3.38	3.55	3.66
District of Columbia	5.66	5.91	6.17	7.36	6.81	7.01	7.19	2.36	2.54	2.77	3.03	3.34	3.51	3.62
Florida	.	.	.	.	.	.	.	.	.	.	.	.	.	.
Georgia	3.69	3.89	3.98	4.39	4.66	4.83	5.01	1.33	1.48	1.67	1.88	2.06	2.19	2.28
Hawaii	7.01	7.17	7.42	8.08	8.42	8.51	8.57	3.42	3.64	3.91	4.21	4.47	4.67	4.80
Idaho	5.74	5.94	6.19	6.40	6.57	6.71	6.82	1.76	2.00	2.31	2.64	2.91	3.09	3.21
Illinois	2.50	2.50	2.50	2.50	2.50	2.50	2.50	1.95	1.98	2.03	2.07	2.11	2.13	2.14
Indiana	2.00	2.00	2.00	2.00	2.00	2.00	2.00	1.60	1.63	1.66	1.69	1.71	1.73	1.74
Iowa	3.25	3.43	3.65	4.31	4.58	4.83	4.62	1.76	1.85	1.98	2.13	2.26	2.35	2.45
Kansas	2.85	3.06	3.34	3.36	3.46	3.65	3.46	1.42	1.49	1.60	1.75	1.87	1.93	2.00
Kentucky	3.47	3.65	3.82	3.99	4.04	4.07	4.07	1.83	1.93	2.06	2.21	2.34	2.43	2.49
Louisiana	1.17	1.22	1.35	1.47	1.46	1.47	1.48	0.12	0.18	0.26	0.35	0.43	0.48	0.51
Maine	3.25	3.51	3.79	4.29	4.45	4.63	4.77	0.92	1.06	1.25	1.48	1.69	1.83	1.92
Maryland	4.83	4.86	4.91	4.97	5.00	5.00	5.00	2.80	2.92	3.06	3.21	3.33	3.40	3.46
Massachusetts	5.06	5.06	5.06	5.06	5.06	5.06	5.06	3.21	3.34	3.50	3.66	3.78	3.85	3.90
Michigan	4.60	4.60	4.60	4.60	4.60	4.60	4.60	3.06	3.16	3.28	3.40	3.49	3.55	3.59
Minnesota	8.19	7.38	12.71	9.95	11.83	14.63	12.86	2.13	2.56	3.04	4.08	4.49	4.91	5.35

State													
Mississippi	1.68	1.94	2.06	2.32	2.80	3.08	3.18	0.29	0.39	0.51	0.66	0.78	0.88	0.96
Missouri	2.20	2.37	2.54	2.76	2.96	3.07	3.17	0.78	0.87	0.99	1.13	1.25	1.33	1.39
Montana	4.74	4.91	5.06	5.35	5.47	5.50	5.59	2.86	2.98	3.12	3.29	3.43	3.53	3.60
Nebraska	3.30	3.07	3.11	3.33	3.48	3.56	3.62	0.76	0.92	1.09	1.27	1.42	1.53	1.60
Nevada														
New Hampshire	0.00	0.00	0.00	0.00	0.00	0.00	0.00	0.11	0.13	0.14	0.15	0.16	0.17	0.18
New Jersey	2.00	2.00	2.00	2.00	2.00	2.00	2.00	0.77	0.85	0.94	1.04	1.11	1.16	1.19
New Mexico	1.36	1.51	1.80	2.10	2.40	2.58	2.72	-0.51	-0.39	-0.23	-0.05	0.12	0.24	0.32
New York	4.61	4.84	4.98	5.37	5.67	6.00	6.24	2.11	2.26	2.46	2.67	2.86	2.99	3.09
N. Carolina	5.04	5.17	5.38	5.67	5.81	5.95	6.07	2.76	2.90	3.07	3.27	3.44	3.56	3.64
N. Dakota	1.86	2.05	2.45	2.91	3.37	3.60	3.77	1.09	1.14	1.21	1.31	1.43	1.52	1.59
Ohio	0.87	0.94	1.15	1.37	1.58	1.80	1.87	0.47	0.50	0.53	0.59	0.64	0.69	0.72
Oklahoma	2.11	2.26	2.53	2.81	3.07	3.26	3.32	0.76	0.84	0.94	1.08	1.21	1.30	1.37
Oregon	2.55	2.65	3.33	3.88	4.36	5.03	5.53	0.17	0.30	0.45	0.67	0.87	1.00	1.09
Pennsylvania	2.17	2.00	2.00	2.00	2.00	2.00	2.00	1.88	1.90	1.90	1.90	1.90	1.90	1.90
Rhode Island	3.91	3.64	3.70	3.96	4.13	4.22	4.30	1.41	1.57	1.74	1.91	2.05	2.16	2.23
S. Carolina	3.93	4.20	4.62	5.09	5.33	5.54	5.64	2.04	2.15	2.31	2.51	2.70	2.83	2.92
S. Dakota														
Tennessee	0.00	0.00	0.00	0.00	0.00	0.00	0.00	0.41	0.41	0.41	0.41	0.41	0.41	0.41
Texas														
Utah	4.74	4.67	4.47	4.48	4.71	4.84	4.92	2.46	2.59	2.74	2.87	2.96	3.03	3.09
Vermont	5.15	4.79	4.86	5.21	5.43	5.56	5.66	1.86	2.08	2.29	2.52	2.71	2.85	2.94
Virginia	3.56	3.83	4.10	4.21	4.31	4.40	4.49	1.40	1.53	1.71	1.92	2.09	2.20	2.28
Washington	0.00	0.00	0.00	0.00	0.00	0.00	0.00	0.00	0.00	0.00	0.00	0.00	0.00	0.00
W. Virginia	2.58	2.74	2.86	3.11	3.32	3.50	3.59	1.72	1.77	1.84	1.93	2.00	2.07	2.11
Wisconsin	5.74	5.87	6.00	6.43	7.04	7.49	7.76	2.90	3.07	3.29	3.52	3.72	3.89	4.01
Wyoming														
Federal	20.61	19.16	19.45	20.83	21.73	22.23	22.63	7.43	8.28	9.14	10.03	10.81	11.36	11.73
Mean	3.27	3.36	3.64	3.82	4.00	4.21	4.27	1.54	1.65	1.79	1.95	2.09	2.19	2.26
Standard deviation	1.66	1.66	2.09	1.98	2.16	2.46	2.37	0.91	0.93	0.96	1.02	1.06	1.10	1.14

158   Daniel R. Feenberg/Harvey S. Rosen

statute changes lead to lower marginal rates for low-income households than would otherwise have been the case. There does not appear to be a simple story to explain this pattern of change. We think that analysis of the dynamics of tax structure modification would be a useful topic for future research.

6.3. Sales Taxes

6.3.1 General Description

State sales tax systems tend to be so complicated—and sometimes eccentric—that there is no simple way to characterize all their provisions. For example, New Jersey has a special asparagus tax; New Mexico levies a tax on dentures, and Maine taxes the proceeds of some (but not all) garage sales. Still, we can summarize the important attributes of the systems. Table 6.7 shows the statutory sales tax rates for 1977–1983. All states except Alaska, Delaware, Montana, New Hampshire, and Oregon levy a sales tax and have done so across the entire period. For states with a general sales tax, rates in 1983 ranged from 2% in Oklahoma to 7.5% in Connecticut. Table 6.7 also indicates each state's tax treatment of food. There is some trend toward the exemption of food: twenty states plus the District of Columbia exempted food in 1977, and by 1983 the figure was twenty-three states plus the District of Columbia. Taken together, the numbers in table 6.7 suggest considerable heterogeneity, just as we found with the income tax.

6.3.2 Methodological Issues

In section 6.2.2 we noted the difficulties inherent in trying to characterize a complex tax system with a single number. The same types of problem crop up here, and our solution is basically the same.

However, a new methodological problem arises in the case of sales taxation. Given that our data come from federal personal tax returns, there is no information on individuals' consumption bundles. Hence, on the basis of our data alone, we can generally calculate neither sales-tax liabilities nor how these liabilities would change with changes in income. It is therefore necessary to impute a sales-tax liability to each household based upon its income and family size.[9]

Our initial plan for doing the imputation was a straightforward three-step procedure. The first step was to compile a detailed history by state of the tax rates applied to each expenditure category. The second was to utilize data from the Consumer Expenditure Survey (CES)[10] to estimate equations for each expenditure category, and use the parameters to estimate expenditures in the various categories for each of the households in our sample. And the third was to multiply each expenditure category by the appropriate tax rate in order to find tax liability.

Unfortunately, we ran into trouble right at the first step. A detailed history by state of sales tax rates and coverage proved impossible to obtain. However, several reference books did show the general rates through time, and also indicated if food was exempt. (This is essentially the information contained in table 6.7.) We therefore used the CES to estimate equations for only two categories: "food" and "goods other than food."

This simplification proved to be unsatisfactory. The results, when multiplied by population weights, simply did not give very good predictions of sales tax revenues by state. While part of the error may have related to our omission of the sales-tax liabilities of firms, we believe that the main problem was that the broadness of the sales-tax base varied significantly across states in a way not captured by the simple food/nonfood distinction.

An alternative method that turned out to be much more successful relied on the "Optional State Sales Tax Tables" which are included by the Internal Revenue Service (IRS) in the standard package of personal income tax instructions (Form 1040). It turns out that since 1978, these tables have been derived from the CES in much the same manner as described above. There is one big difference, however—the Internal Revenue Service had the benefit of a set of questionnaires filled out each year by the states detailing their laws, and was able to divide coverage into twenty-four categories rather than the two categories we used.

The IRS calculations do have several limitations from our point of view. First, they exclude sales-tax liabilities on cars, boats, and mobile homes. Second, certain states tax liquor and a few other items at a different rate from the general rate. Such taxes are not deductible on the federal return and are not included in the IRS computations. Third, the calculation takes no account of the possible impact of interstate differences in relative prices. Fourth, no allowance is made for inflation.

Of these problems, the fourth is certainly the most important, and is easily corrected by adjusting all amounts by the change in the Personal Consumption Deflator. Given the importance of automobile expenditures in the sales tax base, we impute them on the basis of a simple regression relating these expenditures to income and family size.[11] We have not tried to account for the other items in the previous paragraph, but believe that they are relatively minor.

The IRS tabulates national data into fourteen income classes for six family sizes. In each of the eighty-four cells average sales-tax liability is calculated from reported expenditures. Where family size seems not to affect the sales-tax liability significantly, adjacent family sizes are

Table 6.7   State Statutory Sales Tax Rates

State	Normal rate							Rate on food						
	1977	1978	1979	1980	1981	1982	1983	1977	1978	1979	1980	1981	1982	1983
Alabama	4.	4.	4.	4.	4.	4.	4.	4.	4.	4.	4.	4.	4.	4.
Alaska														
Arizona	4.	4.	4.	4.	4.	4.42	5.	4.	4.	4.	3.	0.	0.	0.
Arkansas	3.	3.	3.	3.	4.	3.	3.	3.	3.	3.	3.	4.	3.	3.
California	6.	6.	6.	6.	6.	6.	6.	0.	0.	0.	0.	0.	0.	0.
Colorado	3.	3.	3.	3.	3.	3.	3.34	3.	3.	3.	0.	0.	0.	0.
Connecticut	7.	7.	7.	7.25	7.50	7.50	7.50	0.	0.	0.	0.	0.	0.	0.
Delaware														
District of Columbia	5.	5.	5.	5.33	6.	6.	6.	0.	0.	0.	0.	0.	0.	0.
Florida	4.	4.	4.	4.	4.	4.33	5.	0.	0.	0.	0.	0.	0.	0.
Georgia	3.	3.	3.	3.	3.	3.	3.	3.	3.	3.	3.	3.	3.	3.
Hawaii	4.	4.	4.	4.	4.	4.	4.	4.	4.	4.	4.	4.	4.	4.
Idaho	3.	3.	3.	3.	3.	3.	4.42	3.	3.	3.	3.	3.	3.	4.42
Illinois	5.	5.	5.	5.	5.	5.	5.	5.	5.	5.	4.	3.	3.	3.
Indiana	4.	4.	4.	4.	4.	4.	5.	0.	0.	0.	0.	0.	0.	0.
Iowa	3.	3.	3.	3.	3.	3.	3.84	0.	0.	0.	0.	0.	0.	0.
Kansas	3.	3.	3.	3.	3.	3.	3.	3.	3.	3.	3.	3.	3.	3.
Kentucky	5.	5.	5.	5.	5.	5.	5.	0.	0.	0.	0.	0.	0.	0.
Louisiana	3.	3.	3.	3.	3.	3.	3.	0.	0.	0.	0.	0.	0.	0.
Maine	5.	5.	5.	5.	5.	5.	5.	0.	0.	0.	0.	0.	0.	0.
Maryland	5.	5.	5.	5.	5.	5.	5.	0.	0.	0.	0.	0.	0.	0.
Massachusetts	5.	5.	5.	5.	5.	5.	5.	0.	0.	0.	0.	0.	0.	0.
Michigan	4.	4.	4.	4.	4.	4.	4.	0.	0.	0.	0.	0.	0.	0.
Minnesota	4.	4.	4.	4.	4.	5.	6.	0.	0.	0.	0.	0.	0.	0.
Mississippi	5.	5.	5.	5.	5.	5.	5.	5.	5.	5.	5.	5.	5.	5.

State	3.13	3.13	3.13	3.13	3.13	3.13	4.13	3.13	3.13	3.13	3.13	3.13	3.13	3.13	3.13	3.13	4.13
Missouri	3.13	3.13	3.13	3.13	3.13	3.13	4.13	3.13	3.13	3.13	3.13	3.13	3.13	3.13	3.13	3.13	4.13
Montana	3.	3.	3.	3.	3.	3.	3.75	3.	3.	3.	3.	3.	3.	3.	3.	3.33	3.75
Nebraska	3.	3.	3.	3.	3.	3.	3.75	3.	3.	3.	3.	3.	3.	3.	3.	3.33	3.75
Nevada	3.50	3.50	3.50	3.50	4.81	3.50	5.75	3.50	3.50	3.50	3.50	3.50	4.81	3.50	3.50	5.75	5.75
New Hampshire																	
New Jersey	5.	5.	5.	5.	5.	5.	6.	5.	5.	5.	5.	5.	5.	5.	5.	5.	6.
New Mexico	3.75	3.75	3.75	3.75	3.62	3.75	3.62	3.75	3.75	3.75	3.75	3.75	3.62	3.50	3.50	3.50	3.62
New York	4.	4.	4.	4.	4.	4.	4.	4.	4.	4.	4.	4.	4.	4.	4.	4.	4.
North Carolina	4.	4.	4.	4.	4.	4.	4.	4.	4.	4.	4.	4.	4.	4.	4.	4.	4.
North Dakota	3.	3.	3.	3.	4.34	3.	3.75	3.	3.	3.	3.	3.	3.	3.	3.	3.	3.75
Ohio	4.	4.	4.	4.	4.	5.	5.	4.	4.	4.	4.	4.	4.34	4.	4.	4.	5.
Oklahoma	2.	2.	2.	2.	2.	2.	2.	2.	2.	2.	2.	2.	2.	2.	2.	2.	2.
Oregon																	
Pennsylvania	6.	6.	6.	6.	6.	6.	6.	6.	6.	6.	6.	6.	6.	6.	6.	6.	6.
Rhode Island	6.	6.	6.	6.	6.	6.	6.	6.	6.	6.	6.	6.	6.	6.	6.	6.	6.
South Carolina	4.	4.	4.	4.	4.	4.	4.	4.	4.	4.	4.	4.	4.	4.	4.	4.	4.
South Dakota	4.	4.	4.50	4.50	4.50	4.	4.	4.	4.	4.50	4.50	4.50	4.50	4.50	4.	4.	4.
Tennessee	3.75	4.50	4.50	4.50	4.50	4.50	4.50	3.75	4.	4.50	4.50	4.50	4.50	4.50	4.	4.50	4.50
Texas	4.	4.	4.	4.	4.	4.	4.	4.	4.	4.	4.	4.	4.	4.	4.	4.	4.
Utah	4.75	4.75	4.75	4.75	4.75	4.75	5.03	4.75	4.75	4.75	4.75	4.75	4.75	4.75	4.75	4.75	5.03
Vermont	3.	3.	3.	3.	3.	3.50	4.	3.	4.	4.	3.	3.	3.	3.	3.50	3.	4.
Virginia	4.	4.	4.	4.	4.	4.	4.	4.	4.	4.	4.	4.	4.	4.	4.	4.	4.
Washington	5.10	5.10	5.05	5.10	5.62	5.94	6.32	5.10	2.60	5.10	5.10	5.10	5.10	5.10	3.63	3.63	3.41
West Virginia	3.	3.	3.	3.	4.	4.	5.	3.	3.	3.	3.	3.	3.	4.	4.	3.	5.
Wisconsin	4.	4.	4.	4.	4.	4.70	5.	4.	3.	3.	3.	3.	3.	4.70	4.	3.63	5.
Wyoming	3.	3.	3.	3.	3.	3.	3.	3.	3.	3.	3.	3.	3.	3.	3.	3.	3.

grouped. This is typically the case where food is exempt. The figures actually reported on form 1040 are then obtained by smoothing with the regression

$$\log(\text{sales tax liability}) = a + b \log(\text{AGI}),$$

which is estimated with fourteen observations for each family size in each state. Although the regression parameters are not published, they are obviously easily recovered from the tables.

To reduce the number of parameters, we fit to the tables an equation that included family size as a regressor instead of estimating a separate equation for each family size. Moreover, to facilitate interpretation of the parameter estimates, we subtracted from log(AGI) the log of $15,800, which was about the median value in 1979; and we substracted from family size its mean, 2.4:

(1) $\log(\text{sales tax liability}) = a + b[\log(\text{AGI}) - \log(15,800)] + c \,(\text{family size} - 2.4).$

Of course, subtracting the constants does not change the values of b and c, but it does allow us to interpret the constant a as the logarithm of the tax liability on a family with "typical" characteristics. We also experimented with a specification that was quadratic in family size. Generally, the squared term was statistically insignificant, suggesting that over the range of family sizes in the data, linearity is a satisfactory approximation.

6.3.3 Results

Table 6.8 shows the results when equation (1) is estimated for each state. Several features of the table require comment. First, the 1977 coefficients look rather different from those for subsequent years. They were presumably not produced by exactly the same procedure described above. Second, c is typically about 0.1 for states taxing food and about 0.05 for the others. Other things being the same, larger families pay more sales tax in states where food is not exempt. Third, the tax is apparently quite regressive with respect to annual income.[12] (In 1983, the lowest value of b was .57 for Hawaii, and the highest was .73 for Pennsylvania.)

As suggested earlier, sales tax systems vary not only by revenue elasticities with respect to income, but also by comprehensiveness. It is useful to have a simple index number that measures the size of the sales tax base in each state. To obtain such a number, we (1) compute the revenues that actual sales tax system would raise if applied to our standard set of taxpayers; (2) compute the revenue that would be raised by an income tax levied on AGI at the same rate as the sales tax; and (3) take their ratio. The higher this ratio, the more comprehensive the sales tax base. It might have been more desirable to include in the denominator the revenue that would have been raised by applying the general rate to all *consumption* rather than AGI. Unfortunately, we do not have consumption data. In any case, we do not think that this will have much of an impact on interstate comparisons.

The results are reported in table 6.9. The variation in the value of the ratio across states—almost three to one from largest to smallest— is quite striking. Interestingly, in 1983, Hawaii, which had the lowest revenue elasticity (recall table 6.8), had the broadest base, while Pennsylvania, with the highest revenue elasticity, had the third smallest base.

6.4 Income and Sales Taxes Considered Together

In this section we consider income and sales taxes as a single "structure." When income increases, how does the *sum* of personal income and sales-tax liabilities change? As noted above, for most states, such information goes a long way in characterizing the *entire* state tax structure.

Table 6.10 shows the income elasticity of combined income and sales-tax liability for each state between 1977 and 1983. As one would expect, as a matter of arithmetic, the combined elasticities are smaller than those associated with the income tax, but larger than the sales tax. The result is a set of income-sales taxes that are close to proportional— the average value of the elasticity in 1983 was 1.09. Two other aspects of table 6.10 are noteworthy:

1. The temporal decline in the elasticity of the combined system is somewhat less marked than the decline in the elasticity of the income tax alone. (The average elasticity of the combined system falls from 1.14 to 1.09, while from table 6.3, the average elasticity of the income tax alone fell from 1.66 to 1.54.) Over time, the fact that a greater proportion of revenue was generated by the relatively elastic income tax tended to counterbalance the fact that the income tax itself was becoming less elastic.

2. The combined system is just about as variable as the income tax system alone. In 1983, the coefficient of variation for the elasticity of combined systems was 0.24; for the income tax alone the figure was 0.25. We have already observed that, viewed individually, the income and sales tax systems differ considerably across states. When the systems are aggregated, these differences do not somehow "cancel out."

Tables 6.11a, 6.11b, and 6.11c show the marginal and average tax rates of the combined system for high-, medium-, and low-income individuals, respectively. For all three income groups, the general tendency has been for marginal and average rates to increase over time.

Table 6.8   IRS State Sales Tax Tables: Regression Parameters
                 Deviations from Means, Real 1979 Dollars

State	1977			1978			1979		
	a	b	c	a	b	c	a	b	c
Alabama	5.47	.65	.122	5.53	.63	.090	5.53	.63	.090
Alaska	.	.	.	.	.	.	.	.	.
Arizona	5.56	.62	.118	5.63	.62	.090	5.63	.62	.091
Arkansas	5.26	.64	.123	5.33	.62	.089	5.32	.62	.089
California	5.71	.72	.058	5.77	.66	.061	5.77	.66	.061
Colorado	5.23	.64	.119	5.28	.62	.089	5.28	.62	.089
Connecticut	5.75	.78	.043	5.72	.73	.064	5.71	.73	.054
Delaware	.	.	.	.	.	.	.	.	.
District of Columbia	5.29	.66	.120	5.36	.64	.091	5.36	.64	.091
Florida	5.32	.73	.068	5.26	.70	.057	5.26	.70	.057
Georgia	5.32	.62	.117	5.37	.60	.095	5.37	.60	.095
Hawaii	5.78	.61	.084	5.86	.57	.059	5.86	.57	.059
Idaho	5.21	.65	.119	5.23	.63	.092	5.23	.63	.092
Illinois	5.68	.64	.126	5.77	.61	.095	5.77	.61	.095
Indiana	5.37	.71	.077	5.45	.65	.065	5.45	.65	.065
Iowa	5.17	.77	.094	5.17	.67	.053	5.17	.67	.053
Kansas	5.34	.64	.122	5.39	.63	.090	5.29	.63	.094
Kentucky	5.59	.72	.059	5.60	.66	.057	5.55	.68	.054
Louisiana	5.08	.78	.058	5.04	.70	.051	5.04	.70	.051
Maine	5.54	.75	.062	5.47	.70	.056	5.45	.70	.057
Maryland	5.45	.73	.062	5.51	.68	.059	5.46	.70	.056
Massachusetts	4.84	.75	.138	5.01	.63	.139	5.16	.72	.092
Michigan	5.34	.74	.060	5.41	.66	.057	5.41	.66	.057
Minnesota	5.10	.73	.045	5.11	.71	.071	5.05	.72	.066
Mississippi	5.86	.63	.116	5.93	.61	.091	5.90	.62	.088
Missouri	5.27	.64	.124	5.37	.61	.089	5.37	.61	.089
Montana	.	.	.	.	.	.	.	.	.
Nebraska	5.30	.63	.126	5.33	.61	.090	5.33	.61	.090
Nevada	5.32	.62	.119	5.35	.63	.091	5.22	.65	.072
New Hampshire	.	.	.	.	.	.	.	.	.
New Jersey	5.29	.78	.031	5.32	.65	.039	5.30	.72	.056
New Mexico	5.66	.64	.113	5.71	.61	.089	5.69	.61	.089
New York	5.44	.78	.073	5.47	.67	.059	5.39	.70	.053
N. Carolina	5.48	.64	.118	5.52	.63	.087	5.52	.63	.087
N. Dakota	5.00	.77	.057	5.01	.69	.050	5.01	.69	.050
Ohio	5.20	.80	.059	5.19	.71	.050	5.19	.71	.050
Oklahoma	4.86	.64	.116	4.91	.62	.084	4.91	.62	.084
Oregon	.	.	.	.	.	.	.	.	.
Pennsylvania	5.28	.82	.028	5.36	.74	.045	5.36	.74	.045
Rhode Island	5.54	.76	.046	5.48	.70	.048	5.48	.70	.048
S. Carolina	5.56	.62	.118	5.62	.61	.085	5.62	.61	.085
S. Dakota	5.59	.65	.118	5.65	.62	.084	5.65	.63	.086
Tennessee	5.61	.63	.118	5.70	.62	.083	5.70	.62	.083
Texas	5.28	.73	.064	5.25	.68	.065	5.19	.70	.063
Utah	5.73	.65	.110	5.75	.63	.081	5.75	.63	.081
Vermont	4.67	.72	.119	4.68	.69	.085	4.68	.69	.085
Virginia	5.43	.64	.123	5.49	.62	.091	5.49	.62	.091
Washington	5.78	.66	.116	5.66	.68	.072	5.53	.71	.058
W. Virginia	5.27	.66	.127	5.29	.65	.082	5.25	.65	.078
Wisconsin	5.41	.74	.065	5.44	.66	.064	5.41	.67	.052
Wyoming	5.32	.66	.125	5.34	.62	.082	5.34	.62	.082

Table 6.8 (continued)

1980			1981			1982			1983		
a	b	c	a	b	c	a	b	c	a	b	c
5.53	.63	.090	5.53	.63	.090	5.53	.63	.090	5.51	.63	.093
.	.	.	.	.	.	.	.	.	.	.	.
5.51	.63	.072	5.42	.66	.060	5.43	.66	.060	5.53	.66	.061
5.32	.62	.089	5.37	.62	.088	5.32	.62	.089	5.32	.62	.089
5.77	.66	.061	5.77	.66	.061	5.77	.66	.061	5.77	.66	.061
4.99	.69	.052	4.95	.71	.056	4.95	.71	.056	4.93	.69	.064
5.76	.72	.043	5.82	.71	.055	5.82	.71	.055	5.82	.71	.055
.	.	.	.	.	.	.	.	.	.	.	.
5.46	.65	.086	5.59	.65	.080	5.59	.65	.080	5.59	.65	.080
5.26	.70	.057	5.26	.70	.057	5.42	.71	.057	5.57	.70	.061
5.37	.60	.095	5.37	.60	.095	5.37	.60	.095	5.37	.60	.095
5.86	.57	.059	5.86	.57	.059	5.86	.57	.059	5.86	.57	.059
5.23	.63	.092	5.23	.63	.092	5.23	.62	.094	5.56	.63	.091
5.73	.62	.087	5.68	.64	.082	5.68	.64	.082	5.68	.64	.082
5.45	.65	.065	5.45	.65	.065	5.45	.65	.065	5.68	.64	.066
5.17	.67	.053	5.17	.67	.053	5.17	.67	.053	5.43	.68	.053
5.26	.65	.095	5.26	.65	.095	5.26	.65	.095	5.26	.65	.095
5.51	.68	.051	5.51	.68	.051	5.50	.68	.054	5.48	.68	.057
5.04	.70	.051	5.04	.70	.051	5.04	.70	.051	5.04	.70	.051
5.45	.70	.057	5.45	.70	.057	5.45	.70	.057	5.45	.70	.057
5.40	.72	.053	5.38	.72	.054	5.38	.72	.054	5.38	.72	.054
5.13	.72	.061	5.13	.72	.061	5.13	.72	.061	5.13	.72	.061
5.41	.66	.057	5.41	.66	.057	5.41	.66	.057	5.41	.66	.057
5.03	.72	.045	5.12	.72	.045	5.32	.69	.056	5.49	.68	.063
5.87	.62	.091	5.87	.62	.091	5.87	.62	.091	5.87	.62	.091
5.30	.63	.082	5.30	.63	.082	5.30	.63	.082	5.57	.63	.082
.	.	.	.	.	.	.	.	.	.	.	.
5.33	.61	.090	5.32	.61	.093	5.43	.60	.093	5.48	.62	.084
5.05	.70	.053	5.39	.70	.055	5.54	.70	.054	5.54	.70	.054
.	.	.	.	.	.	.	.	.	.	.	.
5.28	.72	.062	5.26	.72	.067	5.26	.72	.067	5.41	.72	.060
5.69	.61	.089	5.65	.61	.089	5.62	.61	.090	5.65	.62	.087
5.39	.70	.053	5.39	.70	.053	5.39	.70	.053	5.39	.70	.053
5.52	.63	.087	5.52	.63	.087	5.52	.63	.087	5.52	.63	.087
5.01	.69	.050	5.02	.69	.058	5.01	.69	.059	5.18	.69	.067
5.20	.71	.058	5.32	.70	.052	5.48	.70	.052	5.47	.70	.053
4.91	.62	.084	4.87	.64	.082	4.87	.63	.080	4.87	.63	.080
5.36	.74	.045	5.36	.74	.045	5.36	.74	.045	5.37	.73	.051
5.48	.70	.048	5.48	.70	.048	5.48	.70	.048	5.48	.70	.048
5.59	.61	.082	5.58	.62	.080	5.58	.62	.080	5.58	.62	.080
5.75	.64	.082	5.70	.64	.068	5.65	.63	.081	5.65	.63	.087
5.70	.62	.083	5.70	.62	.083	5.70	.62	.083	5.70	.62	.083
5.19	.70	.063	5.19	.70	.063	5.19	.70	.063	5.19	.70	.063
5.75	.63	.081	5.75	.63	.081	5.75	.63	.081	5.79	.63	.082
4.68	.69	.085	4.68	.69	.085	4.81	.73	.074	4.93	.71	.076
5.49	.62	.091	5.49	.62	.091	5.49	.62	.091	5.50	.60	.085
5.53	.72	.052	5.55	.71	.052	5.86	.66	.080	5.94	.68	.074
5.17	.68	.065	5.32	.71	.051	5.47	.73	.047	5.57	.71	.051
5.34	.70	.047	5.34	.70	.047	5.50	.70	.049	5.57	.70	.048
5.34	.62	.082	5.34	.62	.082	5.34	.62	.082	5.34	.62	.082

Table 6.9   Comprehensiveness of State Sales Taxes[a]

State	1977	1978	1979	1980	1981	1982	1983
Alabama	.285	.294	.294	.293	.294	.294	.289
Alaska	.	.	.	.	.	.	.
Arizona	.303	.321	.324	.284	.266	.245	.239
Arkansas	.305	.318	.316	.316	.249	.316	.316
California	.251	.251	.251	.251	.251	.251	.251
Colorado	.296	.303	.303	.238	.232	.232	.201
Connecticut	.235	.219	.216	.216	.221	.221	.221
Delaware	.	.	.	.	.	.	.
District of Columbia	.191	.201	.201	.208	.210	.210	.210
Florida	.258	.235	.235	.235	.235	.257	.257
Georgia	.320	.326	.326	.326	.326	.326	.326
Hawaii	.370	.387	.387	.387	.387	.387	.387
Idaho	.294	.289	.289	.289	.289	.288	.272
Illinois	.277	.295	.295	.284	.274	.274	.274
Indiana	.267	.273	.273	.273	.273	.273	.274
Iowa	.311	.277	.277	.276	.277	.277	.285
Kansas	.330	.340	.309	.304	.305	.305	.305
Kentucky	.267	.257	.245	.237	.237	.235	.231
Louisiana	.283	.251	.251	.251	.251	.251	.251
Maine	.259	.233	.228	.228	.228	.228	.228
Maryland	.233	.237	.229	.219	.216	.216	.216
Massachusetts	.133	.142	.175	.168	.168	.168	.168
Michigan	.263	.262	.262	.262	.262	.262	.262
Minnesota	.204	.205	.194	.189	.207	.197	.195
Mississippi	.330	.345	.338	.329	.330	.330	.330
Missouri	.297	.315	.315	.300	.300	.300	.298
Montana	.	.	.	.	.	.	.
Nebraska	.314	.316	.316	.316	.312	.311	.294
Nevada	.273	.281	.250	.218	.224	.216	.216
New Hampshire	.	.	.	.	.	.	.
New Jersey	.207	.191	.198	.194	.191	.191	.186
New Mexico	.362	.370	.360	.360	.361	.361	.361
New York	.302	.284	.268	.267	.268	.268	.268
North Carolina	.283	.289	.289	.289	.289	.289	.289
North Dakota	.257	.242	.242	.242	.244	.242	.232
Ohio	.242	.222	.222	.224	.231	.235	.232
Oklahoma	.307	.314	.314	.314	.304	.302	.302
Oregon	.	.	.	.	.	.	.
Pennsylvania	.175	.177	.177	.177	.177	.177	.179
Rhode Island	.219	.195	.195	.195	.195	.195	.195
South Carolina	.303	.315	.315	.308	.305	.305	.305
South Dakota	.318	.327	.330	.328	.307	.330	.331
Tennessee	.343	.307	.307	.307	.307	.307	.307
Texas	.248	.229	.219	.219	.219	.219	.219
Utah	.310	.306	.306	.306	.306	.306	.304
Vermont	.181	.175	.175	.175	.175	.176	.173
Virginia	.270	.281	.281	.281	.281	.281	.276
Washington	.305	.271	.245	.250	.249	.283	.269
West Virginia	.314	.311	.302	.281	.336	.295	.257
Wisconsin	.285	.272	.265	.255	.255	.254	.256
Wyoming	.329	.321	.321	.321	.321	.321	.321

a. This table includes local sales taxes for only those states in which over 90% of the population is covered.

Table 6.10   **Elasticity of Combined Income Income and Sales Tax Liability**

State	1977	1978	1979	1980	1981	1982	1983
Alabama	0.99	0.96	0.95	0.93	0.92	0.92	0.92
Alaska	1.54	1.94	.	.	.	.	.
Arizona	1.07	1.05	1.06	1.21	1.26	1.28	1.25
Arkansas	1.24	1.21	1.23	1.22	1.20	1.20	1.19
California	1.42	1.38	1.38	1.44	1.43	1.42	1.42
Colorado	1.19	1.16	1.13	1.01	1.15	1.20	1.13
Connecticut	0.79	0.73	0.74	0.73	0.72	0.72	0.72
Delaware	1.70	1.65	1.65	1.37	1.57	1.55	1.44
District of Columbia	1.36	1.34	1.32	1.14	1.26	1.25	1.18
Florida	0.72	0.69	0.69	0.69	0.69	0.70	0.69
Georgia	1.26	1.23	1.22	1.10	1.18	1.14	1.14
Hawaii	1.18	1.14	1.18	0.95	1.31	1.17	1.01
Idaho	1.35	1.33	1.31	1.31	1.28	1.26	1.18
Illinois	0.88	0.85	0.85	0.86	0.86	0.86	0.88
Indiana	0.91	0.87	0.84	0.89	0.88	0.88	0.90
Iowa	1.28	1.14	1.14	1.05	1.13	1.15	1.12
Kansas	1.09	1.07	1.12	1.00	1.15	1.14	1.07
Kentucky	1.05	1.02	1.02	0.81	1.00	1.01	0.94
Louisiana	1.16	1.09	1.06	1.07	1.12	1.14	1.16
Maine	1.39	1.41	1.41	1.42	1.42	1.40	1.40
Maryland	1.08	1.05	1.04	0.95	1.05	1.04	0.94
Massachusetts	1.16	1.11	1.10	1.10	1.16	1.14	1.14
Michigan	1.18	1.08	1.11	1.16	1.15	1.14	1.14
Minnesota	1.63	1.77	1.79	1.27	1.98	1.55	1.64
Mississippi	1.03	1.01	1.02	0.94	1.03	1.03	1.07
Missouri	1.12	1.09	1.08	1.03	1.09	1.10	1.04
Montana	1.44	1.40	1.50	1.21	1.42	1.48	1.37
Nebraska	1.34	1.33	1.38	1.36	1.35	1.31	1.27
Nevada	0.61	0.62	0.64	0.69	0.70	0.70	0.70
New Hampshire	1.45	1.41	1.40	1.39	1.40	1.37	1.35
New Jersey	1.09	1.02	1.05	1.05	1.05	1.05	1.01
New Mexico	1.38	1.34	1.36	1.35	1.30	1.39	1.46
New York	1.39	1.37	1.40	1.31	1.34	1.35	1.32
North Carolina	1.16	1.15	1.14	1.14	1.14	1.13	1.12
North Dakota	1.34	1.32	1.11	1.09	1.25	1.26	1.20
Ohio	1.16	1.14	1.14	1.13	1.10	1.14	1.26
Oklahoma	1.43	1.41	1.42	1.30	1.41	1.44	1.37
Oregon	2.21	2.13	2.18	2.15	2.02	1.95	1.83
Pennsylvania	1.00	0.94	0.92	0.89	0.89	0.87	0.88
Rhode Island	1.25	1.27	1.28	1.29	1.29	1.28	1.31
South Carolina	1.19	1.16	1.16	1.17	1.16	1.15	1.15
South Dakota	0.64	0.61	0.62	0.63	0.63	0.63	0.62
Tennessee	0.68	0.66	0.66	0.66	0.66	0.66	0.66
Texas	0.72	0.67	0.69	0.69	0.69	0.69	0.69
Utah	1.03	1.00	0.99	0.86	0.95	0.95	0.90
Vermont	1.47	1.50	1.50	1.50	1.49	1.44	1.40
Virginia	1.17	1.14	1.14	1.06	1.11	1.10	1.06
Washington	0.65	0.67	0.70	0.71	0.71	0.65	0.67
West Virginia	1.12	1.13	1.15	1.05	1.17	1.15	1.21
Wisconsin	1.60	1.50	1.63	1.44	1.48	1.42	1.31
Wyoming	0.65	0.61	0.61	0.61	0.61	0.61	0.61
Federal	1.78	1.79	1.84	1.80	1.78	1.73	1.72
Mean	1.14	1.11	1.11	1.08	1.11	1.10	1.09
Standard deviation	0.28	0.28	0.29	0.27	0.29	0.27	0.26

Table 6.11a   Average and Marginal Tax Rates at $40,000 AGI (1979 Dollars) (Combined Income and Sales)

State	Marginal rate							Average rate						
	1977	1978	1979	1980	1981	1982	1983	1977	1978	1979	1980	1981	1982	1983
Alabama	3.96	3.85	3.81	3.67	3.61	3.70	3.80	4.79	4.83	4.90	4.91	4.92	4.89	4.95
Alaska	5.28	5.39	0.00	0.00	0.00	0.00	0.00	3.46	3.01	0.00	0.00	0.00	0.00	0.00
Arizona	5.47	5.38	5.31	5.02	4.82	5.07	5.32	5.08	5.25	5.06	4.44	4.14	4.18	4.56
Arkansas	7.36	7.35	7.52	7.52	7.55	7.53	7.54	5.55	5.70	5.86	6.04	6.25	6.26	6.30
California	10.52	10.58	11.01	10.37	10.40	10.25	10.43	6.42	6.43	6.54	6.11	6.16	6.01	6.24
Colorado	5.35	5.21	4.63	4.39	4.05	5.02	5.22	4.39	4.38	4.00	3.74	3.52	4.06	4.19
Connecticut	1.15	0.97	0.96	0.97	1.02	1.02	1.02	3.09	2.81	2.76	2.81	2.99	2.99	2.99
Delaware	8.34	8.35	8.69	8.68	8.79	9.03	9.26	4.42	4.57	4.87	4.92	5.10	5.21	5.30
District of Columbia	9.31	9.48	9.65	10.13	10.47	10.66	10.75	6.24	6.44	6.67	7.08	7.53	7.67	7.77
Florida	0.66	0.57	0.57	0.57	0.57	0.68	0.76	1.76	1.57	1.56	1.56	1.57	1.86	2.13
Georgia	6.53	6.51	6.51	6.51	6.52	6.53	6.53	4.97	5.05	5.18	5.31	5.40	5.51	5.50
Hawaii	9.24	9.36	9.51	9.58	9.65	9.74	9.87	7.51	7.63	7.79	7.78	7.93	7.87	8.09
Idaho	8.03	7.99	7.99	7.99	8.00	8.00	8.18	5.92	5.97	6.10	6.09	6.21	6.27	6.87
Illinois	3.25	3.24	3.24	3.23	3.22	3.22	3.72	4.52	4.61	4.62	4.57	4.52	4.53	4.95
Indiana	2.66	2.58	2.28	2.48	2.48	2.48	3.73	3.59	3.55	3.29	3.43	3.44	3.45	4.88
Iowa	5.26	5.10	5.07	5.08	5.21	5.62	6.10	4.55	4.31	4.37	4.45	4.52	4.73	5.37
Kansas	4.96	4.90	5.03	4.85	4.76	5.03	5.23	3.98	4.00	4.01	3.97	4.01	4.20	4.37
Kentucky	4.68	4.48	4.50	4.31	4.28	4.48	4.63	4.84	4.72	4.76	4.74	4.78	4.89	4.99
Louisiana	1.93	1.74	2.23	2.51	1.64	1.92	2.68	2.21	1.99	2.09	2.15	1.76	1.83	2.09
Maine	8.73	8.57	9.20	9.53	9.74	9.75	9.75	5.33	5.05	5.40	5.75	6.02	6.20	6.32
Maryland	5.74	5.68	5.68	5.68	5.68	5.68	5.68	5.42	5.41	5.38	5.37	5.39	5.42	5.44
Massachusetts	5.78	5.71	5.88	5.85	5.84	5.82	5.78	6.53	6.59	6.92	6.79	6.50	6.52	6.48
Michigan	5.28	5.17	5.17	5.17	5.17	5.67	6.92	5.53	5.48	5.54	5.59	5.64	6.10	7.21
Minnesota	10.36	10.11	9.97	9.52	9.39	10.29	10.78	8.64	8.62	8.41	8.24	8.21	9.21	9.90
Mississippi	4.63	4.68	4.74	4.71	4.71	4.71	5.49	4.52	4.68	4.75	4.80	4.74	4.81	5.06

Missouri	4.05	4.00	4.01	3.94	3.91	4.13	4.44	3.50	3.60	3.72	3.74	3.76	3.90	4.49
Montana	5.50	5.55	5.52	5.40	4.84	5.13	5.45	3.39	3.50	3.39	3.37	3.26	3.35	3.51
Nebraska	5.95	6.19	7.05	6.38	6.58	7.24	7.49	3.93	3.96	4.28	3.92	4.05	4.54	4.74
Nevada	0.50	0.51	0.48	0.46	0.65	0.75	0.75	1.56	1.58	1.42	1.27	1.79	2.07	2.07
New Hampshire	·	·	·	·	·	·	·	·	·	·	·	·	·	·
New Jersey	3.25	3.03	3.14	3.13	3.12	3.12	3.23	3.55	3.33	3.54	3.55	3.58	3.61	3.92
New Mexico	5.53	5.72	5.96	6.38	5.09	6.82	8.99	3.56	3.69	3.73	3.98	3.38	4.06	5.00
New York	13.26	13.10	13.26	12.57	11.60	11.50	11.46	8.20	8.15	8.36	8.50	8.48	8.48	8.57
N. Carolina	7.39	7.49	7.52	7.60	7.62	7.66	7.66	6.17	6.28	6.42	6.51	6.60	6.68	6.74
N. Dakota	6.03	6.04	3.26	3.20	3.19	3.98	4.26	3.97	3.98	2.78	2.83	2.62	3.26	3.86
Ohio	3.56	3.47	3.47	3.56	3.80	4.78	6.79	3.41	3.25	3.33	3.45	3.70	4.56	5.69
Oklahoma	5.71	5.61	5.82	5.73	5.81	6.20	6.14	3.23	3.40	3.69	3.88	4.01	4.11	4.27
Oregon	7.64	8.19	7.09	8.16	8.53	9.20	9.10	1.60	1.74	1.47	1.66	1.83	2.45	2.75
Pennsylvania	2.78	2.89	2.89	2.89	2.85	2.89	3.14	3.84	3.99	3.98	3.98	3.98	3.98	4.25
Rhode Island	7.36	7.49	7.65	8.18	8.55	8.89	9.97	5.26	5.02	4.99	5.23	5.43	5.65	6.08
S. Carolina	7.12	7.15	7.29	7.45	7.5·	7.52	7.57	5.21	5.36	5.53	5.67	5.82	5.91	5.98
S. Dakota	0.70	0.67	0.68	0.79	0.72	0.69	0.68	2.11	2.09	2.12	2.39	2.21	2.13	2.12
Tennessee	0.69	0.70	0.70	0.70	0.73	0.70	0.70	2.94	3.03	3.02	3.02	3.03	3.03	3.03
Texas	0.64	0.53	0.52	0.52	0.52	0.52	0.52	1.69	1.51	1.46	1.46	1.46	1.46	1.46
Utah	5.75	5.57	5.61	5.39	5.22	5.66	5.93	5.72	5.67	5.79	5.80	5.82	5.97	6.25
Vermont	8.87	9.25	8.72	9.37	9.68	9.37	9.44	5.05	5.08	4.70	4.98	5.17	5.22	5.29
Virginia	5.92	5.91	6.01	6.04	6.22	6.26	6.24	4.44	4.53	4.64	4.75	4.85	4.91	4.88
Washington	0.88	0.80	0.75	0.77	0.79	0.94	1.06	2.60	2.28	2.06	2.09	2.13	2.76	3.03
W. Virginia	4.96	5.15	5.34	5.63	6.37	6.29	8.75	3.87	3.88	3.97	4.02	4.45	4.84	5.59
Wisconsin	11.35	9.54	8.18	9.24	9.25	9.34	10.40	7.77	7.10	6.28	5.70	5.71	5.98	7.04
Wyoming	0.56	0.49	0.49	0.49	0.49	0.49	0.49	1.66	1.53	1.53	1.53	1.53	1.53	1.53
Federal	34.07	35.73	36.55	39.38	40.71	37.38	34.64	16.17	16.57	16.39	17.62	18.42	17.16	15.64
Mean	5.66	5.57	5.59	5.51	5.43	5.58	5.95	4.71	4.67	4.70	4.67	4.69	4.84	4.84
Standard deviation	3.79	3.75	3.82	3.64	3.52	3.48	3.48	1.93	1.95	2.00	1.96	1.96	1.94	1.99

Table 6.11b   Average and Marginal Tax Rates at $20,000 AGI (1979 Dollars) (Combined Income and Sales)

State	Marginal rate							Average rate				
	1977	1978	1979	1980	1981	1982	1983	1979	1980	1981	1982	1983
Alabama	4.64	4.58	4.62	4.56	4.52	4.39	4.49	5.18	5.26	5.33	5.22	5.28
Alaska	4.44	4.58	0.00	0.00	0.00	0.00	0.00	0.00	0.00	0.00	0.00	0.00
Arizona	5.51	5.66	5.29	4.90	4.57	4.60	4.92	4.75	4.02	3.68	3.69	4.04
Arkansas	5.92	6.06	6.50	6.71	6.92	6.99	7.04	4.84	5.06	5.34	5.37	5.46
California	7.18	7.20	7.33	6.96	6.99	6.75	7.06	5.20	4.83	4.87	4.78	4.94
Colorado	5.15	5.40	4.51	4.36	4.06	4.86	5.07	3.68	3.37	3.19	3.59	3.69
Connecticut	1.32	1.15	1.13	1.15	1.23	1.22	1.22	3.10	3.20	3.40	3.39	3.39
Delaware	6.98	7.12	7.79	7.67	7.97	7.99	8.04	3.50	3.64	3.86	4.04	4.14
District of Columbia	8.17	8.33	8.50	8.93	9.10	9.24	9.33	5.54	6.17	6.69	6.85	6.95
Florida	0.78	0.68	0.68	0.68	0.68	0.81	0.92	1.86	1.86	1.86	2.18	2.53
Georgia	6.27	6.48	6.59	6.64	6.71	6.65	6.65	4.48	4.71	4.88	5.23	5.05
Hawaii	9.48	9.15	9.47	9.61	9.94	9.10	9.16	7.54	7.51	7.70	7.58	7.92
Idaho	7.98	8.04	8.06	8.12	8.18	8.11	8.33	5.11	5.12	5.35	5.50	6.27
Illinois	3.43	3.43	3.43	3.43	3.42	3.40	3.90	5.00	4.92	4.84	4.85	5.25
Indiana	2.79	2.73	2.43	2.64	2.64	2.63	3.90	3.56	3.68	3.69	3.70	5.16
Iowa	5.36	5.28	5.15	5.31	5.32	5.58	6.04	3.97	4.10	4.21	4.37	5.02
Kansas	3.90	3.99	4.24	4.37	4.37	4.65	5.05	3.65	3.57	3.67	3.82	3.95
Kentucky	5.09	5.04	5.12	5.15	5.11	5.18	5.32	4.79	4.82	4.92	5.03	5.11
Louisiana	2.21	2.05	2.18	2.25	1.93	2.11	2.32	2.08	2.15	1.61	1.70	1.98
Maine	5.67	5.56	6.25	7.54	7.77	8.16	8.51	4.05	4.34	4.62	4.83	4.96
Maryland	5.88	5.83	5.62	5.70	5.76	5.77	5.80	5.23	5.22	5.27	5.32	5.35
Massachusetts	5.70	5.64	5.71	5.78	5.69	5.65	5.65	6.09	5.95	5.60	5.67	5.61
Michigan	5.40	5.31	5.31	5.33	5.34	5.81	7.06	5.36	5.45	5.53	5.96	6.96
Minnesota	11.94	11.62	11.40	11.10	10.69	11.69	12.30	6.77	6.94	7.14	8.06	8.82

State														
Mississippi	4.33	4.35	4.47	4.58	4.57	4.63	4.97	4.23	4.50	4.56	4.65	4.48	4.58	4.69
Missouri	3.67	3.79	3.98	4.15	4.16	4.40	4.79	3.14	3.33	3.45	3.49	3.58	3.72	4.41
Montana	5.15	5.26	5.30	5.48	4.97	5.51	5.74	2.90	3.04	2.75	2.72	2.81	2.82	2.90
Nebraska	4.38	4.49	4.84	4.39	4.58	5.07	5.17	3.28	3.28	3.51	3.23	3.33	3.76	4.01
Nevada	0.62	0.64	0.59	0.55	0.78	0.90	0.90	1.92	1.96	1.74	1.51	2.12	2.44	2.44
New Hampshire														
New Jersey	2.85	2.68	2.82	2.93	3.01	3.07	3.26	3.20	3.10	3.26	3.23	3.26	3.30	3.70
New Mexico	3.83	4.05	4.17	4.63	3.76	4.88	6.33	2.90	3.07	3.06	3.29	2.92	3.31	3.91
New York	9.32	9.97	10.81	12.66	14.49	14.88	15.28	5.73	5.73	5.83	6.10	6.36	6.36	6.51
N. Carolina	6.71	6.86	7.07	7.22	7.43	7.41	7.46	5.55	5.72	5.89	5.99	6.11	6.23	6.31
N. Dakota	4.07	4.63	2.79	2.93	3.14	4.00	4.28	2.89	2.95	2.45	2.51	2.12	2.78	3.57
Ohio	2.93	2.95	3.08	3.26	3.55	4.41	6.11	2.81	2.72	2.82	2.96	3.27	4.02	4.65
Oklahoma	3.58	4.10	4.59	5.12	5.58	5.83	6.22	2.28	2.44	2.63	2.85	3.01	3.05	3.25
Oregon	5.68	5.95	5.60	5.60	5.73	6.56	6.76	1.17	1.34	1.24	1.40	1.54	2.11	2.52
Pennsylvania	2.88	3.01	3.01	3.01	3.04	3.01	3.26	4.04	4.29	4.29	4.28	4.28	4.27	4.55
Rhode Island	5.49	5.47	5.32	5.65	5.95	6.23	6.81	4.64	4.36	4.34	4.50	4.63	4.77	5.06
S. Carolina	5.89	6.05	6.49	6.72	6.53	7.01	7.10	4.64	4.83	5.01	5.16	5.31	5.44	5.52
S. Dakota	0.86	0.84	0.86	0.98	0.50	0.87	0.86	2.57	2.60	2.63	2.94	2.73	2.61	2.62
Tennessee	0.86	0.88	0.88	0.88	0.88	0.88	0.88	3.01	3.18	3.18	3.17	3.17	3.16	3.16
Texas	0.75	0.64	0.63	0.63	0.63	0.63	0.63	1.96	1.81	1.74	1.74	1.74	1.73	1.73
Utah	6.57	6.43	6.51	6.43	6.36	6.50	6.78	5.81	5.91	6.08	6.21	6.32	6.49	6.78
Vermont	6.28	6.46	5.80	6.20	6.49	6.36	6.31	3.92	3.86	3.62	3.81	3.94	4.04	4.17
Virginia	5.34	5.43	5.62	5.87	6.10	6.14	6.18	4.31	4.47	4.60	4.77	4.93	5.03	5.05
Washington	1.08	0.97	0.90	0.92	0.94	1.15	1.29	3.13	2.74	2.45	2.46	2.51	3.33	3.62
W. Virginia	4.00	4.06	4.23	4.37	4.71	5.04	6.09	3.72	3.73	3.74	3.71	4.12	4.52	4.96
Wisconsin	9.43	8.42	7.10	8.11	8.17	8.25	9.34	6.23	6.16	5.44	4.74	4.78	5.14	6.10
Wyoming	0.68	0.61	0.61	0.61	0.61	0.61	0.61	1.99	1.91	1.91	1.91	1.91	1.90	1.90
Federal	23.47	24.34	23.57	25.32	26.56	24.58	22.31	10.85	10.81	10.74	11.57	12.13	11.34	10.36
Mean	4.80	4.83	4.90	5.09	5.26	5.42	5.81	4.15	4.20	4.21	4.21	4.27	4.42	4.73
Standard deviation	2.74	2.81	2.93	3.24	3.60	3.66	3.74	1.33	1.41	1.42	1.42	1.46	1.45	1.51

Table 6.11c Average and Marginal Tax Rates at $10,000 AGI (1979 Dollars) (Combined Income and Sales)

State	Marginal rate							Average rate						
	1977	1978	1979	1980	1981	1982	1983	1977	1978	1979	1980	1981	1982	1983
Alabama	4.06	4.36	4.31	4.55	4.66	4.45	4.51	4.33	4.63	4.83	4.96	5.09	5.11	5.15
Alaska	4.03	3.38	0.00	0.00	0.00	0.00	0.00	2.13	0.89	0.00	0.00	0.00	0.00	0.00
Arizona	5.13	5.43	4.76	4.49	4.07	3.93	4.30	4.63	4.98	4.69	3.47	3.00	2.97	3.32
Arkansas	3.94	4.22	4.43	4.83	5.17	5.24	5.25	3.23	3.51	3.63	3.79	4.04	4.04	4.12
California	5.13	5.14	5.25	5.21	5.00	4.84	5.06	3.96	4.15	4.23	3.71	3.80	3.75	3.88
Colorado	4.23	4.32	3.90	3.56	3.38	3.99	4.17	3.61	3.75	3.47	3.18	2.99	3.30	3.34
Connecticut	1.44	1.26	1.26	1.31	1.37	1.37	1.37	3.40	3.21	3.20	3.36	3.55	3.55	3.55
Delaware	5.30	5.63	5.93	6.36	6.65	6.84	6.99	2.22	2.38	2.54	2.69	2.91	3.07	3.18
District of Columbia	6.37	6.66	6.91	8.19	7.75	7.96	8.14	4.11	4.43	4.62	5.07	5.66	5.80	5.90
Florida	0.85	0.77	0.77	0.77	0.77	0.91	1.04	2.15	2.02	2.02	2.01	2.02	2.38	2.76
Georgia	4.38	4.59	4.68	5.09	5.35	6.23	5.67	3.25	3.49	3.66	3.85	4.01	4.79	4.10
Hawaii	8.08	8.26	8.51	8.92	9.39	9.02	9.02	6.38	6.89	7.13	7.11	6.96	7.07	7.48
Idaho	6.38	6.63	6.84	6.88	7.05	7.17	7.49	3.43	3.73	3.94	4.03	4.28	4.45	5.30
Illinois	3.49	3.56	3.56	3.54	3.52	3.52	4.02	4.65	5.02	5.06	4.98	4.91	4.93	5.32
Indiana	2.86	2.84	2.54	2.74	2.74	2.74	4.05	3.68	3.88	3.69	3.64	3.67	3.70	5.09
Iowa	4.02	4.09	4.58	4.86	5.07	5.08	5.52	3.43	3.51	3.45	3.58	3.70	3.85	4.51
Kansas	3.57	3.70	3.89	3.94	4.06	4.57	4.45	3.35	3.51	3.44	3.36	3.47	3.57	3.69
Kentucky	4.57	4.67	4.73	4.95	5.08	5.20	5.28	4.47	4.58	4.61	4.64	4.77	4.87	4.92
Louisiana	1.89	1.84	2.07	2.20	1.46	1.47	1.87	1.83	1.81	1.99	2.07	1.68	1.73	1.91
Maine	4.33	4.23	4.62	5.07	5.22	5.41	5.54	3.52	3.34	3.49	3.70	3.89	4.00	4.09
Maryland	5.79	5.80	5.35	5.46	5.52	5.58	5.60	4.99	5.18	4.96	4.94	4.99	5.06	5.10
Massachusetts	5.57	5.55	5.74	5.74	5.71	5.71	5.71	4.18	4.49	4.96	5.06	4.23	4.35	4.32
Michigan	5.47	5.42	5.42	5.42	5.42	5.92	7.17	4.97	5.18	5.28	5.39	5.48	5.88	6.81
Minnesota	8.87	8.04	12.66	10.89	16.03	16.57	17.31	3.68	3.06	3.03	3.37	3.87	5.45	6.20

Mississippi	2.86	3.19	3.30	3.53	3.33	3.59	3.63	3.76	4.13	4.16	4.18	4.00	4.07	4.14
Missouri	2.86	3.07	3.22	3.48	3.71	3.95	4.41	2.65	2.96	3.10	3.10	3.18	3.31	4.04
Montana	4.74	4.93	4.86	5.02	4.81	4.84	5.03	2.60	2.71	2.51	2.40	2.48	2.35	2.39
Nebraska	3.96	3.75	4.79	3.92	3.75	4.20	4.35	2.66	2.88	2.98	2.87	2.98	3.38	3.69
Nevada	0.68	0.72	0.67	0.62	0.88	1.02	1.02	2.02	2.14	1.91	1.65	2.32	2.67	2.67
New Hampshire														
New Jersey	2.92	2.76	2.82	2.80	2.78	2.78	2.92	2.86	2.92	2.96	2.98	3.01	3.05	3.45
New Mexico	2.35	2.54	2.63	2.95	2.49	3.16	4.09	2.40	2.71	2.69	2.86	2.63	2.79	3.16
New York	5.63	5.69	5.77	6.10	6.43	6.73	7.02	4.34	4.48	4.46	4.61	4.77	4.50	4.57
N. Carolina	5.85	6.02	6.24	6.49	6.53	6.75	6.82	4.88	5.15	5.30	5.39	5.53	5.65	5.72
N. Dakota	2.52	2.64	2.04	2.11	1.32	2.98	3.77	2.57	2.61	2.35	2.37	1.67	2.10	3.15
Ohio	1.71	1.67	1.88	2.10	2.39	3.19	4.30	2.37	2.35	2.38	2.44	2.76	3.33	3.47
Oklahoma	2.56	2.73	3.02	3.31	3.54	3.81	4.05	1.98	2.14	2.27	2.39	2.46	2.46	2.57
Oregon	2.55	2.57	2.64	2.88	3.41	4.66	5.12	0.16	0.21	0.17	0.24	0.31	0.64	0.91
Pennsylvania	3.12	3.10	3.10	3.10	3.10	3.10	3.35	3.86	4.16	4.16	4.16	4.17	4.16	4.40
Rhode Island	5.04	4.61	5.30	5.06	4.90	5.17	5.70	4.02	3.91	3.83	4.06	4.22	4.32	4.57
S. Carolina	4.80	5.08	5.36	5.93	6.21	6.44	6.53	4.42	4.74	4.90	5.01	5.14	5.25	5.34
S. Dakota	0.93	0.96	0.97	1.11	1.05	0.99	0.97	2.66	2.87	2.89	3.21	3.07	2.89	2.89
Tennessee	0.93	1.01	1.01	1.01	1.01	1.01	1.01	3.08	3.41	3.41	3.41	3.42	3.42	3.42
Texas	0.82	0.73	0.71	0.71	0.71	0.71	0.71	2.07	1.98	1.88	1.88	1.88	1.88	1.88
Utah	5.82	5.77	5.63	5.66	5.92	6.19	6.47	5.32	5.54	5.71	5.83	5.94	6.16	6.42
Vermont	5.57	5.21	5.67	5.37	5.13	5.11	5.16	2.77	2.92	2.68	2.96	3.12	3.24	3.43
Virginia	4.34	4.65	4.92	5.03	4.76	4.92	5.03	3.53	3.84	4.00	4.19	4.49	4.57	4.63
Washington	1.15	1.08	1.01	1.03	1.05	1.29	1.44	3.23	2.96	2.65	2.67	2.73	3.62	3.93
W. Virginia	3.27	3.44	3.55	3.77	4.14	4.48	5.27	3.49	3.62	3.63	3.57	3.98	4.40	4.72
Wisconsin	6.68	6.39	5.54	5.87	5.86	5.96	6.81	4.99	5.16	4.74	2.77	2.79	3.16	4.17
Wyoming	0.72	0.71	0.71	0.71	0.71	0.71	0.71	2.03	2.12	2.12	2.12	2.13	2.13	2.13
Federal	20.60	19.19	22.84	21.57	20.49	19.21	17.70	6.74	7.24	6.83	8.04	8.74	8.14	7.61
Mean	3.81	3.82	3.95	4.02	4.14	4.32	4.64	3.57	3.71	3.73	3.67	3.72	3.87	4.12
Standard deviation	1.87	1.87	2.15	2.07	2.49	2.54	2.63	1.02	1.13	1.16	1.16	1.16	1.15	1.23

In 1983, for high-income individuals the highest marginal tax rate was in New York (11.46%); the highest average tax rate was in Minnesota (9.90%). For middle-income taxpaying units, the highest marginal rate was again New York's (15.28%); Minnesota again had the highest average rate (8.82%). For low-income taxpayers in 1983, the highest marginal rate was in Minnesota (17.31%), and the highest average rate in Hawaii (7.48%).

To facilitate across-state comparisons, table 6.12 records marginal and average rates for the three income groups for the year 1983.

So far in our calculations we have ignored the fact that taxpayers who itemize on their federal returns can deduct all state income and general taxes taxes. In table 6.13 we exhibit the impact of federal deductibility on the effective rates of the combined income–sales tax structures. Unlike previous tables, for this exercise we used the actual income distribution of taxpayers in each state, not the synthetic distribution described above. For this particular exercise to be interesting, *federal* marginal tax rates must differ across states, and of course they cannot if the states have the same income distributions. As one would expect, the proportion by which gross and net tax rates differ varies considerably from state to state. Presumably, such differences should be taken into account in studies of the state demand for public goods.

6.5 Concluding Remarks

We have computed a number of summary measures characterizing state personal income and general sales tax systems over the period 1977–83. We believe that the availability of such measures will be of use to both academic researchers and policymakers. Still, we should reemphasize some caveats:

1. Although personal income and sales taxes constitute *most* of state tax revenues, they do not constitute *all* of the revenues. Differences in corporate income, property, and other taxes could alter our results.

2. All the measures use annual income as the point of reference. For many problems, some indicator of permanent income is more appropriate.

3. The measures tell us only the statutory incidence of the various taxes. Standard theoretical considerations suggest that the economic incidence may be quite different. Having pointed this out, we hasten to add that any serious study of the economic incidence of state tax systems must begin with careful measures of their structures.

4. We have not considered the role of local public finance. It might be that ignoring how localities raise their money leads to a misleading picture of the overall tax structure facing each state's citizens. Again, however, a good start on this problem requires an adequate representation of the state systems.

Table 6.12   **Combined Income and Sales Tax Rates, Summary for 1983**

State	Marginal rate			Average rate		
	$10,000	$20,000	$40,000	$10,000	$20,000	$40,000
Alabama	4.51	4.49	3.80	5.15	5.28	4.95
Alaska	0.00	0.00	0.00	0.00	0.00	0.00
Arizona	4.30	4.92	5.32	3.32	4.04	4.56
Arkansas	5.25	7.04	7.54	4.12	5.46	6.30
California	5.06	7.06	10.43	3.88	4.94	6.24
Colorado	4.17	5.07	5.22	3.34	3.69	4.19
Connecticut	1.37	1.22	1.02	3.55	3.39	2.99
Delaware	6.99	8.04	9.26	3.18	4.14	5.30
District of Columbia	8.14	9.33	10.75	5.90	6.95	7.77
Florida	1.04	0.92	0.76	2.76	2.53	2.13
Georgia	5.67	6.65	6.53	4.10	5.05	5.50
Hawaii	9.02	9.16	9.87	7.48	7.92	8.09
Idaho	7.49	8.33	8.18	5.30	6.27	6.87
Illinois	4.02	3.90	3.72	5.32	5.25	4.95
Indiana	4.05	3.90	3.73	5.09	5.16	4.88
Iowa	5.52	6.04	6.10	4.51	5.02	5.37
Kansas	4.45	5.05	5.23	3.69	3.95	4.37
Kentucky	5.28	5.32	4.63	4.92	5.11	4.99
Louisiana	1.87	2.32	2.68	1.91	1.98	2.09
Maine	5.54	8.51	9.75	4.09	4.96	6.32
Maryland	5.60	5.80	5.68	5.10	5.35	5.44
Massachusetts	5.71	5.65	5.78	4.32	5.61	6.48
Michigan	7.17	7.06	6.92	6.81	6.96	7.21
Minnesota	17.31	12.30	10.78	6.20	8.82	9.90
Mississippi	3.63	4.97	5.49	4.14	4.69	5.06
Missouri	4.41	4.79	4.44	4.04	4.41	4.49
Montana	5.03	5.74	5.45	2.39	2.90	3.51
Nebraska	4.35	5.17	7.49	3.69	4.01	4.74
Nevada	1.02	0.90	0.75	2.67	2.44	2.07
New Hampshire	.	.	.	.	.	.
New Jersey	2.92	3.26	3.23	3.45	3.70	3.92
New Mexico	4.09	6.33	8.99	3.16	3.91	5.00
New York	7.02	15.28	11.46	4.57	6.51	8.57
North Carolina	6.82	7.46	7.66	5.72	6.31	6.74
North Dakota	3.77	4.28	4.26	3.15	3.57	3.86
Ohio	4.30	6.11	6.79	3.47	4.65	5.69
Oklahoma	4.05	6.22	6.14	2.57	3.25	4.27
Oregon	5.12	6.76	9.10	0.91	2.52	2.75
Pennsylvania	3.35	3.26	3.14	4.40	4.55	4.25
Rhode Island	5.70	6.81	9.97	4.57	5.06	6.08
South Carolina	6.53	7.10	7.57	5.34	5.52	5.98
South Dakota	0.97	0.86	0.68	2.89	2.62	2.12
Tennessee	1.01	0.88	0.70	3.42	3.16	3.03
Texas	0.71	0.63	0.52	1.88	1.73	1.46
Utah	6.47	6.78	5.93	6.42	6.78	6.25
Vermont	5.16	6.31	9.44	3.43	4.17	5.29
Virginia	5.03	6.18	6.24	4.63	5.05	4.88

Table 6.12   (continued)

State	Marginal rate $10,000	$20,000	$40,000	Average rate $10,000	$20,000	$40,000
Washington	1.44	1.29	1.06	3.93	3.62	3.03
West Virginia	5.27	6.09	8.75	4.72	4.96	5.59
Wisconsin	6.81	9.34	10.40	4.17	6.10	7.04
Wyoming	0.71	0.61	0.49	2.13	1.90	1.53
Federal	17.70	22.31	34.64	7.61	10.36	15.64
Mean	4.64	5.81	5.95	4.12	4.73	5.18
Standard deviation	2.63	3.74	3.48	1.23	1.51	1.99

Table 6.13   **Average and Marginal State Tax Rates after Federal Deduction: 1979 Law and Actual Incomes**

State	Percentage itemizers	Average rates gross	net	Marginal rates gross	net
Alabama	22.10	5.07	4.34	3.80	3.55
Alaska	37.72	0.01	0.01	0.00	0.00
Arizona	31.92	5.11	4.21	3.87	3.48
Arkansas	24.61	5.34	4.58	5.05	4.63
California	36.12	6.18	4.12	5.86	4.91
Colorado	41.82	3.94	3.07	3.73	3.25
Connecticut	31.07	3.13	2.63	1.06	0.98
Delaware	17.91	4.27	3.49	5.15	4.69
District of Columbia	30.44	6.52	4.91	7.11	6.21
Florida	24.06	1.97	1.74	0.70	0.66
Georgia	28.52	4.87	3.98	4.51	4.04
Hawaii	26.80	8.01	6.60	7.50	6.83
Idaho	37.42	5.48	4.45	5.92	5.20
Illinois	27.02	4.98	4.19	3.40	3.14
Indiana	23.59	3.72	3.23	2.37	2.22
Iowa	22.82	4.55	3.77	3.58	3.25
Kansas	27.18	4.18	3.57	3.55	3.20
Kentucky	25.66	5.08	4.34	4.18	3.87
Louisiana	19.28	2.73	2.33	2.52	2.33
Maine	18.54	4.71	4.07	4.04	3.68
Maryland	35.70	5.57	4.27	4.87	4.23
Massachusetts	32.28	6.05	4.90	5.09	4.60
Michigan	43.63	5.54	4.28	5.40	4.73
Minnesota	32.03	5.61	4.17	7.52	6.65
Mississippi	19.68	5.03	4.36	2.71	2.48
Missouri	21.46	3.75	3.26	2.96	2.75
Montana	31.88	3.00	2.55	4.02	3.68
Nebraska	23.02	3.96	3.26	3.97	3.59
Nevada	26.39	1.81	1.56	0.53	0.50
New Hampshire	19.22	0.20	0.17	0.00	0.00

Table 6.13   (continued)

State	Percentage itemizers	Average rates gross	net	Marginal rates gross	net
New Jersey	27.51	3.55	2.82	2.27	2.02
New Mexico	21.05	3.65	3.07	2.93	2.63
New York	35.31	7.13	5.34	7.33	6.13
North Carolina	23.33	6.19	5.20	5.72	5.25
North Dakota	26.59	2.92	2.48	2.00	1.81
Ohio	23.24	3.18	2.67	2.29	2.06
Oklahoma	28.35	3.28	2.75	3.56	3.20
Oregon	33.65	1.54	1.19	3.38	2.88
Pennsylvania	25.49	4.35	3.75	2.93	2.72
Rhode Island	27.41	5.03	4.02	4.39	3.85
South Carolina	29.76	5.56	4.69	5.17	4.69
South Dakota	13.86	2.91	2.72	0.97	0.94
Tennessee	21.30	3.19	2.84	1.42	1.38
Texas	22.17	1.78	1.55	0.63	0.59
Utah	31.19	6.20	5.11	5.39	4.92
Vermont	21.02	3.98	3.27	4.31	3.89
Virginia	31.30	4.93	3.94	4.30	3.74
Washington	24.10	2.42	2.10	0.82	0.77
West Virginia	26.11	4.34	3.66	4.02	3.62
Wisconsin	34.43	5.17	3.98	7.81	7.10
Wyoming	16.25	1.92	1.75	0.67	0.64
Average	28.80	4.60	3.64	3.94	3.48

Notes

1. Calculated from Tax Foundation, Inc. 1983, 26.

2. There are also nontax forms of revenue such as user charges, revenues from state-owned liquor stores, etc. These are not considered in this paper.

3. "The extent of reliance on income taxation should provide a reasonable approximation to the relative elasticity of the tax structure" (Oates 1975, 147).

4. See Musgrave and Thin (1948) and Formby and Sykes (1984). An analogous problem arises in trying to summarize the degree of inequality in an income distribution. See, e.g., Atkinson 1970.

5. We compute the average tax rate as the average of each individual's average tax rate. Marginal tax rates and elasticities are computed analogously.

6. Specifically, take the grouped data on rent and income presented in table 16 of U.S. Department of Labor 1977 and estimate the regression: Rent = 1750 + 0.1 Income. Because the constant term in the regression applies to 1972–73 data, it is inflated to 1979–83 levels.

7. The calculations for each income level involve the returns of households within a range of those levels. The ranges are $8,000–12,000 for the $10,000 level; $16,000–24,000 for the $20,000 level; and $32,000–48,000 for the $40,000 level.

8. Partial indexing of the federal personal income tax is due to begin in 1984 with respect to taxes due in 1985. At one time or another, seven states had some provisions for indexing their personal income taxes.

9. A general discussion of the problems involved in using one data set to impute values for another is provided by Feenberg and Rosen 1983.

10. The 1972–73 CES was used. As of mid-1984 this was the only comprehensive source of individual consumption data. However, a 1982 survey should become available soon. As an alternative to using actual tax returns with imputed consumption data, we might use the CES as a source of both income, deduction, and consumption data. The CES is not, however, a satisfactory source of income data for high-income individuals.

11. The regression, based on cross-tabulations in Bureau of Labor Statistics (1978), is: log(expenditure) = 6.74 + .687 Income + .052 (Family Size). (The expenditures include autos, trucks, and boats.).

12. Of course, we are referring to the statutory incidence of the sales tax. Tax shifting could, in principle, affect the ultimate distributional implications of the tax.

References

Advisory Commission on Intergovernmental Relations. 1979. *State-local finances in recession and inflation—An economic analysis*, A–70. Washington, D.C.: Government Printing Office.

Atkinson, A. B. 1970. On the measurement of inequality. *Journal of Economic Theory* 2:244–63.

Bradbury, K. R., A. Downs, and K. A. Small. 1982. *Urban decline and the future of american cities*. Washington, D.C.: The Brookings Institution.

Bureau of Labor Statistics. 1978. *Consumer expenditure survey series: Interview survey 1972–73, bulletin 1985*. Washington, D.C.: Government Printing Office.

Congressional Budget Office. 1980. *Indexing the individual income tax*. Washington, D.C.: Government Printing Office.

DiLorento, T. J. 1982. Tax elasticity and the growth of local public expenditure. *Public Finance Quarterly* 10, no. 3:385–92.

Feenberg, D. R., and H. S. Rosen. 1983. Alternative tax treatments of the family: Simulation methodology and results. In M. S. Feldstein, ed., *Behavioral simulation methods in tax policy analysis*. Chicago and London: University of Chicago Press.

Formby, J. P., and D. Sykes. 1984. State income tax progressivity. *Public Finance Quarterly* 12, no. 3:153–66.

Gold, S. D. 1983. Recent developments in state finances. *National Tax Journal* 36, no. 1:1–30.

Greytak, D., and J. Thursky. 1979. Functional form in state income tax elasticity estimation. *National Tax Journal* 32, no. 2:195–200.

Maxwell, J. A., and J. R. Aronson. 1979. *Financing state and local governments*. 3d ed. Washington, D.C.: The Brookings Institution.

Musgrave. R. A., and T. Thin. 1948. Income tax progression 1929–1948. *Journal of Political Economy* 56:498–514.

Oates, W. E. 1975. 'Automatic' increases in tax revenues—The effect on the size of the public budget. In Wallace E. Oates, ed., *Financing the new federalism*. Baltimore: The Johns Hopkins University Press.

Tax Foundation, Inc. 1983. *Facts and figures on government finance—22nd biennial edition 1983*. Washington, D.C.
U.S. Department of Labor, Bureau of Labor Statistics. 1977. Consumer expenditure survey series: Interview survey 1972 and 1973. Report 455.

Comment   George R. Zodrow

This paper is an important one because it makes a significant first step toward filling an obvious void in the public finance literature—the lack of a comprehensive characterization of the tax structures of the fifty states, complete with a supporting data base. Gold (1983, 1) notes that "state finances have received surprisingly little attention in the academic literature" and, although the Advisory Council on Intergovernmental Relations (ACIR) publishes a great deal of informative data relevant to state public finance issues, the information and results presented by Feenberg and Rosen are considerably more sophisticated than the data on tax structures and tax rates issued by the ACIR in publications like its Significant Features of Fiscal Federalism series. Thus, in calculating income elasticities and marginal and average tax rates for all state income taxes, income elasticities and a measure of base comprehensiveness for all state sales taxes, and income elasticities and marginal and average tax rates for the combined income–sales tax systems for all fifty states, Feenberg and Rosen have accomplished a formidable and useful task.

The procedure used by Feenberg and Rosen is straightforward. They use federal tax return data on personal income, exemptions, and deductions to construct a synthetic data base that is representative of the distribution of income in the United States rather than any specific state, use data on the details of state income and sales tax codes to calculate tax burdens for each state for this synthetic distribution, and characterize these nonlinear tax structures using the summary measures described above.

The goal of the paper is "to develop and implement a coherent methodology for characterizing the structures of state tax systems" which can be used by researchers in studying familiar public finance questions such as the effects of state taxes on individual and firm migration decisions, the nature of interstate tax competition, and the changes in state taxes induced by income growth and inflation. I shall make four general comments on the extent to which the authors have met this goal and then briefly examine their results.

George R. Zodrow is assistant professor of economics at Rice University and is currently on temporary assignment as a financial economist on the Fundamental Tax Reform Project at the U.S. Treasury Office of Tax Analysis.

First, all of the results presented in the paper, with the exception of the final table 6.13, are based on the synthetic income distribution constructed by the authors. The primary advantages of the use of a synthetic distribution rather than the actual state distributions of income are that the data requirements are reduced and the comparison of state tax structures abstracts away from differences in state income distributions. However, there are some troublesome problems with this approach. The authors stress the considerable heterogeneity of state tax structures found in their analysis and note that this implies that previous characterizations of state tax structures using indicators such as the proportion of revenues raised with income taxes are inadequate. However, the distributions of incomes in the states are also rather heterogeneous—1981 data issued by the ACIR indicate a per capita annual income range of $7,408 to $13,763 about a mean of $10,491 with a standard deviation of $1,480—so that the use of a synthetic distribution masks significant income differences across states; this implies the results presented by Feenberg and Rosen are subject to a similar criticism.

This problem seems especially relevant in terms of the research questions listed above. For example, data on average and marginal tax rates at specific income levels, rather than at income levels of a synthetic distribution, would be of concern to researchers studying business or individual migration or the extent to which tax structures are affected by the fiscal policies of nearby states. Similarly, since data on actual state income elasticities would be of concern to researchers studying the effects of inflation or growth on a single state or region, the Feenberg and Rosen data might be misleading; for example, if in a relatively high-tax state there were fewer high-income and more low-income people than implied by the synthetic income distribution (as some would predict would be implied by mobility considerations), the income elasticity calculated by the authors would likely be too high (the degree of variation might also be overstated). Also, questions regarding how the presence of special interest groups or other economic and demographic characteristics affect the nature of the tax structure (such as whether homogeneous states are more likely to use broad-based proportional taxes and if reforms are more likely to involve large-scale changes in nonhomogeneous states as the dominant interest group changes over time) require specific information about the income distribution in the state.

Feenberg and Rosen do use actual state income distributions in the construction of table 6.13, which is limited to aggregate marginal and average combined sales—income tax rates for 1979. Since the authors have the data required to compile all of their summary measures of state taxes on the basis of actual state income distributions, such an extension of their results would seem to be worthwhile, especially in light of the relevant state public finance questions they cite. It would at least be interesting to compare the tax rates calculated on the basis of the actual state income distributions with those calculated on the basis of the synthetic distribution; such a comparison is impossible without information beyond that presented in the paper.

Second, all of the results presented in the paper, again with the exception of table 6.13, do not take into account the fact that taxpayers who itemize on their federal returns can deduct state income and sales taxes. Although reasonable for the elasticity calculations, this procedure is troublesome for the calculation of state average and marginal tax rates. State public finance questions that focus on individual and firm migration decisions or the nature of interstate tax competition hinge on effective state tax differentials, which include the effects of federal deductibility of state taxes. Accordingly, another useful extension of the results would be to calculate the state tax rates allowing for deductibility, as is done in the limited results presented in table 6.13.

Third, the authors describe their state income and sales tax parameters as "characterizing the structures of state tax systems," arguing that all other state revenue sources account for only one-quarter of revenues. This position seems somewhat overstated, as one-quarter is not an insignificant fraction for the average amount of revenues ignored and there are significant deviations about the average (for example, eight states receive over 20% of revenues from severance taxes alone). Moreover, the state corporate and severance taxes omitted from consideration are growing as a fraction of state revenues and are likely to be the critical factors in analyses of business migration decisions, interstate tax competition, and the effects of state tax structure on the level of state expenditures. Accordingly, a description of the results simply as characterizing state income and sales tax structures would be more appropriate and in no way diminish their significance.

Fourth, the caveats listed by the authors are worth emphasizing. The analysis considers only statutory incidence and may be misleading for state income and sales taxes, although arguably less so than a similar analysis for property or corporate income taxes; for example, high state sales taxes will have a smaller impact on individual migration decisions if they are exported to a substantial extent. Also, the lack of information about the nature of state expenditures implies that the results are incomplete in terms of explaining individual and firm migration decisions as well as the nature of interstate competition. Since most studies that address similar issues also note the importance of benefits but then ignore them, any attempt by the authors to incorporate an analysis of the expenditure side of state budgets in their analysis would be a welcome and important extension.

Turning to the calculation of the state income tax parameters, Feenberg and Rosen estimate: (1) the income elasticity by increasing all income sources and deductions by 1% and calculating the effect on revenues; (2) the average tax rate by dividing revenues by reported income; and (3) the marginal tax rate by increasing only wage income by $1,000, holding deductions constant, and calculating the effect on revenues; the tax rates are calculated for low-, middle-, and high-income levels of the synthetic distribution. The rationale for the asymmetry in the methods of calculating the income elasticities and the marginal tax rates is not entirely convincing. Even if one were concerned only about tax distortions in net wage rates across states, an additional $1,000 of wage income is likely to lead to an increase in deductions, which should not be ignored since it will reduce the associated increase in taxes paid. Since the nature of the deductions allowed may vary widely across states, a procedure that neglects changes in deductions will not capture a perhaps important factor in determining interstate income tax differentials.

More importantly, a marginal tax rate with respect to both capital and wage income rather than wage income alone would be relevant for many questions. For example, individual migration decisions would be affected by such a "total" marginal tax rate, as would a firm's decision to relocate its headquarters (and transfer high-income employees). Since this calculation would involve only manipulation of the income elasticity data at the relevant income levels, it would appear to be a straightforward and useful extension of the analysis. It would also be interesting to document the extent to which the states tax capital income.

The most striking features of the income tax results are the large variations in the parameters across states and the calculated declines in income elasticities and increases in marginal tax rates. Two sets of manipulations of the results on changes in tax rates over time would be informative. First, it might be useful to have a finer division of income classes than the low-middle-high breakdown utilized by Feenberg and Rosen, especially at the highest income levels. For example, in the version of the paper presented at the conference, the authors noted that the mean marginal state income tax rate on individuals in the top decile declined from 6.78% in 1977 to 4.70% in 1983. This rather dramatic reduction in rates is not reflected in the marginal tax rate change experienced by the high-income group, where the mean rate increased from 5.56% to 5.89%.

Second, it would be interesting to devise a summary measure of the magnitude of interstate tax differentials based on the Feenberg and Rosen data, and then determine changes over time in the measure.

Such a statistic would shed some light on whether interstate tax competition is increasing over time.

Feenberg and Rosen also separate the effects of statutory tax changes and nominal income changes on their parameters by doing the same calculations holding the state tax codes constant at their 1977 configuration. Results here imply that the statutory changes made the state tax systems more elastic than they would have been, raised marginal rates for high-income individuals, but lowered marginal tax rates for middle- and low-income individuals. The authors offer no explanation for the slightly odd combination of higher income elasticities and lower marginal rates on middle- and low-income individuals, and an example or two from specific states might be enlightening. The result may occur partly because of the way the income elasticities and marginal tax rates are defined. For example, states may have tightened provisions for the personal taxation of capital income (this certainly occurred with respect to corporate taxation of capital income as twenty-six of the forty-four states with a corporate income tax increased corporate taxes relative to the national level after the 1981 Economic Recovery Tax Act), while lowering marginal rates on wage income in response either to "tax revolt" public pressure for income tax relief (fifteen states lowered income tax rates between 1978 and 1980) or to lower service levels (despite generally increasing budgets, state revenues as a percentage of GNP declined slightly from 1977 to 1982). The last comment suggests that in general it might be useful to attempt to examine the changes in state tax structures after controlling for the size of the budget if an acceptable procedure could be devised.

The state sales tax results are based on IRS estimates of sales tax liability as a function of adjusted gross income and family size. The basic approach used by the IRS is straightforward; data from the Consumer Expenditure Survey are used to predict consumption in twenty-four different categories and details of state sales tax codes are then used to calculate sales tax liability on the predicted consumption pattern. Note that it would be interesting to check the IRS compilations to see if the common perception of downward bias of sales tax liability is valid.

The calculations again indicate a considerable degree of heterogeneity across states. The most striking result is a large degree of regressivity—income elasticities range from 0.55 to 0.75; note, however, that the familiar argument that progressivity should be measured with respect to some measure of permanent income applies here. Feenberg and Rosen also demonstrate that the nature of the sales tax base is quite important—tax liabilities increase twice as fast with respect to family size in states that do not exempt food. They measure the "comprehensiveness" of the base as the ratio of actual revenue to revenue with an income tax at the same rate and again note large variation. One interesting feature of the results is that over the 1981–83 period, the comprehensiveness of the sales tax base increased in roughly one-third of the states. This contrasts with previous experience; Gold (1983) documents a plethora of base changes that reduced comprehensiveness over the 1971–81 period while only three states increased comprehensiveness. It would be interesting to determine if the change to increased coverage is a real phenomenon or an artifact of the definition of comprehensiveness (actual total consumption should be in the denominator rather than income) or some other facet of the compilations.

Note also that the heterogeneity of coverage of the sales tax base has implications for the current debate regarding the relative desirability of a national value-added tax or a national retail sales tax. Proponents of the latter argue that the existence of a collection mechanism is a strong point in their favor; the heterogeneity of the sales tax bases reduces the strength of this argument somewhat as states would probably be reluctant to change their laws to conform to a national base, thus lowering the administrative cost advantage of a national sales tax. Feenberg and Rosen also note that base exclusions are, at least in some cases, effective in vertical equity terms—states with many exemptions, presumably chosen to exclude commodities purchased disproportionately by the poor, are in fact characterized by more income-elastic sales tax structures. This fact suggests that it is quite feasible to reduce the regressivity of a national value-added tax with a judicious choice of exempt commodities.

The final set of calculations presented by the authors combines the two tax systems. Results here indicate that heterogeneity is not significantly reduced, the decline over time of the income elasticity of the combined tax structure is small as the declining elasticity of the income tax is offset by increased use of income taxation relative to the much more regressive sales tax, that marginal and average tax rates have increased over time, and that the common perception of an approximately proportional tax structure is accurate on average although there are certainly deviations about the average.

In summary, this paper provides a wealth of new results on the nature of state income and sales taxes. Subject to the caveats noted above, this information will be very useful to practitioners in state and local public finance. In addition to the specific questions cited above, the data accumulated suggest an important possibility for incidence theory. To the extent that the Feenberg and Rosen analysis indicates increased interstate tax competition (through lower income elasticities or perhaps through increases in an "interstate tax competition" summary measure as described above), it suggests that incidence theories that rely on implicit collusive exploitation of capital through widespread use of corporate taxes or industrial property taxes must take such competitive behavior into account.

Reference

Gold, S. D. 1983. Recent developments in state finances. *National Tax Journal* 36, no.1:1–29.

7   Education, Welfare and the "New" Federalism: State Budgeting in a Federalist Public Economy

Steven G. Craig and Robert P. Inman

7.1 Introduction

The United States public economy is a federalist economy. Public services are financed and purchased by federal, state, and local governments each with autonomous decision-making authority, but each intimately connected to the others through an elaborate network of grants-in-aid and regulations. Historically, it has been an evolving structure marked by significant shifts in responsibilities and control.[1] Most recently the trend in financial responsibility has been upward, toward the federal level, while the state-local sector has become the primary provider of (nondefense) public services.[2] The decade 1965–75, called the period of "creative federalism," marked a significant acceleration in those trends. During this period the number of federal grants to the state-local sector went from 160 separate aid programs in 1965 to 412 by 1976. Federal to state-local aid grew from about $66 per capita in 1960 to $192 per capita in 1980, both measured in 1972 dollars.[3] Almost all of these transfers imposed significant federal regulation and spending requirements upon the recipient state and local governments; the one exception is General Revenue Sharing, which comprised only 8 % of all aid transferred in 1980.

In January 1982, President Reagan proposed a significant reform in our current fiscal structure. Under the label of the "new federalism," Reagan has offered a three-part reform package whose objectives were to decentralize fiscal choice through a consolidation of grants and a relaxation of federal requirements, and to shrink the size of federal

Steven G. Craig is assistant professor of economics at the University of Houston. Robert P. Inman is professor of finance and economics at the Wharton School, University of Pennsylvania, and a research associate of the National Bureau of Economic Research.

government spending through a gradual reduction in overall dollar support. First, sixty-one federal programs in education, community development, transportation, and social services will be returned to the states for state financing and administration. To help defray the costs of these programs, a $28 billion federal trust fund supported by existing federal excise taxes will be established. The trust fund will be fully funded until 1988, at which time it will be reduced in four equal steps until, by 1992, no additional federal support will be offered. However, the supporting federal excise taxes will be discontinued as federal taxes, and the states may, if they wish, institute these taxes as their own after 1992. Second, the federal government will turn over to the states for state financing and administration the present Aid for Families with Dependent Children (AFDC) program. To help the states assume this financial obligation, the federal government will, third, assume full financial and administrative responsibility for the current state-run and state-supported Medicaid program. As initially calculated, the dollars flowing to the states from the trust fund and the federal assumption of Medicaid would just equal the added program costs to the states of AFDC and the sixty-one released federal programs. The initial effects of the exchange would leave the fiscal structure basically unchanged; one redistribution program (Medicaid; health care for the poor) would be traded for another (AFDC), and block grants (the trust fund) would replace categorical aid (the sixty-one existing programs). In the long run, however, the Reagan administration hopes to "cap" and reform the current health insurance system (including Medicaid), to phase out the trust fund aid, and to foster interstate competition to discourage the growth of the state-local sector. If this program is successful, the end result will be a more decentralized public sector and perhaps a smaller one as well.

Will the new federalism succeed? There is the first question, of course, of whether the new federalism will even emerge from Congress sufficiently intact to have its intended effects. We shall not make political predictions here.[4] In this paper, we are interested in the economic—i.e., allocative—consequences of Reagan's reforms *assuming* they do become law. Our work here extends our previous analysis of the new federalism (Craig and Inman 1982) in two important directions. First, the previous work studied the effect of the fiscal reforms on one important state-local service, education. Here we include a second major program area—welfare—which is in many ways the linchpin of the new federalism. Second, in order to model two public services it is crucial that we specify how grants will influence both services and allow for the possibility of cross-effects between program areas. To do so we must specify more carefully than has been done in past research (our own included) just how multiservice fiscal allocations are decided. As in our prior work, however, we will continue to assume federal fiscal policy is exogenously set and concentrate instead on the effects of that policy on fiscal choices in the state-local sector. It is from this analysis that we hope to understand the likely consequences of President Reagan's proposed reform of our current federalist fiscal structure.

7.2   A Model of State-Local Fiscal Choice in a Federalist Economy

From the early simple linear determinant models of state-local fiscal choice to the more recent median voter specifications, the emphasis in the empirical analysis of state-local budgetary allocations has been on voter preferences and the fiscal constraint that defines the set of feasible public budgets. Figure 7.1 illustrates the now familiar story.

One resident will be chosen as the representative or "typical" resident whose preferences for state and/or local services are decisive in the budgetary process. This resident's preferences are represented by a utility function over after-tax private income (y) and public goods (g), denoted $U(g, y)$, and are shown as a set of indifference curves in figure 7.1. Public services (g) are generally assumed to flow from a per capita sharing of a public facility (x) with a population of size n: $g = x/n$. The public facility—e.g., a park or school—is produced by a constant-returns-to-scale technology; x costs c dollars per unit. Total expenditures to provide a facility of size x is cx. Residents may not be required to pay all of cx for these local services. In a federalist public economy, the federal government often assists states and localities by either paying a fraction (m) of those total expenditures directly or by offering the locality a lump-sum payment (z) that can be used to cover local service costs. Residents therefore need pay taxes that total only $(1 - m)cx - z$, the government's net expenditure after deducting federal "matching aid" (m is the matching rate) and federal "lump-

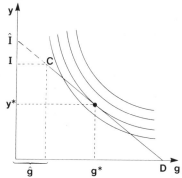

Fig. 7.1   Resident preferences and budget constraint.

sum aid." The total tax payment—$T = (1 - m)cx - z$—will be shared by all residents within the community. If local taxes are proportional taxes, then each resident's share (denoted ϕ) will equal the resident's share of his or her tax base (b) in the total tax base of the locality: $\phi = b/(B \cdot n)$, where B is the aggregate tax base per resident in the locality. A typical local resident therefore pays a tax (t) equal to

$$t = \phi T = (b/B) \{(1 - m)(cx/n) - (z/n)\} \text{, or}$$

since $g = (x/n)$,

$$t = (b/B) \{(1 - m)cg - (z/n)\} .$$

To define after-tax income for the typical resident, we simply subtract t from pretax income (I), with one further adjustment. Since most residents can deduct their state or local taxes from their federal income tax payments, a dollar of local taxes will not cost the resident a full dollar. For each dollar of local taxes paid the resident saves a fraction, q, of that dollar in federal tax payments, where q is the resident's marginal federal tax rate. The portion of local taxes actually lost from pretax income will be $\pi = (1 - q)$. Net local tax payments are therefore πt, and after tax income, y, is equal to $I - \pi t$. This definition of y allows us to define the typical resident's budget constraint when purchasing private goods (y) and public services (g). From $y = I - \pi t$, and the definition of t, we have:

$$y = I - \{\pi(b/B)(1 - m)c\}g + \pi(b/B)(z/n),$$

or, upon rearranging terms:

$$y + p \cdot g = \hat{I},$$

where p is called the "tax price" of local public services and equals $\{\pi(b/B)(1 - m)c\}$ and where $\hat{I}$ is called "full fiscal income" and equals $I + \pi(b/B)(z/n)$. The budget constraint is drawn in figure 7.1 as the line ICD. The kink in the budget line at point C reflects the fact that exogenous, lump-sum aid is generally restricted to be spent only on g and cannot be given directly to households; points along the dashed extension of the budget line to I are not legally available to the typical resident. From the point of view of the resident, lump-sum aid is equivalent to a free gift of $\hat{g}$ units of the public good.[5] From point C, the resident is then free to buy additional units of g at a "tax price" of $p \{= \pi(b/B)(1 - m)c\}$ dollars per unit of g.

The preferred allocation of the representative resident will be that combination of g and y which maximizes $U(g, y)$ subject to the constraint. This is point (g^*, y^*) in figure 7.1. As is true in most economic models of this form, an increase in full fiscal income ($\hat{I}$) or a fall in the price of $g(p)$ will stimulate the resident's demand for the public good.

$\hat{I}$ rises either because before-tax income increases (I) or lump-sum aid per capita increases (z/n). The price, p, falls either because costs (c) fall, or the matching rate (m) rises, or more local taxes become deductible (π falls), or there is an exogenous increase in the average level of the locality's tax base (B rises). The effects of change in each of these variables is captured in the representative resident's demand curve for public services:

(1) $g = f(p, \hat{I}|\text{Tastes})$,

where the comparative statics of price and income changes (normally) predicts $\partial g/\partial p \leq 0$ and $\partial g/\partial \hat{I} \geq 0$. The taste variables (Tastes) are assumed to be those of the "typical" resident who is decisive in budgetary allocations.

This specification of state-local fiscal choice has been used extensively to analyze allocation in a federalist economy; see Inman (1979) for a review. However, there has been one matter left unresolved in almost every application of this approach. Who exactly is the typical resident whose demand curve is estimated? Vague, but generally unsubstantiated, references to some average income voter are seen to suffice. Only recently have there been efforts to give a precise answer to this important question. That literature draws its inspiration from the classic paper of Howard Bowen (1943) on the role of the median voter in fiscal politics.[6]

In the special case where only one public service level is being decided and decisions are made by a simple majority rule process— school spending by local districts is the usual example—the political process will select that level of services preferred by the voter with the median (fiftieth percentile) demand for the public good. If a service level greater than that demanded by the median voter is offered, the median voter and all voters with lower demands will vote against it. If a service level less than that demanded by the median voter is offered, the median voter and all voters with higher demands will vote against it. That level of services demanded by the median voter will defeat all other service levels in majority-rule comparisons. The median demand voter is decisive and becomes the natural candidate for the "typical" resident in the economic model of fiscal choice.

Tests of the median voter model against recent experiences of U.S. and European local governments support at least two of the model's central predictions: the demand for local services declines as the median voter's tax price increases ($\partial g/\partial p < 0$), and the demand for local services increases as the median voter's full fiscal income rises ($\partial g/\partial \hat{I} > 0$).[7] Yet one central prediction of the model is rejected. The two components of full fiscal income—private income (I) and lump-sum aid per capita (z/n)—should have identical effects on local service demands if $\pi(b/B) \equiv 1$; alternatively, if $\pi(b/B) < 1$ the effect of income should be greater than the effects of exogenous aid.[8] In fact, the empirical evidence is uniformly against this proposition: (z/n) has almost always had a larger impact, sometimes twenty times as great, on local service demands than I. The large effect of aid on local service demand compared to the small effect of income has been called the "flypaper effect." Since private income belongs initially in private hands and public aid is given initially into public hands, it appears that dollars "stick" where they first land. Yet the demand model predicts dollars are fully transferable between public and private uses. Something more than the demand model is needed if we are to rationalize these empirical results.

That something more is politics.[9] The existence of a "flypaper effect" implies the presence of a wedge between what fully informed, utility-maximizing residents would prefer and what they finally receive from the state-local fisc. They would prefer to have lump-sum aid spent as private income; what they get is lump-sum aid spent almost entirely on public services. Who or what is the wedge that stands between public allocations and resident preferences? Romer and Rosenthal (1979; 1982 with Filimon) have argued that it is a budget-maximizing politician-bureaucrat—a "typical" state-local official—who is insulated from resident control. A desire to maximize the public budget means the bureaucrat-politician wants to spend all aid.[10] Insulation from voter control gives him the freedom to do so. In essence, what Romer and Rosenthal have done is introduce a second player into the game of fiscal choice—a "typical" state-local official—whose preferences for how public dollars are allocated differs dramatically from the preferences of our first player—the "typical" resident. We have a conflict that must be resolved. It is politics, the process of conflict resolution, that will balance these competing interests, and it is the analysis of politics that is so far missing from our formal models of fiscal choice.

The Romer-Rosenthal analysis sees the public allocation process as a bargaining game between the politician-bureaucrat and the resident voter. The voter retains the ultimate right to veto any budgetary proposal but the politician retains the right to offer proposals. The game is played a finite number of times and if no agreement is reached, a "reversion level" or fall-back budget is automatically adopted. Politicians and voters can talk to each other—there are budget hearings—and they will seek to strike the best compromise subject to the rules of bargaining. The model predicts two outcomes that can distinguish it from the strict, resident-only demand model: (1) lump-sum aid and private income need no longer have identical effects, and (2) the compromise will likely balance the competing interests of the typical voter and the typical state-local official.[11] The empirical evidence supports both predictions. First, Filimon, Romer, and Rosenthal (1982) find a significant flypaper effect—like most other studies of local budgeting—which they attribute to the inability of voters to monitor what public officials do with lump-sum aid (a "fiscal illusion"). Second, they find the bargaining process between the voter and the bureaucrat leads to a local budget that is approximately 15% larger than that desired by the median voter were he or she decisive alone.

While one need not embrace all the details of the Romer-Rosenthal analysis, their basic point seems hard to ignore. Politics matters. They have introduced the state-local official as a second player along with the utility-maximizing resident voter into the game of state and local fiscal choice. Each player is given the "right to play" and must negotiate an outcome. Suddenly, it is not just preferences and a budget constraint that determine local fiscal allocations; the rules of the game matter too. Who are the players? What are their standing and rights within the budgetary game? How will conflicts be resolved? These are political questions and they require political analysis for answers. The simple analytics of budgetary choice so neatly captured by equation (1) will be inadequate when policy choices involve many players and many possible public programs.

Yet the formal analysis of conflict resolution within a democratic process faces a troubling contradiction of theory and fact. In his famous (Im)possibility theorem, Kenneth Arrow (1963) proves that there is no democratic process involving more than two players and more than two options that will always yield a determinate outcome. Either matters are indeterminate—essentially "cycling" from one policy option to another—or there is a dictator who decides the final allocation. Only in very special and unlikely circumstances (Plott 1967 and Kramer 1973) will it be theoretically possible for a democratic choice process to give a determinate outcome. No equilibrium is the most likely result. Yet as a factual matter, our democratic fiscal system does arrive at equilibrium allocations of services and taxes. How can we resolve this apparent conflict of theory with the facts? The answer must lie in a richer theory. Recent advances in the theory of political institutions provide us with what we need.

Figure 7.2 illustrates the central analytic problem for the simple case of two fiscal options—e.g., spending on education (g_1) and welfare (g_2)—and three coalitions—e.g, poor (P), rich (R), and middle-class (M) voters. Each coalition is *assumed* to have well-defined preferences over g_1 and g_2. These preferences differ, however, and a conflict arises that must be resolved. The poor want large welfare expenditures and

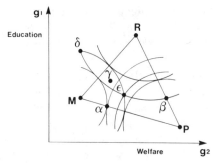

Fig. 7.2   Majority rule disequilibrium.

relatively low education outlays. The rich want modest welfare expenditures and large education outlays. The middle class are assumed
to want modest expenditures on education and low welfare outlays.[12]
The conflict resolution process is assumed to be a democratic majority
rule process in which each coalition has one equal vote.[13] Coalition
preferences are represented by a "bliss point" or an ideal allocation—
points P, R, and M—and a set of indifference curves about the bliss
points representing decreasing levels of well-being as we move away
from the ideal allocation. The indifference curves are depicted as cir-
cular for simplicity. The solid lines connecting the bliss points are the
"contract lines" marking the tangencies of the indifference curves
between the various pairs of coalitions. The area within the three contract lines defines the set of Pareto points for this allocation problem.
A move from an allocation within the Pareto set (e.g., point ϵ) to a
point outside the set (e.g., point δ) will make members of at least one
coalition worse off (e.g., coalition P). Conversely, there is always a
point within the Pareto set (e.g., point γ) that will make all voters better
off compared to its alternative outside the Pareto set (e.g., point δ).
The important point, however, is there is no stable majority-rule winner
in this game. As any point outside the Pareto set will be defeated
unanimously by some point within the set, we can focus our analysis
on alternatives such as α, β, γ, and ϵ. In pairwise comparisons by
majority rule, β (favored by P and R) beats α (favored by M), α (favored
by M and P) beats γ (favored by R), but now note that γ (favored by
M and R) beats β (favored by P). Point ϵ, which is inside the Pareto
set, is also caught in a voting cycle. Point ϵ wins over point α as voters
P and R prefer ϵ; point α defeats γ as M and P prefer α; but γ beats
ϵ as M and R prefer γ. There is no equilibrium winner among the
alternatives in figure 7.2.

To obtain an equilibrium outcome for this allocation game further
political structure in addition to majority rule is needed. Shepsle (1979)
has described and analyzed various legislative institutions that are sufficient to produce stable, majority-rule allocations. The final allocations
in a Shepsle equilibrium—often called a structure-induced equilibrium—are conditioned by the status quo and the constitutional rules
that determine legislative structures. Shepsle adds three new structural
features to the majority-rule allocation game: (1) a *committee structure*
that identifies who is allowed to offer proposals for consideration by
the full legislature; (2) a *jurisdiction structure* that defines which proposals may be considered by the committee and the legislature; and
(3) an *amendment structure* that describes how the committee's proposals to the legislature may be altered. Together, these three additional
rules can ensure a stable allocation.

Figure 7.3 illustrates one possible case. The committee structure
identifies that group which is permitted to submit proposals for consideration; assume for the example it is group R, the rich. In figure 7.3
the jurisdiction structure limits voters to consider only education pro-
posals; if $(\hat{g}_1, \hat{g}_2)$ is the status quo point (denoted β), only policies along
the line at $g_2 = \hat{g}_2$ can be considered.[14] The amendment structure
permits voters to consider only the committee's proposal against the
status quo; the amendment process is "closed."[15] Group R, which we
call the "agenda setter" in this example, will propose the g_1 alternative
along the line at $\hat{g}_2$ that maximizes R's utility subject to the constraint
that it will be approved by a majority in a pairwise comparison with
the status quo point. R needs one more vote in addition to its own.

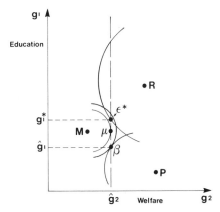

Fig. 7.3   Single jurisdiction equilibrium.

That vote will come from the middle class (M), and the final allocation will be at point $\epsilon^* = (g_1^*, \hat{g}_2)$. Point ϵ^* is just inside M's indifference curve through the status quo—the position needed to win M's support—and is the best that R can do as an agenda setter subject to these structural constraints. If group M were the agenda setter from the committee structure, the final equilibrium would be at point μ with M and R voting for approval and the poor (P) against. If P were the agenda setter, the final allocation would remain at the status quo point, β, for group P could not do better and still win support needed from groups M or R to defeat β.

Figure 7.4 extends the analysis to a case where the jurisdiction structure allows the committee and the voters to consider both dimensions of fiscal choice simultaneously. Again, allow R to be the agenda setter and point β to be the status quo. R seeks, as before, to maximize its utility subject to the structural constraints and the status quo. R can attract group P into a majority-winning coalition with any proposal along the contract line between points P and δ.[16] Group P is just indifferent between the status quo and proposal δ; allocations closer to point R along the contract line (which group R prefers) will be rejected by P in favor of β. If R chooses to align with group M, points along the R-to-M contract line between allocations γ and ϵ^{**} are available; allocations between points M and γ are rejected by group R while allocations between R and ϵ^{**} are rejected by group M. Therefore, the possible winning allocations available to agenda-setter R are on the heavy-line segments $\gamma\epsilon^{**}$ and $P\delta$ in figure 7.4. R will select that allocation on one of these line segments which maximizes the coalition's utility; e.g., allocation ϵ^{**} in figure 7.4. In this example, policy is set by the middle and rich coalitions. A similar analysis will show that point P is the winning allocation if group P is the agenda setter and

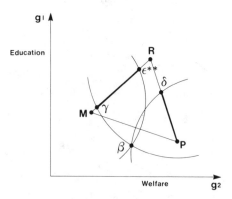

Fig. 7.4   Open jurisdiction equilibriums.

that point γ is the winning allocation if group M is the agenda setter. All three allocations are stable equilibriums provided the political structure, including the status quo point, remains fixed.[17]

The concept of a structure-induced equilibrium provides an important element in the needed theoretical framework to begin the analysis of fiscal allocations in a federalist economy. Since budget allocations are stable over time, it is essential that we have a theory of political choice that gives a well-defined equilibrium prediction. Further, the theory must generate equilibrium outcomes even when there is conflict and the issues are multidimensional. The theory of structure-induced equilibriums does just that. To apply the theory of structure-induced equilibriums, however, we must close two gaps in the analysis. First, we must specify the determinants of voter preferences in the policy space from a general, underlying preference structure over public and private goods. Second, the political theory is a partial equilibrium theory providing predictions of budget allocations *given* the status quo point and the relevant political institutions. Applications of the theory of structure-induced equilibrium must specify which institutions are relevant and exactly how those institutions will influence budgetary choices.

The starting point for the specification of voter preferences over fiscal policies is the individual utility maximization model of fiscal choice that defined the individual voter demand curves in (1).[18] Generalized to the case of multiple public goods ($t = 1, \ldots, G$), the utility-maximizing demand model would define a vector of preferred allocations, the typical element of which is $g_t = f(p_1, \ldots, p_G, \hat{I}|\text{Tastes})$. The optimal level of private goods (y) will be what is left over after the resident pays for the preferred bundle of public goods. For each voter or coalition, the vector of preferred public allocations defines the voters' bliss points—e.g., point R, M, and P, in figures 7.3 and 7.4 for the case of two public goods.[19] The starting point for specifying the influence of political institutions on budgetary choices is the fact that in models of structure-induced equilibriums final allocations will be weighted averages of the (just specified) voter bliss point—e.g., points ϵ^{**}, γ, or P in figure 7.4. The institutional structure—status quo, committee, jurisdiction, and amendment structures—will define the weights. If we allow S to represent political structure and β the status quo point, then the final budgetary allocations of public goods can be specified as

$$(2) \quad g_t^* = \alpha^R(S, \beta) \cdot g_t^R(p_R, \hat{I}_R|\text{Tastes}) + \alpha^M(S, \beta) \cdot g_t^M(p_M, \hat{I}_M|\text{Tastes})$$
$$+ \alpha^P(S, \beta) \cdot g_t^P(p_p, \hat{I}_P|\text{Tastes}) \qquad (t = 1, \ldots, G)$$

where p_i is the vector of tax prices, $\hat{I}_i$ is the full fiscal income respectively of each voter group i ($= R, M, P$) and where $\alpha^R(\cdot)$ is the political weight on the rich coalition, $\alpha^M(\cdot)$ is the political weight on the coalition of middle-class voters, and α^P ($\equiv 1 - \alpha^R - \alpha^B$) is the political weight on poor voters. Variables that might be included in the vector of political structure include controlling interests (chairmanship, majority) of the key legislative committees that set the agenda, jurisdiction, and budgetary rules on how dollars can be allocated, size of voting blocs within the legislature or community, political allegiance of those with veto power over final allocations (e.g., governor, mayor), and amendment rules that might allow proposals to be submitted from at-large interests.[20]

Once estimated, equation (2) gives us exactly what is needed to begin to analyze the effects of changes in public dollars and political structures on fiscal allocations in a federalist economy. Section 7.3 outlines one application of this methodology to state government spending for welfare, education, and "other services."

7.3 State Spending for Education, Welfare, and "Other" Services

President Reagan's new federalism offers a fundamental reorganization of our current federalist fiscal economy, decentralizing many of the new federally mandated fiscal activities of the state and local sector. Central elements in the reform are the current federal aid programs in education and public welfare. These programs now constitute 49.5 % of all federal to state-local assistance. It seems useful, therefore, to begin our analysis of fiscal allocations in a federalist economy by focusing on a major, new reform package and on the central components of that package. We do so by specifying and estimating a four-equation budgetary model of state allocations for education, welfare, "other services," and revenues. The model is based upon the conceptual analysis of fiscal choice summarized by equation (2) above, and is estimated for a sample of the forty-eight mainland states over the period 1966–80.

Three voter coalitions—a rich/upper middle class (R; defined as the percentage of families with income > \$25,000), a middle class (M; percentage of families with incomes between \$5,000 and \$25,000), and a poor class (P; percentage of families with incomes less than \$5,000)— are assumed to determine state budgetary allocations over three expenditure categories and nondebt, current state revenues (SREV). Expenditures include state aid to local elementary-secondary education (SAE), state payments to low-income families for all state-run welfare programs (SWL), and "other" current account state expenditures (OEXP). SAE includes all direct state to local educational aid as well as all federal education aid given to the states with the requirement that it be "passed through" to the local units. SWL includes state AFDC payments, state Medicaid payments, state general assistance payments, and the many small state-run supplemental welfare programs. All federal aid dollars that are given directly to the states to help defray these welfare costs are included in SWL. OEXP includes all other state expenditures supported from nondebt state revenues (SREV), while SREV includes all state tax revenues as well as revenues from state user fees and licenses. The model is specified as four behavioral equations and a current accounts budget identity:

$$
(3) \quad \left. \begin{array}{l} \text{SAE} \\ \text{SWL} \\ \text{OEXP} \\ \text{SREV} \end{array} \right\} = f_t(\underline{p}_R, \; \underline{p}_M, \; \underline{p}_P, \; \hat{I}_R, \; \hat{I}_M, \; \hat{I}_P; \; \text{Tastes}_R, \; \text{Tastes}_M, \; \text{Tastes}_P; \; S, \; \beta; \; v_t)
$$

where t = SAE, SWL, OEXP, SREV, and

$$
(4) \quad \text{SAE} + \text{SWL} + \text{OEXP} \equiv (1 + \phi e)\text{SREV} + \text{LSGRS} + \text{LSEA} + \text{CEM} + m\theta\text{SWL} + \text{LSWA} + \text{OFA},
$$

where tax prices (p_i, $i = R, M, P$), full fiscal income ($\hat{I}_i$, $i = R, M, P$), voter tastes (Tastes_i, $i = R, M, P$), the political structure (S) and the budgetary status quo (β) are defined as in our previous discussion of equation (2) above, and where v_t captures the effects of all unmeasured determinants of SAE, SWL, OEXP, or SREV. Equation (4) is the state's budget identity, which relates total expenditures to total current account revenue from the state's own revenues and from the federal-to-state grants-in-aid. Our analysis provides a careful disaggregation of the effects of federal aid; these aid programs are central to our understanding of fiscal allocations in a federalist economy and to predicting the likely effects of the new federalism. Disaggregated federal assistance includes: (1) federal general revenue sharing measured by the program's two component parts—a lump-sum, general revenue sharing grant (LSGRS) and a tax effort component that gives states more money (at a rate, e) for each dollar raised from a state income tax (which constitutes the share ϕ of total state revenues);[21] (2) lump-sum education aid (LSEA, including Elementary and Secondary Education Act, Title I for the educationally deprived, Title VI for the handicapped, and vocational education aid); (3) closed-ended matching aid for education and welfare (CEM, including school lunch, breakfast, and milk programs and all low-income commodity assistance aid); (4) open-ended welfare matching aid at the federal matching rate m for eligible expenditures (AFDC and Medicaid outlays are eligible for matching aid and constitute a share θ of SWL); (5) lump-sum welfare aid (LSWA, including aid for social services, child nutrition, maternal and child health care); and (6) other federal aid for current expenditures (OFA, excluding highway construction aid but inclusive of other federal-to-state aid not already included in revenue-sharing, education, or welfare aid). Since the budget identity defines an exact relationship between each of the three expenditure categories—SAE, SWL, and OEXP—and own-state revenues (SREV) given federal-to-state aid, we need only estimate three of the four behavioral equations in (3). We choose to estimate the SAE, SWL, and SREV equations and infer OEXP from the budget identity.

The estimation of the SAE, SWL, and SREV equations requires the approximation of several of the independent variables in (3). Specifically, we do not have individualized tax prices or individualized full fiscal incomes for the rich, middle-class, and poor coalitions, nor do we have measures of the determinants of coalition tastes. We do have measures of the components of those tax prices and fiscal incomes, and plausible correlates with coalition preferences. Coalition tax prices have two elements: open-ended federal matching aid programs and relative population usage. The open-ended matching programs are revenue sharing (e) and welfare (m); while relative population usage of education services is measured by the percentage of school-age children who attend private schools (PRIV), and population usage of welfare is measured by the percentage of families with a head over sixty-five (OLD), or headed by a female (FHH).[22] Per capita state income (INC), exogenous federal aid to state governments (LSGRS, LSEA, CEM, LSWA, OFA), exogenous federal aid to local governments (educational impact aid [IMPA] and low-income housing aid [LHA]), and federal assistance given directly to households (earned income tax credit [EITC] and food stamps [FS]), are used to specify, collectively, the coalitions' full fiscal incomes.[23] Two variables are included to specify coalitions' tastes for education—percentage of high school graduates (HS) and the average number of children per family (KIDS)—and three variables are used to measure coalitions' tastes for low-income assistance including the exposure to poverty or to the risks of poverty: percentage of population in urban areas (METRO), the state unemployment rate (UE), and percentage of state population employed in manufacturing (MAN).

Political structure is defined by the percentage of the population in each voter coalition—R and P, with M omitted from the regressions to avoid singularity—and by the percentage of population that is white (WHT) as a proxy for possible political discrimination and/or relative voter participation. We also include a vector of state dummy variables to control for the many institutional differences in the budgetary process across states.[24] Finally, the state's budgetary status quo is represented by a lagged vector of educational services—lagged school personnel per public school enrollee (PER_{-1}), lagged wages per public school employee (WAG$_{-1}$), and lagged nonpersonnel expenditures per public enrollee (NPEXP$_{-1}$)—and by lagged state welfare expenditures per capita (SWL$_{-1}$). All fiscal variables and state income are measured in per capita units and are deflated by a state cost of living index.[25]

The error term specification of our model assumes that our state dummy variables will capture all systematic effects across states that are correlated with the included exogenous variables. Previous analysis (Craig and Inman 1982) suggests that a time trend may also be appropriate with this sample to control for the systematic upward drift in state spending. With both state dummy variables and a time trend included as exogenous variables we feel that the remaining unmeasured determinants of taxes and spending captured by $v_t(t =$ SAE, SWL, and SREV) are randomly distributed across states and time. This least-squares dummy variable estimation procedure has been shown to approximate closely two-way error components estimation (see Baltagi 1981). We do, however, permit error term interdependence across revenue and spending within states and years. Such cross-equation interdependence is to be expected in budgetary models; estimation by generalized least squares (GLS) is appropriate.[26]

The model as estimated is clearly a reduced-form specification of the structural model given in equations (3) and (4). Thus we cannot identify the relative importance of the various coalitions in state budgetary policy, nor the exact role political structure plays in setting spending or taxes. We can, however, identify the effects of federal aid on state budgetary outcomes, and that is our central concern here.[27] Section 7.4 summarizes our results based upon GLS estimation of the budget model.

7.4 State Fiscal Policy

Table 7.1 summarizes our estimates of a state budgetary model for state assistance for education (SAE), state welfare spending (SWL), state revenue (SREV), and, via the budget identity, other state expenditures financed from current revenues (OEXP). The results across all three estimated equations tell a consistent, and upon reflection a not too surprising, story: education assistance, welfare spending, and broad-based tax relief are not the favored outlets for state dollars. State politicians prefer to spend state public dollars on OEXP, the treasure chest of many small, favored public projects that keep constituents from all corners of the state content. If the federal government wishes to stimulate state spending on human services—education and low-income assistance—it must impose strong spending regulations and matching requirements on federal aid, and even these requirements will not keep some dollars from leaking into OEXP.

Table 7.1   **GLS Estimation Results**

Variable	SAE	SWL	SREV
CONSTANT	282.71*	33.33	290.13*
	(43.26)	(25.00)	(76.95)
ln(LSGRS)	−.24	−.25*	.26
	(.18)	(.10)	(.30)
e	17.42	−36.48*	−14.34
	(26.85)	(15.52)	(46.09)
LSEA	.43	.23	−.39
	(.36)	(.21)	(.60)
CEM	.98*	.05	.61
	(.26)	(.15)	(2.14)
CEM* INC	—	—	.00035
			(.00069)
(1-m)	35.71*	−22.95*	−30.05
	(16.86)	(9.74)	(50.71)
(1-m) INC	—	—	.024*
			(.014)
LSWA	−.20*	.076	−.12
	(.08)	(.048)	(.14)
OFA	−.16*	−.06	.005
	(.07)	(.04)	(.12)
ln (EITC)	1.37*	.74*	1.47*
	(.28)	(.16)	(.47)
FS	.34	.12	.69*
	(.22)	(.13)	(.37)
IMPA	1.16	.95*	3.24*
	(.98)	(.57)	(1.63)
LHA	−.76	−.32	.12
	(.51)	(.29)	(.85)
INC	.0033	.0078*	.025*
	(.0034)	(.002)	(.008)
OLD	72.12	−43.11	−346.94
	(206.39)	(119.27)	(345.78)
PRIV	−12.78	1.00	−4.98
	(17.46)	(10.09)	(29.15)
FHH	−7.98*	−2.85*	−9.17*
	(1.22)	(.70)	(2.14)
HS	−263.28*	6.03	−312.30*
	(91.35)	(52.78)	(152.42)
KIDS	−5.53	16.29*	27.77*
	(8.01)	(4.63)	(13.34)
METRO	−25.16	5.48	−70.35*
	(17.68)	(10.22)	(29.53)
UE	−.73	.34	−3.46*
	(.51)	(.29)	(.84)
MAN	−228.28*	−140.79*	−415.90*
	(97.01)	(56.06)	(163.34)

Table 7.1   (continued)

Variable	SAE	SWL	SREV
POOR (P)	1.88	1.63	11.07
	(12.82)	(7.41)	(21.39)
RICH (R)	−73.60	17.89	70.93
	(67.78)	(39.17)	(112.92)
WHT	−.95*	−.43*	−.37
	(.34)	(.20)	(.58)
PER$_{-1}$	1.36*	1.11*	4.54*
	(.68)	(.39)	(1.14)
WAG$_{-1}$	.0031*	.0001	.0086*
	(.0014)	(.0008)	(.0023)
NPEXP$_{-1}$	.009	−.005	−.01
	(.01)	(.009)	(.02)
SWL$_{-1}$	.17*	A.746*	.47*
	(.05)	(.03)	(.09)
TIME	6.64*	.92	10.21*
	(1.29)	(.75)	(2.16)
SDUMS[a]	—	—	—
R^2[b]	.90	.97	.95

Standard errors in parentheses.
*Indicates significance at 10% level.
a. Individual state dummy variables. See appendix 7A.2 for parameter estimates.
b. From OLS. Estimation is by GLS.

Nothing reveals this pattern more clearly than an analysis of the initial impact effects of the major federal-to-state aid programs, beginning with the least restrictive grant—general revenue sharing—and moving to the most regulated grant—open-ended categorical matching aid.

1. *General Revenue Sharing.* The marginal effects of a dollar of lump-sum revenue-sharing aid (LSGRS) on each of the two estimated expenditure items—SAE and SWL—are negative and, in the case of SWL, statistically different from zero. Estimated at the mean value of LSGRS (= $2.84/capita), a dollar of GRS aid will reduce state education aid by $.08 and state welfare spending by $.09. LSGRS is estimated to increase state revenues by $.09, but the effect is not statistically significant. OEXP is clearly the net recipient of GRS funds. From the budget identity—equation (4)—we can estimate the average effect of a small change in LSGRS on OEXP as $\Delta OEXP = \Delta LSGRS - \Delta SAE - (1-m\theta)\Delta SWL + (1 + \phi e)\Delta SREV = 1 - (-.08) - (.4)(-.09) + (1 + .01)(.09) = \$1.21$.[28]

The "tax effort" component of revenue-sharing (e) has only tiny effects on the state budget; the estimated coefficients are insignificant, except for SWL, and the implied elasticities of spending and revenue with respect to e never exceed .01. What small budget effects result from an increase in the effort rate favor SAE and OEXP.

2. *Categorical, Lump-Sum Aid.* There are three categorical, lump-sum grants considered here, one for each expenditure category: LSEA (education), LSWA (welfare), and OFA (OEXP). These grants are nominally restricted to be spent only on the specified programs. However, states can comply with the terms of the grant by spending the aid dollar as specified but then cutting back on their own expenditures on closely related state-funded projects. Some, or perhaps even all, of the categorical aid dollars can thereby be "released" for allocations elsewhere in the budget. This is in fact what happens with LSWA and LSEA assistance. A dollar of federal lum-sum welfare aid (LSWA) increases state welfare spending by only $.076, of which the state pays only the fraction $(1 - m\theta)$ or $.03 (= .4 \times .076)$. LSWA also *lowers* state education aid spending by $.20. This decline in SAE is not surprising since many of targeted programs in LSWA assistance are for low-income, school-age children. The total "released" dollars for each dollar of federal LSWA is $1.17, $.97 from welfare and $.20 from education. However, only $.12 of these released dollars are allocated to revenue relief; $\partial SREV/\partial LSWA = -.12$. OEXP receives the remaining $1.05.

LSEA is somewhat more productive when it comes to keeping federal aid dollars within the target category, perhaps because a major component of LSEA is Title I school assistance for low-income children and this program has been closely monitored by federal auditors. Approximately $.43 of each LSEA dollar remains in SAE; $\partial SAE/\partial LSEA = .43$.[29] Welfare spending rises by $.23 as well, perhaps because of a regulatory spillover onto child welfare programs. Not all of the LSEA dollars remain in human services, however. Each dollar of aid increases education plus the state share of welfare spending by $.52 (= .43 + .23(1 - m\theta) = .43 + (.23 \times .4))$ so $.48 is allocated to tax relief and OEXP. The coefficient of LSEA on SREV suggests tax relief receives $.39 per dollar of aid, leaving $.09 for OEXP.

Other federal aid (OFA) helps only OEXP. A dollar of OFA leads to a $.16 reduction in SAE, a $.057 reduction in SWL with a state share of $.025 (= .057(1 - m\theta) = .057 \times .4)$ and a $.005 rise in SREV; overall OEXP rises by $1.19 (= 1 + .16 + .025 + .005)$.

3. *Categorical, Closed-ended Matching Aid.* A prominent form of categorical federal assistance is to require the state to "match" a fixed amount of federal aid with some corresponding number of state dollars at a given mark-up—e.g., $2 of state money for each dollar of federal aid. (The fact that the amount of federal aid is fixed distinguishes these programs as "closed-ended" matching grants.) The federal hope is that

these levered dollars will stay within the program area. However, in the case of education and welfare aid (school breakfast and lunch assistance and low-income commodity assistance) there is only partial retention; again OEXP captures the spillover. The average required mark-up of federal aid dollars can be estimated from the SREV equation as the increase in state revenues induced by a dollar increase in CEM aid: $\partial \text{SREV}/\partial \text{CEM} = .61 + .00035 \cdot \text{INC}$. Evaluated at the mean income in our sample (INC = \$2950/capita) the implicit state match for the CEM program is 1.64. The rate of mark-up rises with state income as is in fact required by the federal law for the programs in CEM. For the average income state, therefore, a dollar of federal aid must be matched by \$1.64 of state money. Thus \$2.64 flows into the categorical program areas in education and welfare. Only \$1.03 remains, however—\$.98 in education spending and \$.05 in welfare assistance. OEXP captures the residual flow of \$1.64 ($= 2.64 - .98 - .05(1 - m\theta) = 1.66 - (.05 \times .4)$). It is clear that the federal match requirement brings more dollars into the target programs, but it also provides state legislators with a reason to increase taxes and to reallocate all of that increase to their favored programs in OEXP.

4. *Open-ended Matching Aid.* The most regulated of the federal aid programs is an open-ended matching grant that operates as a tax-price subsidy. Aid is only received when dollars are spent on the targeted program, and further, additional state spending is rewarded with additional federal aid. The net effect of such assistance is to lower the per unit costs to taxpayers of providing the aided service. If m is the open-ended federal matching rate and θ is the share of state spending covered by aid, then $(1 - m\theta)$ is the share of expenditures that must be paid by taxpayers. The major open-ended matching grants now used by the federal government are for the state provision of welfare spending on AFDC and Medicaid. For all states participating in the program, the rate m varies from a low of .5 for the richer states (INC $\geq$ national average income) to a high of .78 for the poorest states. The share of total welfare spending in AFDC and Medicaid (θ) is $\simeq .8$ for states in our sample. We have estimated the effects of $(1 - m\theta)$ on state spending and revenues.[30] Calculated at the means, the implied tax price elasticities for $(1 - m\theta)$ are $+ .22$ for SAE (a positive cross-price effect), $- .17$ for SWL (a negative own-price effect), $- .08$ for OEXP (a negative cross-price effect), and $+ .07$ for SREV (implying a negative cross-price elasticity of $- .001$ for private income). Welfare and education are (loosely speaking) substitutes in the state budget, while welfare, private income, and other expenditures are complements. If states transfer more income to the poor, they apparently transfer more income to other income classes also. The transfers are facilitated by a reduction in the education budget and increased federal aid. In fact, the dollar

flows to the middle- and upper-income groups may exceed those to the poor. Again, we do our calculations for the average state. A rise in the average state's effective matching rate ($m\theta$) from .60 to .615 will bring in $1/capita more in welfare matching aid. This additional dollar will initially be spent on the targeted activity increasing state welfare expenditures by $.34. The additional $.34 of SWL brings in an additional $.21 (= .615 · .34) of aid. As m increases, (1 − $m\theta$) falls and SAE falls, too—by approximately $.54. SREV also falls by an estimated $.63. OEXP rises, however, by $.78 ($\equiv$ $1 − ΔSAE − ΔSWL(1 − .615) + ΔSREV = $1 + .54 − .34(.385) − .63). Again, other expenditures and tax relief are the favored outlets for federal assistance, even when that assistance is targeted to the poor.

This pattern of state spending, which allocates new, marginal dollars towards OEXP, is also observed in how states react to federal assistance that bypasses the state and is paid to local governments and to households directly. Such federal aid will still be available to state legislators if they are willing to tax back some or all of the aid through an increase in state revenues. For the earned income tax credit (EITC) and food stamps (FS) paid directly to low-income households, and for federal impact school aid (IMPA) paid to school districts, this seems to be what happens. We do not observe a statistically significant tax-back effect with low-income housing aid (LHA) paid to local governments. For a state with the average EITC grant (= $2.91/capita), a dollar of EITC assistance triggers a $.50 increase in state revenues, which is allocated entirely to school aid ($.47) and state welfare ($.25, of which the state pays .25(1 − $m\theta$) = .25 × .4 = $.10); here OEXP seems to lose on average (−$.07). There is a similar tendency to tax back food stamp assistance. A dollar of food stamp aid to the household sector is offset in part by a $.69 increase in SREV, which is spent on SAE ($.34), on welfare ($.12, which requires $.05 from the state = .12(1 − $m\theta$) = .12 × .4) and on OEXP ($.30). School impact aid (IMPA) has the most pronounced effect on SREV—$3.22 for each dollar of federal-to-local school aid (!)—and OEXP is a main beneficiary, receiving $1.68 after the SAE ($1.16) and SWL ($.95), with a state share = .95 × .4 = .38) allocations. We have difficulty rationalizing the size of this effect of IMPA on SREV, however, particularly since our earlier work (Craig and Inman 1982) for a shorter, but largely overlapping sample period (1965–77) found a large, negative effect of this aid on state taxes. We can only suggest a cautious use of the IMPA results. Finally, a dollar of federal-to-local housing aid (LHA) has a modest positive, but not statistically significant, effect on SREV ($.12) and depressing, but not significant, effects on SAE (−$.76) and SWL (−$.32); if we accept these coefficients as measuring average effects, OEXP spending rises by $1.01 for each dollar of LHA. Over all four bypass aid programs considered here, a dollar of increased federal aid to each program will stimulate a full tax-back of $4.53, allocated to $1.21 to SAE, $1.00 to SWL (of which the state pays $.40 due to $m\theta$ aid), and $2.92 to OEXP.

Increases in average state income (INC) stimulate a larger state budget, with low-income assistance and "other expenditures" as the favored outlets. A dollar of INC increases SREV by $.025, which induces a $.003 rise in SAE, a $.008 rise in SWL (though the state share is only .0032), and a .019 rise in OEXP. The private income elasticity of demand for state education assistance is .13, .45 for state welfare assistance, .26 for "other expenditures," and .32 for state revenues. Our results also confirm the presence of a flypaper effect on state budgets. Most all of private income stays in the private sector; most all public aid dollars stay in the public sector.

The nonaid variables included in the analysis to reflect across-state-and-time changes in voter coalition bliss points and political structure reveal no major surprises. The three tax price variables—OLD, PRIV, and FHH—are either insignificant or, as in the case of FHH in the SWL equation, significant and of the correct sign. The coefficients for the five "taste" variables—HS, KIDS, METRO, UE, MAN—reveal a revenue-spending pattern that favors OEXP and tax relief over human services (SAE, SWL) in those states with a large number of existing manufacturing jobs, which are heavily urbanized, with relatively high rates of unemployment (though SWL does increase in response to UE), fewer children per family, and more high school graduates.[31] These states tend to be the older, urbanized states of the east, south, and midwest. One plausible explanation for this observed spending pattern is that these are also the states under intense fiscal pressure as they struggle to retain mobile capital and jobs. What business wants is tax relief and "other expenditures," not school aid and welfare, and the states seem to be responsive.

The political structure variables—R, P, WHT, and the individual state constant terms—show state fiscal policy is not responsive to the income class divisions as measured here, once we have accounted for the effects of average income. While income class seems unimportant, racial divisions are not. As the percentage of the state's population becomes more white, fewer dollars are allocated to SAE and to SWL, the human service portion of the state budget. Quantitatively, the effects of major swings in the racial composition of the state are important; states one standard deviation below the mean percentage white spend approximately $24/capita more on human services and $13/capita less on OEXP than states one standard deviation above the mean percentage white.[32] The individual state constant terms meant to capture the idiosyncratic nature of state political structures are reported in appendix 7A.2.

As we emphasized in section 7.2, state budgetary politics is a dynamic process. Our results illustrate the importance of these dynamics. First, from the coefficient on TIME we observe a continual upward drift in *real* state spending and revenue over time, favoring SAE ($6.64/capita per year) and OEXP ($3.20/capita per year = ΔSREV − ΔSAE − ΔSWL(1 − $m\theta$) = 10.21 − 6.64 − .92(.4)). Second, our theory of budgetary politics predicts an important role for the level of last year's services in this year's budgeting (the status quo) and our empirical analysis confirms this prediction. We have modeled the dynamics of the political process by including lagged service levels for education (PER$_{-1}$, WAG$_{-1}$, and NPEXP$_{-1}$) and welfare (SWL$_{-1}$) in each of the three estimated budget equations; the lagged service variables are always statistically significant as a set.[33] Further, the implied dynamic adjustment process has important implications for the final disbursement of fiscal resources. While the feedback effects of lagged school services on state spending and taxes are modest with most effects of a fiscal change felt in the first year, lagged welfare spending has a quantitatively important impact—particularly on SWL, SREV, and OEXP—that takes from four to six years to be fully felt.[34] There is an inertia in state welfare budgeting, as legislators seem reluctant to expand or cut welfare spending too quickly, perhaps because they are concerned about the reaction of neighboring states (see Gramlich 1982). Table 7.2 summarizes our estimates of the equilibrium effects of changes in each of the exogenous fiscal variables in our model allowing for the dynamic adjustments to the budget through lagged education and welfare services.[35] The table reports the equilibrium effects of an additional $1 of federal assistance paid either directly to the states or as "bypass" assistance to households and local governments. The calculation for federal bypass aid allocates $.25 to each of the four bypass programs in our study (EITC, FS, LHA, and IMPA). We also show the equilibrium allocation of an additional dollar of state private income. Quali-

Table 7.2   **Equilibrium Effects of Federal Aid**

$1 of aid as:	ΔSAE	ΔSWL	ΔOEXP[a]	ΔSREV
LSGRS	−.15	−.34	1.20	−.09
LSEA	.66	.94	.13	.17
LSWA	−.16	.28	1.04	−.01
OFA	−.21	−.22	1.17	−.12
CEM	1.07	.22	1.72	1.88
m	−.33	1.35	.79	−.02
Bypass	.49	.98	.79	1.67
INC	.008	.031	.021	.041

a. In all cases, ΔOEXP is calculated as the residual change necessary to balance the state budget after equilibrium adjustments in SAE, SWL, and SREV.

tatively, the equilibrium effects of aid and income parallel the impact effects described above: (1) OEXP is generally favored, but (2) the more regulated federal aid is, the more likely it is to remain within the target expenditure category. Quantitatively, the equilibrium effects of aid on the human resource portion of the state budget exceed the impact effects of aid, primarily because of lagged adjustments to welfare spending. Positive "shocks" to the human resource budget (via m, CEM, LSEA, LSWA, and INC) increase SAE and SWL over time while negative shocks (via LSGRS and OFA) decrease SAE and SWL over time. OEXP is largely unaffected; it is SREV that adjusts to the changes in SAE and SWL.

Overall, both the impact and the dynamic equilibrium analyses of federal assistance to the state-local sector reveal the same essential pattern to desired state spending: federal dollars that flow into the state via grants-in-aid are allocated disproportionately toward OEXP and away from the human services components—SAE and SWL—of the state budget. It is important to know why. This analysis cannot answer that question—structural, not reduced form, models are needed—but we will offer one hypothesis that, on its face, we find persuasive. Like their counterparts in Washington, state legislators are rewarded with reelection when they deliver publicly funded programs to their constituents *and* when those additional public dollars can be explicitly linked to the efforts of the elected official.[36] Public expenditures that are most conducive to district-by-district, constituent-by-constituent allocations are those outlays that can be allocated by legislative or bureaucratic choice, not formula. Both welfare assistance and school aid are disbursed according to preestablished formulas.[37] The real battles for state dollars are fought in the nonformula expenditures—that is, in OEXP. Thus the more money to OEXP the better, for it makes all legislators better off.[38] The major state services provided by OEXP dollars include state highway maintenance (potholes and jobs), state hospitals and medical centers (health care and jobs), universities (educational opportunity and jobs), parks (recreation and jobs), and state bureaucracies (services and jobs). Each of these programs permits discretion in dollar allocations. From these OEXP programs, alternative omnibus spending bills can be fashioned to ensure majority approval of the state budget. OEXP is the grease or "pork" that keeps the wheels of state politics in motion. In such a world, it is not surprising that federal aid dollars are rechanneled whenever possible into "other expenditures."

Nor is it surprising that those interested in reducing the size of government should wish to reduce and/or restructure the federal aid system. President Reagan's "new federalism" reforms can be viewed as one attempt to curtail the flow of federal aid dollars into state treasuries.

The likely impact of the Reagan reforms on state budgets is described in section 7.5. The president will not be disappointed with the results.

7.5 The Budgetary Effects of the New Federalism

President Reagan's new federalism is a three-step reform package whose primary intention—Washington rhetoric aside—is to reduce federal and state-local government spending. Step 1 of the reform is to turn the AFDC and food stamp programs over to the states for financing and administration. In step 2 the federal government will assume full responsibility for Medicaid. Step 3 gives the states financial responsibility for sixty-one domestic aid programs in exchange for a lump-sum transfer per capita from a newly established trust fund, with trust fund payments reduced gradually until, by 1992, no further federal lump-sum aid will be paid to the states. Table 7.3 summarizes the predicted equilibrium effects of these reforms on the allocation of state budgets to SAE, SWL, OEXP, and SREV.

The baseline for our simulation is the "average" in each budget category for our sample states in 1980; see table 7.3. This average prereform budget for 1980 is then adjusted by the equilibrium budgetary responses to changes in federal grants-in-aid for each of two major components of the new federalism reform: the welfare exchange of AFDC and food stamps for Medicaid and the exchange of trust fund aid for sixty-one categorical programs. First, the simulations assume each component of the reform is done separately—the columns labeled "welfare exchange" and "trust fund exchange" in table 7.3—and then simulations are performed for the entire new federalism package with

Table 7.3	The Fiscal Effects of the New Federalism[a]				
	SAE	SWL	OEXP[b]	SREV	Federal to State Aid
Prereform (1980)	$ 77.30	$60.59	$235.74	$266.33	$107.30
(1) welfare exchange	$ 99.92	$21.47	$261.75	$306.31	$ 76.83
(2) trust fund exchange	$ 73.81	$40.52	$233.54	$251.46	$ 96.41
(3) new federalism (1988)	$ 96.42	$ 1.39	$259.57	$291.44	$ 65.94
(4) new federalism (1992+)	$105.55	$23.32	$168.20	$297.07	≡ 0

a. All dollar figures are in real 1966 dollars per capita.
b. In all simulations, OEXP is calculated as the residual category to balance the state budget.

full trust fund aid (the column labeled "new federalism, 1988") and then without trust fund aid (labeled "new federalism, 1992+"). For each simulation, we assume that (1) the effect of requiring state responsibility is equivalent to setting federal aid equal to zero for the affected programs, (2) trust fund aid is equivalent to a lump-sum grant-in-aid, and (3) the federal assumption of Medicaid payments will induce state budget responses equivalent to those now observed for a similar existing federal-to-poor-household aid program, food stamps. We also assume the earned income tax credit (EITC) will be unaffected by reform.[39]

The transfer of food stamp aid and AFDC to the states and of Medicaid to the federal level is functionally equivalent to setting the welfare matching rate (m) to zero, food stamp aid (FS) to zero, and establishing Medicaid assistance as a federal-to-household bypass aid program. The combined effects of these reforms are dominated by the change in the welfare matching rate from $m = .6$ to $m = 0$. Equilibrium welfare spending falls by 65%. State-own revenues rise somewhat to offset the fall in federal-to-state aid; these dollars along with the state dollars released from the welfare budget are allocated to education aid and other state expenditures. The exchange of trust-fund aid for categorical aid has a somewhat different pattern of effects, and favors tax relief. State assumption of federal categorical aid implies all federal-to-state aid (LSEA, CEM, LSWA, OFA) and all federal-to-local aid (IMPA, LHA) in our model now receive zero funding. In their place, states receive a lump-sum grant from the federal trust fund approximately equal to the value of the lost categorical aid.[40] Under this component of the new federalism package, state education and welfare spending fall, other expenditures remain the same, and state revenues and federal aid decline. Again, we observe that once the categorical "strings" of federal human resource aid are untied, dollars leave this portion of the state budget; in this case they go to state tax relief. Reagan's new federalism package combines the welfare exchange and the trust fund exchange. The policies' joint effects are not additive, however, because of the interaction of aid and spending levels in the equilibrium model. When full trust-fund aid is paid to the states (the new federalism to 1988), SAE and OEXP are the clear net gainers, while state taxes rise and state welfare falls to almost nothing. The welfare exchange plus the strong negative effect of LSGRS on state welfare spending (see tables 7.1 and 7.2) are responsible for this large fall in SWL. When federal trust fund aid is removed in 1992, we observe a increase in state own revenues, SAE and SWL, and a sizable fall in OEXP.

While the exact dollar predictions in table 7.3 must be interpreted with care, we feel the overall impression left by these simulations is valid. In the end, the new federalism reforms will reduce welfare spending, increase education spending, reduce state expenditures on "other" goods and services, and increase state revenues. The combined size of federal-state-local government will also decline. Though state (and possibly local) government revenues increase (by about $30/capita in table 7.3), federal spending is reduced by the amount of saved federal aid ($107.30/capita) less any increases in federal Medicaid spending ($\approx$ $17/capita, if 1980 average state Medicaid spending is maintained).

On balance, it appears the new federalism of President Reagan will achieve its objectives. Government, and particularly pork-barrel government, is smaller. The possible price we pay is less public assistance for low-income households.[41]

7.6   A Concluding Comment

The U.S. federalist public economy has evolved to the point where today the federal government is the primary provider of public dollars and the state-local sector is the primary provider of public services. There are good reasons to doubt the efficiency of such a fiscal structure, particularly if the wedge between the revenue and spending responsibility is large. Grants-in-aid is the source of that wedge. Efforts to reform our current system of grants-in-aid require a careful understanding of the effects of aid on state and local fiscal choice: first, to answer the question of whether federal aid is a cause of inefficiency, and, if so, to then fashion a reform policy to improve resource allocations.[42] The formal analysis of state-local fiscal choice must recognize the fact that state and local governments are *political institutions*, however, and that the grants-in-aid system is an integral part of that institutional structure. This first analysis confirms the importance of grants as a structural determinant of state budgetary choice. The task before us now is to reveal more fully just how this structure works and to exploit that knowledge to improve public sector resource allocations.

Appendix 7A.1
Data Description

Dependent variable	Definition	Mean	Standard deviation
SAE	State education spending, deflated, per capita	65.78	23.05
SWL	State welfare spending, deflated, per capita	52.75	23.11
SREV	State-own source revenues, deflated, per capita	233.20	54.66

Dependent variable	Definition	Mean	Standard deviation
Independent variable			
LSWA	Federal-state lump sum welfare aid, equals total federal-state welfare aid minus AFDC, Medicaid, and SSI after 1973, deflated, per capita	9.74	7.77
LHA	Federal-local welfare aid, equals housing aid, deflated, per capita	2.97	2.25
FS	Food Stamps, deflated, per capita	6.53	5.94
EITC	Earned Income Tax Credit, deflated, per capita	1.44	1.74
$(1-m)$	State share of federal matching aid	.403	.088
OFA	Other federal aid, excluding welfare, education, highway, and general revenue sharing aid, deflated, per capita	39.44	16.97
LSGRS	Lump-sum component of general federal-state revenue sharing, deflated, per capita	1.76	1.99
e	State effort index for revenue sharing	.03	.03
INC	Per capita income, deflated	2950.49	436.34
LSEA	Lump-sum federal-state education aid, including vocational and handicapped aid, and Title I, deflated, per capita	5.82	2.66
CEM	Closed-end matching federal-state aid, included school breakfast and lunch and commodity distribution, deflated, per capita	4.31	2.63
IMPA	Impact federal education aid to local governments, deflated, per capita	1.91	1.59
HS	Percentage that completed high school	.59	.09
KIDS	Average number of children per household	1.18	.18
POOR(P)	Percentage below $5,000 annual income	.14	.075
OLD	Percentage 65 years old and over	.10	.014
RICH(R)	Percentage above $25,000 annual income	.03	.018
METRO	Percentage that lives in a metropolitan area	.55	.26
UE	Percentage unemployed	5.59	1.88
MAN	Percentage of the population working in manufacturing	.086	.033
FHH	Percentage of families headed by a female	9.52	2.40
WHT	Percentage white	90.1	8.83
PRIV	Percentage of school-age children in private school	.094	0.58
PER_{-1}	School personnel per enrollee lagged one year	11.31	1.58
WAG_{-1}	Wages per school personnel lagged one year, deflated	5966.78	795.66
$NPEXP_{-1}$	Nonpersonnel expenditures per capita lagged one year, deflated	60.69	29.82
SWL_{-1}	State welfare expenditure lagged one year, deflated, per capita	50.17	23.03

Appendix 7A.2
State Dummy Variables[a]

	SAE	SWL	SREV	OEXP[b]
AR	−34.48*	−.63	−39.65*	−4.92
	(6.09)	(3.52)	(10.14)	
CA	46.15*	8.68	58.92*	9.30
	(16.26)	(9.40)	(27.07)	
CO	29.89	−12.12	17.86	−7.18
	(18.72)	(10.82)	(31.26)	
CT	34.98*	10.69	52.31*	13.05
	(14.04)	(8.11)	(23.54)	
DE	57.98*	1.64	175.97*	117.33
	(13.15)	(7.60)	(21.92)	
FL	24.00	−9.78	13.30	−6.79
	(13.07)	(7.55)	(21.82	
GA	8.16	−.27	−25.93*	−33.93
	(6.58)	(3.80)	(10.99)	
ID	.16	−10.29	−12.50	−8.54
	(18.65)	(10.78)	(31.24)	
IL	15.60	7.04	.81	−17.61
	(10.00)	(5.78)	(16.68)	
IN	6.34	.24	22.47	16.93
	(10.61)	(6.13)	(17.89)	
IO	7.55	−2.88	−2.34	−8.74
	(13.57)	(7.84)	(22.66)	
KS	−3.73	−8.59	−20.81	−13.64
	(14.34)	(8.29)	(23.92)	
KY	−29.01*	4.20	−17.01	10.32
	(6.62)	(3.82)	(11.06)	
LA	−4.13	−11.79*	27.76*	36.61
	(7.87)	(4.55)	(13.37)	
ME	15.66	14.21*	17.95	−3.39
	(11.88)	(6.86)	(19.77)	
MD	18.41	−7.08	45.63*	30.05
	(11.97)	(6.92)	(19.94)	
MA	36.96*	22.58*	56.99*	11.00
	(13.30)	(7.69)	(22.27)	
MI	29.14*	10.74	54.42*	20.98
	(19.09)	(6.99)	(20.20)	
MN	36.31*	−1.14	61.09*	25.24
	(12.13)	(7.01)	(20.34)	
MS	−10.21	.30	−7.32	2.77
	(9.97)	(5.76)	(16.68)	
MT	−5.37	−16.53	−38.03	−26.05
	(18.18)	(10.50)	(30.43)	
NE	−47.21*	−11.78	−37.20	14.72
	(15.25)	(8.81)	(25.45)	

	SAE	SWL	SREV	OEXP[b]
NV	40.60*	−20.12	20.78	−11.77
	(20.21)	(11.68)	(33.68)	
NH	−13.16	8.37	−33.65	−23.84
	(13.90)	(8.03)	(23.18)	
NJ	16.68	4.74	−.53	−19.11
	(10.66)	(6.16)	(17.89)	
NM	31.28	−25.58*	79.72	58.67
	(17.47)	(10.09)	(29.23)	
NY	57.49*	16.29*	86.08*	22.07
	(10.43)	(6.03)	(17.51)	
NC	27.59*	3.93	3.18	−25.98
	(6.72)	(3.89)	(11.28)	
ND	−41.82*	−18.44*	−8.53	40.67
	(12.12)	(7.01)	(20.33)	
OH	26.56*	3.87	−5.96	−34.07
	(11.02)	(6.37)	(18.44)	
OK	−11.22	−6.61	2.93	16.79
	(9.41)	(5.44)	(15.72)	
OR	15.35	1.49	33.70	17.75
	(14.06)	(8.13)	(23.49)	
PA	30.86*	13.01*	40.97*	4.91
	(9.46)	(5.47)	(15.89)	
RI	11.27	28.30*	56.12*	33.53
	(12.36)	(7.14)	(20.85)	
SD	−59.14*	−16.89*	−87.87*	−21.97
	(14.18)	(8.19)	(23.71)	
TN	−23.59*	3.53	−38.13	−15.95
	(6.39)	(3.69)	(10.65)	
UT	64.74*	−16.00	50.97	−7.37
	(22.27)	(12.87)	(37.30)	
VT	9.89	9.61	36.94	23.21
	(15.93)	(9.21)	(26.53)	
VA	−5.73	−11.54*	−19.72	−9.37
	(8.44)	(4.88)	(14.07)	
WA	46.83*	−5.93	71.54*	27.08
	(17.23)	(9.96)	(28.77)	
WI	6.68	8.59	76.81*	66.69
	(10.82)	(6.25)	(18.18)	
WY	−1.96	−24.79	34.73	46.61
	(25.27)	(14.60)	(42.30)	

Standard errors are in parentheses.
*Indicates significance at the 5% level.
a. These estimates are from the model presented in table 7.1. Seven states are excluded: Alabama is the base state, Arizona and Texas have no observations, Missouri and South Carolina have only one observation, and Alaska and Hawaii have unique fiscal situations that suggest excluding them from our general analysis.
b. Calculated from the point estimates.

Notes

The authors would like to thank the NBER for partial funding for this research, the Center for Public Policy and a Research Initiation Grant at the University of Houston that supported a portion of Craig's research, and the NSF (under grant SES-8112001), which supported a portion of Inman's research. The comments of Helen Ladd, Ron Fisher, and the participants at the Bureau's conference on state and local finance (June 15–16, 1984) pushed us to revise significantly and extend our initial research. We hope this new product does justice to their excellent comments.

1. For a description of the historical evolution of our federalist public economy, see Scheiber (1966).
2. The federal share of all nondefense, government spending has grown from 28.5% in 1902 to 48.8% by 1983. The source of this growth has been the increase in federally funded transfer programs to families and to governments. The state-local sector has always been the main *producer* of public services. The state-local sector's share of nontransfer, nondefense government spending has grown from 71% in 1902 to 84.6% by 1983. Financial control has become more centralized; production has become less centralized. Bridging the widening gap between the financing and provision of public services are grants-in-aids; see Inman (1985).
3. See Inman (1985).
4. See Inman (1985) for some thoughts on this issue based upon the political history of our existing fiscal system.
5. The level of free g ($= \hat{g}$) made available by lump-sum aid is $(z/n)/c(1 - m)$. As z dollars of aid buys $z/c(1 - m)$ units of x and x provides x/n units of g, $\hat{g} = (x/n) = (z/n)/c(1 - m)$. The assumption in this calculation is that expenditures from z aid can be "leveraged" further by matching aid.
6. See the work of Bergstrom and Goodman (1973) and Inman (1978).
7. See Inman (1979) for a review of the U.S. experience and Jackman and Papadachi (1981) and Pommerehne (1978) for examples of applications of the median voter model to fiscal choice in European communities.
8. The theory predicts that the effects of I and (z/n) work only through full fiscal income, $\hat{I}$. While a dollar more of I increases $\hat{I}$ by one dollar, a dollar more of (z/n) increases $\hat{I}$ by $\pi(b/B)$, which generally is not equal to 1. If $\pi(b/B) < 1$, a dollar of private income (I) should have a greater stimulative effect on the demand for g than a dollar of lump-sum aid per capita (z/n). If $\pi(b/B) \equiv 1$, then I and (z/n) should have equal effects on g.
9. Two alternative explanations have been offered for the flypaper effect. Moffitt (1984) argues that the flypaper effect may be due to a misspecification of the resident's budget constraint by failing to allow for nonlinearities of the constraint, e.g., the kink in the constraint at point C in figure 7.1. Moffitt explicitly allows for such kinks and bends in the resident's budget constraint when estimating a budgetary model for state welfare programs and finds that after such a correction the effects of the lump-sum component of such aid cannot be statistically distinguished from the effects of residential income, i.e., there is no flypaper effect. While such nonlinearities are important in welfare aid, and Moffitt is clearly correct to allow for these, most other federal and state aid programs for which the flypaper effect has been found do not involve nonlinear budget constraints over the relevant range of local fiscal choice. For most programs, full fiscal income, $\hat{I}$, or its components I and (z/n), are the correct independent variables.

Hamilton (1983) has also argued that the flypaper effect is due to an error in specification, now of the technology of local service provision. Resident income plays two roles, not one. Income defines the resident's available resources, but income also is a determinant (or a very good proxy for the true determinants) of local service production. It is generally less expensive to provide a given level of services, g, in rich towns than in poor towns. Local service costs (c) depend on I; as I increases, c declines. Resident income therefore plays two roles: (1) as a part of full fiscal income ($\hat{I}$), and (2) as a part of the production function and local service costs (c). If income increases and c falls, then the local tax price falls, and we demand more g (Hamilton's output effect). But the fall in c means it is cheaper to produce any g and thus we need spend less on public inputs (Hamilton's substitution effect). If the substitution effect dominates the output effect, then the total effect of I through the production relationship on public input use will be negative. Thus while resident income and lump-sum aid may have nearly identical effects on local spending because of their effects on full fiscal income $(\hat{I})$, resident income may have an additional, possibly negative effect because of its role in the production of local services. The effect of I on local spending will be less than the effect of (z/n) on local spending. Hamilton tests his model for plausible parameter values and finds that it accounts for about half of the observed flypaper effects. But "the parameter values required to explain the entire flypaper effect appear to be implausible" (Hamilton 1983, 355). Hamilton's hypothesis, while interesting, cannot really save the resident utility maximization explanation of state-local fiscal choice. Something more is needed.

10. See Niskanen (1975) for the motivation behind this objective of politician-bureaucrat behavior.

11. See Filimon, Romer, and Rosenthal (1982) or Inman (1981) for alternative model specifications.

12. This particular positioning of each coalition's preferred allocations is only illustrative; the analysis that follows holds equally well for alternative combinations of preferences. Implicit in this particular configuration is the view that education and a concern for the less fortunate are both normal goods with respect to income and that all income classes also have a social insurance motive for supporting low-income assistance programs. Even Boeing engineers have need for food stamps every once in a while. The social insurance motive dominates the altruism motive for the poor leading to a high welfare demand for this coalition, while the altruism motive is relatively strong for the upper-income groups inducing a relatively high demand for welfare by this coalition. The blue-collar middle class, motivated by neither altruism nor a need for public income insurance, has a low demand for welfare.

13. The relative voting strength of the three coalitions need not be equal for the analysis that follows. All that really is required is that no one coalition hold an absolute majority by itself, for then the analysis reduces to a study of a dictator and the fiscal model behind equation (1) will be sufficient.

14. Examples of such jurisdictional structures are special districts that can decide allocations on only one policy dimension, taking the allocation of other special districts as given. In our example, a school district decides on g_1 and a welfare district sets g_2. We will not consider the interaction between special districts that sets the joint allocation of g_1 and g_2, but see Shepsle (1979) or Inman (1986).

15. A fully open amendment process where any proposal can be considered would undo the committee and jurisdictional structures and return the decision process to the majority-rule-only case and its prediction of no stable equilibrium.

16. Points off the contract line will always be rejected in favor of points on the contract line by the $R–P$ coalition, so we need consider only points on the line.

17. If the status quo point is not fixed then a new equilibrium point will emerge. Specifically, if the budgeting process is a dynamic one in which the last period's budget is the next period's status quo, then it is possible to show that the group that controls the agenda can move the budget allocation arbitrarily close to its ideal point over time. For example, if we repeat the analysis above using ϵ^{**} as the status quo, the new, next period allocation will be on the $R–P$ contract line closer to the ideal point, R, than ϵ^{**}.

18. See also Denzau and Parks (1979), who provide a general treatment of the problem of specifying voter preferences for policy outcomes from a basic preference structure over primary goods and services.

19. The analysis here assumes the coalitions in conflict are three consumer groups who have demands for the public services. While this is reasonable, the model can be extended to allow industry groups or even public employees to have a direct say in the final allocations. To formally include such groups in the analysis we must define their preferences for outcomes. Niskanen (1975), Inman (1981), and Courant, Gramlich, and Rubinfeld (1979) offer such models for public employees, while Stigler (1971) and Peltzman (1976) have specified profit-maximization models of firm or industry preferences for public service allocations.

20. The Romer-Rosenthal analysis can be seen as a special case of this more general structure. Specifically, Romer and Rosenthal consider the one jurisdiction case in which the high-spending coalition is the agenda setter. In terms of our analysis, this corresponds to figure 7.3 with the rich coalition as the agenda setter. The allocation of ϵ^* results, which exceeds the allocation that would have emerged from a median voter model (point μ). Point β, our status quo, corresponds to Romer and Rosenthal's so-called reversion level.

21. See Reischauer (1975) for estimates of e.

22. Our original definition of the tax price in section 7.2 above assumed all taxpayers used the public service. A simple recalculation of p will show that if n people pay taxes (so $B \cdot n$ is still the aggregate tax base) but only u people use the public service (so $g = x/u$), then the definition of p becomes $\pi(b/B)(u/n)(1 - m)c$, where the new term (u/n) is the percentage of population that uses the public service. As PRIV rises, (u/n) falls and the tax price for education falls, while for welfare if OLD or FHH rises, (u/n) rises and the tax price for welfare rises.

23. Aid programs explicitly for the elderly, such as Social Security and Medicare, have been excluded. Only means-tested programs are included in order to confine the analysis to political choice over a common set of goals. Similarly, unemployment and training programs such as CETA have been excluded because they are motivated by a different set of coalition determinants.

24. Since our continuous aid, income, and demographic variables are likely to capture most systematic differences across states in coalitions' preferences—the bliss points— we are reasonably confident that our state dummy variables will capture the systematic effects of state political and institutional differences on fiscal allocations. Exploring exactly what these differences might be is the task for later research.

25. The cost-of-living index used in this study is an update of an index we created in our previous study of federal-state-local finance of education. See Craig-Inman (1982, 545).

26. See Zellner (1962) and Hausman (1978).

27. For specialists in state-local finance, our reduced-form equations will appear (as they are) to be "old wine in a new bottle." The variables are familiar ones used in most previous budgetary models. We have given them a potentially new interpretation, however, an interpretation we find more compelling for reasons outlined in section 7.2 above.

One note of caution must be sounded before presenting our results. Like all reduced form budget studies, we must assume that a change in a policy variable—e.g., federal aid—does not alter the basic political structure that defines spending or revenues. For example, less federal aid for the poor does not lead to more or less political influence for the poor in state budgeting. If so, the reduced form model will be misspecified. The assumption of no structural change is probably valid for small adjustments in federal assistance, or for the first few years following large changes in assistance. Our results must be interpreted with this caveat in mind.

28. All marginal effects are calculated at the means. The decision to use a logarithmic specification for LSGRS reflects the fact that such aid has generally been found to have nonlinear effects on spending and revenues; see Inman (1979).

29. LSEA is comparable to "pass-through education aid" of our previous paper (Craig and Inman 1982). Comparing the results here to those of our earlier paper shows that this aid has a smaller effect on SAE than previously estimated. Additional years and a more complete specification in this study lead us to favor these results.

30. The estimation of the effects of matching aid is problematic. The voters' budget constraints need not be straight lines, but can have complicated "kinks" depending on whether the state enrolls under one aid formula or another. The AFDC formula is a subtle combination of open-ended and close-ended grants and requires a rather involved nonlinear estimation procedure; see Moffitt (1984). The Medicaid formula, however, does not involve such "kinks" and by 1974 most states were using this simpler aid formula. We have chosen to restrict our analysis to the sample of states that use the Medicaid formula, and then to address the problem of selection bias such a restricted sample may impose upon our results. We have adopted the procedure of Olsen (1980) for the correction of selection bias. In the SAE and SWL equations the variable to correct for selection bias was not significant, implying no bias. The variable was significant in the SREV equation, though the degree of bias in coefficients was small. We

could not apply the procedure to all years in our original sample, however, because of data limitations. We have chosen, therefore, to present the uncorrected results in table 7.1, under the (largely substantiated) assumption that the bias will be small.

31. OEXP will rise if the decline in SAE and SWL dominate any decline in SREV.

32. The mean percentage white for our sample is 90.07 (s.e. = 8.83). The change in percentage white from a low state to a high state is 17.66 % inducing a change in SAE of $-\$16.42$, a change in SWL of $-\$7.24$, and a change in SREV of $-\$6.53$. The resulting change in OEXP from the state budget identity is $\$12.79$ ($= \Delta$SREV $- \Delta$SAE $- (1 - m\theta)\Delta$SWL).

33. The fact that education services are provided by local school districts leads us to use local school personnel per enrollee (PER), local school payroll per employee (WAG), and nonpersonnel expenditures per enrollee (NPER) as our measures of education services. State welfare services as social insurance or as a redistributive public good are assumed to be available to all residents equally, so lagged SWL is used to measure welfare service levels.

An F test as to the joint significance of lagged PER, WAG, NPEXP, and SWL in the SAE, SWL, and SREV equations leads us to reject the null hypothesis of no significance in each case. The value of the respective F statistics are 6.33 (for SAE), 160 (for SWL), and 17.54 (for SREV).

34. We have calculated the dynamic structure for changes in state education aid using a local fiscal model previously estimated in Craig and Inman (1982) that specifies the effects of SAE on PER, WAG, and NPEXP. A change in SAE_{-1} changes PER_{-1}, WAG_{-1}, and NPEXP_{-1}, which in turn influence SAE, SWL, and SREV today. Tracing through the dynamic influences of last year's SAE on this year's SAE, SWL, and SREV, we can estimate the influence of one dollar of SAE_{-1} as .059 on SAE, as .007 on SWL, and .134 on SREV. Thus the dynamic effects of last year's state education aid on this year's state budget are small. These results should be contrasted to the effect of a dollar of SWL_{-1} on SAE (.17), SWL (.75), and SREV (.47). These large marginal effects will take several years before adjustment is complete.

35. The equilibrium effects of exogenous aid changes on SAE, SWL, and SREV were estimated by solving this three equation dynamic model:

$$\text{SAE} = \phi X + .17 \text{ SWL}_{-1} + .059 \text{ SAE}_{-1},$$
$$\text{SWL} = \beta X + .75 \text{ SWL}_{-1} + .007 \text{ SAE}_{-1}, \text{ and}$$
$$\text{SREV} = \theta X + .47 \text{ SWL}_{-1} + .134 \text{ SAE}_{-1},$$

where the impact coefficients ϕ, β, θ for the exogenous aid variable (X) and the coefficients on SWL_{-1} are as reported in table 7.1, and the coefficients on SAE_{-1} are as reported in note 34 above. The dynamic equilibrium of aid changes on OEXP were calculated from the state budget identity. The interpretation of these dynamic results is subject to the caveats of note 27 above.

36. See for example Fiorina (1977).

37. How these formulas are chosen is itself an important question that we hope to address in future research.

38. The presumption here is that there is no effective tax relief coalition within the state that can divert dollars from OEXP to tax relief on a regular basis. The sporadic success of the state tax limitation movements seems to be evidence on this point.

39. Before discussing the simulation results we must emphasize that the numbers in table 7.3, which look precise, are not. In calculating equilibrium effects we used all estimated aid coefficients in our model, many of which are statistically insignificant (see table 7.1). Further, the policy changes we are simulating can hardly be considered "small" changes that fall within the range of current sample variation. Whether the observed fiscal behavior holds outside the sample is an unanswered question. At best table 7.3 provides only a first impression of what may happen under the new federalism.

40. The new federalism reform agreed to pay approximately 90% of the lost categorical aid, which was about $73/capita. Thus lump-sum aid from the trust fund will be $65.94.

41. It is also possible the form of the remaining assistance will change. See Craig and Kohlhase (1985).

42. The Reagan administration's reform is only one alternative. See Gramlich (1985) for another proposal of merit.

References

Arrow, K. J. 1963. *Social choice and individual values.* 2d ed. New York: John Wiley.

Baltagi, B. H. 1981. Pooling: An experimental study of alternative testing and estimation procedures in a two-way error component model. *Journal of Econometrics* 17: 21–49.

Bergstrom, T. C., and R. P. Goodman. 1973. Private demands for public goods. *American Economic Review* 63: 280–96.

Bowen, H. 1943. The interpretation of voting in the allocation of economic resources. *Quarterly Journal of Economics* 58: 27–48.

Courant, P. N., E. M. Gramlich, and D. L. Rubinfeld. 1979. Public employee market power and the level of government spending. *American Economic Review* 69: 806–17.

Craig, S. G., and R. P. Inman. 1982. Federal aid and public education: An empirical look at the new fiscal federalism. *Review of Economics and Statistics* 64: 541–52.

Craig, S. G., and J. Kohlhase. 1985. Why there is not a unified welfare system: Fiscal federalism from an agency approach. In J. Quigley, ed., *Perspectives on local public finance and public policy, II.* Greenwich, JAI Press.

Denzau, A. T., and R. P. Parks. 1979. Deriving public sector preferences. *Journal of Public Economics* 11: 335–52.

Filimon, R., T. Romer, and H. Rosenthal. 1982. Asymmetric information and agenda control: The basis of monopoly power in public spending. *Journal of Public Economics* 17: 51–70.

Fiorina, M. 1977. *Congress: Keystone of the Washington establishment.* New Haven: Yale University Press.

Gramlich, E. 1982. An econometric examination of the new federalism. *Brookings Papers on Economic Activity* 2: 327–60.

———. 1985. Reforming U.S. federalism arrangements. In J. Quigley and D. Rubinfeld, eds., *Urban America and the Reagan budget.* Berkeley: University of California Press.

Hamilton, B. 1983. The flypaper effect and other anomalies. *Journal of Public Economics* 22: 347–62.

Hausman, J. A. 1978. Specification tests in econometrics. *Econometrica* 46: 1251–71.

Inman, R. P. 1978. Testing political economy's 'as if' proposition: Is the median income voter really decisive? *Public Choice* 33: 45–65.

———. 1979. The fiscal performance of local governments: An interpretative review. In Mieszkowski and Straszheim, eds., *Current issues in urban economics.* Baltimore: John Hopkins University Press.

————. 1981. Wages, pensions and employment in the local public sector. In Mieszkowski and Peterson, eds., *Public sector labor markets*. Washington, D.C.: Urban Institute Press.

————. 1985. Fiscal allocations in a federalist economy: Understanding the new federalism. In J. Quigley and D. Rubinfeld, eds., *Urban America and the Reagan budget*. Berkeley: University of California Press.

————. 1986. Markets, governments and the 'new' political economy. In A. Auerbach and M. S. Feldstein, eds., *Handbook of public economics* 2. Amsterdam: North-Holland, forthcoming.

Jackman, R., and J. Papdachi. 1981. Local authority education expenditure in England and Wales. In M. J. Bowman, ed., *Collective choice in education*. The Hague: Martinus Nijhoff.

Kramer, G. H. 1973. On a class of equilibrium conditions for majority rule. *Econometrica* 41: 285–97.

Moffitt, R. 1984. The effects of grants-in-aid on state and local expenditures: The case of AFDC. *Journal of public economics* 23: 279–306.

Niskanen, W. 1975. Bureaucrats and politicians. *Journal of Law and Economics* 18: 617–43.

Olsen, R. J. 1980. A least squares correction for selectivity bias. *Econometrica* 48: 1815–20.

Peltzman, S. 1976. Toward a more general theory of regulation. *Journal of Law and Economics* 19: 211–40.

Plott, C. R. 1967. A notion of equilibrium and its possibility under majority rule. *American Economic Review* 57: 787–806.

Pommerehne, W. W. 1978. Institutional approaches to public expenditures: Empirical evidence from Swiss municipalities. *Journal of Public Economics* 9: 255–80.

Reischauer, R. 1975. General revenue sharing—The program's incentives. In W. Oates, ed., *Financing the new federalism*. Baltimore: Johns Hopkins University Press.

Romer, T., and H. Rosenthal. 1979. Bureaucrats vs. voters: On the political economy of resource allocation by direct democracy. *Quarterly Journal of Economics* 93: 562–87.

Scheiber, H. N. 1966. The condition of American federalism: An historian's view. Subcommittee on Intergovernmental Relations to the Committee on Government Operations, U.S. Senate, 15 October 1966.

Shepsle, K. 1979. Institutional arrangements and equilibrium in multidimensional voting models. *American Journal of Political Science* 23: 27–59.

Stigler, G. J. 1971. The theory of economic regulation. *Bell Journal of Economics* 2: 3–21.

Zellner, A. 1962. An efficient method of estimating seemingly unrelated regressions and tests for aggregation bias. *Journal of the American Statistical Association* 57: 348–68.

Comment   Helen F. Ladd

This paper follows in the tradition of the authors' pioneering paper on federal aid for public education (Craig and Inman 1982). Like its predecessor, the paper estimates the magnitude of governmental responses to federal aid in order to simulate the effects of recent proposals to reform the U.S. federal system. It differs from the earlier paper by the addition of a theoretical framework that incorporates the role of politics in governmental decision making and by the simultaneous focus on three types of services—welfare, education, and all other current spending—with attention to the cross-effects of aid to one category on expenditures in the other categories. It is similar to the earlier paper in terms of the carefully specified intergovernmental aid variables and associated income and price effects.

My comments are organized into three main areas: the conceptual framework and its relationship to the estimated equations; the empirical findings; and the simulated effects of the new federalism proposals. Though many of my comments are critical, they are not intended to belittle the contribution of this type of analysis. Sorting out intergovernmental fiscal interactions is a complex problem. The authors have made a reasonable first step in conceptualizing the problem in a way that can be examined empirically. I doubt that they will disagree with my judgment that their paper raises as many questions as it answers and that it should not be viewed as the definitive analysis of state responses to federal aid. At the same time, it sets a high standard in terms of specification of the key economic variables and should inspire others to pursue some of the political aspects of the modeling problem in future research.

The Theoretical Model and Its Relationship to the Estimated Equations

The median voter model typically serves as the theoretical foundation for empirical models of state and local governmental spending. Correctly criticizing this model for its oversimplification of the political

Helen F. Ladd is associate professor at the John F. Kennedy School of Government, Harvard University.

process, Craig and Inman enrich the model by introducing a bargaining process among coalitions of voters. This leads to a model in which spending outcomes are weighted averages of the bliss points of the major coalitions. The weights reflect the political power of the various coalitions, and the bliss points reflect the standard determinants of individual demand functions, namely tax prices, tastes, and income, appropriately defined to include intergovernmental lump-sum aid. This conceptual formulation implies that estimating equations should include tax prices and income by voting coalition, measures of political power, and status quo service levels as measures of the reversion levels of spending.

Correctly specified, this approach would lead to a set of estimating equations that differ in significant ways from those derived from a more traditional model. The reported equations, however, resemble only slightly the theoretical model, at least so far as the political aspects of the model are concerned. First, the voter coalitions are not very carefully defined. Consistent with the authors' presentation of the conceptual model (though not necessarily consistent with political reality), the three coalitions incorporated into the equations are rich, middle-class, and poor households. The political power of these groups is measured simply by the proportion of households in each category. Given the empirical definitions, the average proportions in the high- and low-income coalitions are only 3% and 14%, respectively. Although people with high income may well exert political power out of proportion to their numbers, the tiny proportion of wealthy households in the empirical analysis argues against viewing them as a powerful political force. Not surprisingly, none of the coefficients of these political power variables is statistically significant in any of the equations.

I suspect that the problem is less one of finding the appropriate income cutoff than one of identifying the appropriate dimension along which to identify coalitions. This is consistent with the finding that another composition variable, the nonwhite percentage of the population, enters the equations with statistically significant and nontrivial coefficients. This issue of identifying the relevant coalitions is a difficult one for economists, but one that cannot be ignored as economists venture further into the world of political economy. Further complicating the estimating process is the possibility that the identity or composition of these coalitions might vary from one state to another.

The only other aspect of the political model explicitly included in the equation is lagged values of service or spending levels. According to the authors' conceptual formulation, these variables should serve as reversion levels, that is, the level to which services will revert if the current budget is not approved. This interpretation leads, I believe, to a predicted negative sign in the relevant spending equation. The lower the reversion level, the greater the spending that can gain majority support from a high-spending agenda setter. Similarly, the higher the reversion level, the lower the spending that can gain majority support from a low-spending agenda setter. Clearly, however, other interpretations of the role of these variables are possible, as the authors discuss in more detail in their 1982 paper. This is fortunate, since most of these variables enter the spending equations with the more commonly predicted positive sign. My point is simply that the equations reported by Craig and Inman do not provide much of a test of the political model so carefully elaborated in the first half of the paper. In this sense, the empirical work is disappointing.

Empirical Findings

In contrast to the limited attention paid to political variables in the equation specifications, the authors devote substantial attention to economic variables such as income and tax prices. As we have come to expect in work by Craig and Inman, tax prices are adjusted for itemizing under the federal income tax (although how they deal with variation across jurisdictions in the frequency of itemizing is not clear from the text); open-ended matching grants are appropriately differentiated from closed-ended matching grants; and revenue sharing is divided into two parts, a lump-sum component and a tax-effort component (defined in a curious way, as pointed out below).

The distinguishing characteristic of this paper is its attention to the multiple effects of federal aid, that is, the effects of aid to a particular category on that category of spending, on other spending categories, and on tax revenues. The basic strategy involves estimating spending equations for two of the three spending categories, welfare and education, and a tax equation, and then to derive the impact on a third spending category, all other spending, by making use of a current operating budget constraint.

The broad conclusions of the empirical analysis seem plausible, namely (1) that the more specific the grant program is, the more likely it is that some of the aid will stay put and (2) that states divert some of the aid intended for social services to other expenditures. At the same time, many of the estimated coefficients are implausible and should not be taken too seriously. This last point can be illustrated with revenue sharing aid.

The results imply that revenue sharing aid reduces welfare spending, reduces state education spending, may slightly increase state taxes, and increases spending on the "all other" category. Specifically, an additional dollar of revenue sharing leads to an increase in spending on all other services of $1.21. I find this impact on other services highly implausible. Unlike narrowly defined categorical grants, revenue sharing serves neither as seed money to promote additional spending nor specifically encourages spending that would lead to additional complementary spending out of own-source revenues. Not directly estimated, this figure of $1.21 is derived from the budget constraint and the somewhat questionable coefficients of revenue sharing aid in the other equations. The authors provide no explanation for the estimated reduction in welfare and school aid; why higher revenue sharing should lead to this response for welfare spending is baffling. Reductions in state school aid are also hard to understand. A possible explanation is that some of the revenue sharing aid goes to local governments who then require less state aid. This explanation would be more compelling, however, if local revenue sharing funds were distributed to local school districts as well as local general-purpose governments.

Revenue sharing is estimated to have a small positive effect on state taxes. Here, reverse causation could be a serious problem. Both the three-factor and the five-factor formulas for distributing revenue sharing include a tax-effort factor so that states with high taxes in relation to income receive larger revenue sharing grants. This relationship leads to a simultaneity problem and implies that the equations probably understate the extent to which revenue sharing aid reduces state taxes. The failure of the authors to consider this simultaneity is curious. They explicitly control for the component of tax effort related to the use of state income taxes, but ignore this more basic component, which is potentially much larger.

The diversion of intergovernmental aid funds to all other spending turns out to be the most pervasive finding of the empirical work. The authors explain this finding by hypothesizing that nonsocial service programs are politically more attractive to state policymakers than social service programs since additional public dollars in these areas can be explicitly linked to the efforts of the elected official. Since other spending plays such an important part in the results, I wish the authors had estimated the equation directly. Why didn't they do this? I suspect the answer is that current spending on other functional categories cannot be readily derived from the data. To the extent that capital spending is financed out of current tax revenue, it becomes difficult to derive a measure of current spending on all other goods. If such a variable could be constructed, I would guess the aid coefficients might be smaller than those derived from the budget constraint. This would then imply that revenue sharing or other aid was used to build up surplus or reduce debt, a conclusion that would reduce the plausibility of the authors' hypothesis that funds are diverted to programs that provide more immediate political gratification.

Simulations of the New Federalism

Three main points need to be made. First, while the simulations probably present a realistic picture at a very general level, the implausible empirical results discussed above quite naturally lead to implausible simulations. The finding that revenue sharing aid decreased welfare spending, for example, means that the simulated effects of switching from categorical grants to lump-sum aid distributed through a trust fund reduce state welfare spending almost to zero, a result that seems highly improbable.

Second, I find it rather odd that the authors discuss President Reagan's 1982 federalism proposals in the present tense, given that state and local officials and Congress have made it clear that they will not accept the main feature of the proposal, namely, the transfer of responsibility for AFDC and food stamps to the states in exchange for federal takeover of the Medicaid program. This makes the simulations simply an exercise in examining what might have been. At one level this is not very useful, especially given the historical trend toward more rather than less centralization of income-support programs. At another level, however, the simulations are important because they help us better understand the generic issue, that is, the question of how state governments are likely to respond to changes in federal aid programs. I would have preferred that the simulations had been discussed in this broader context.

This leads me to my third and most important point. How appropriate is it to use past behavior to simulate the effects of major changes in our intergovernmental system? Predicting effects of changes that are large relative to the changes observed historically is always worrisome but one that we cannot usually do anything about. Here, however, there is additional cause for concern. Throughout the 1960s and 1970s, state governors played a much larger role than state legislatures in allocating federal aid money. Indeed, some federal programs prohibited legislative involvement, presumably based on the argument that the states were simply acting as the administrative arm of the federal government. With the recent shift to block grants and the pressure on state service levels related to cutbacks in federal aid, however, state legislatures have started to play a much larger role (see Doolittle 1984). Any federalism reform of the scope of that proposed by President Reagan would presumably accelerate this shift of power to the legislature. To the extent that economists are serious about introducing political elements into expenditure models, this changing mix of political power at the state level should not be ignored.

References

Craig, S. G., and R. P. Inman. 1982. Federal aid and public education: An empirical look at the new fiscal federalism. *The Review of Economics and Statistics* 64:541–52.

Doolittle, F. C. 1984. State legislatures and federal grants: An overview. *Public Budgeting and Finance* 4:7–23.

List of Contributors

Paul N. Courant
Institute of Public Policy Studies
1512 Rackham Building
University of Michigan
Ann Arbor, MI 48109

Steven G. Craig
Department of Economics
University of Houston
Houston, TX 77004

Daniel Feenberg
National Bureau of Economic
    Research
1050 Massachusetts Avenue
Cambridge, MA 02138

Roger H. Gordon
Department of Economics
University of Michigan
Ann Arbor, MI 48109

Douglas Holtz-Eakin
Department of Economics
Columbia University
New York, NY 10027

Robert P. Inman
Department of Finance/The Wharton
    School
University of Pennsylvania
Philadelphia, PA 19104

Helen F. Ladd
Kennedy School of Government
Harvard University
79 Boylston Street
Cambridge, MA 02138

Sharon Berstein Megdal
Arizona Corporation Commission
1200 W. Washington
Phoenix, AZ 85007

Peter Mieszkowski
Department of Economics
Rice University
Houston, TX 77251

James M. Poterba
Department of Economics,
    E52-262C
Massachusetts Institute of
    Technology
Cambridge, MA 02139

Harvey S. Rosen
Department of Economics
Princeton University
Princeton, NJ 08544

Joel Slemrod
Department of Economics
University of Minnesota
Minneapolis, MN 55455

Kenneth A. Small
School of Social Sciences
University of California
Irvine, CA 92715

Michelle J. White
Law School
University of Michigan
Ann Arbor, MI 48109

Clifford Winston
Brookings Institution
1775 Massachusetts Avenue, NW
Washington, DC 20036

George R. Zodrow
Department of Economics
Rice University
Houston, TX 77251

Author Index

231

Subject Index

233